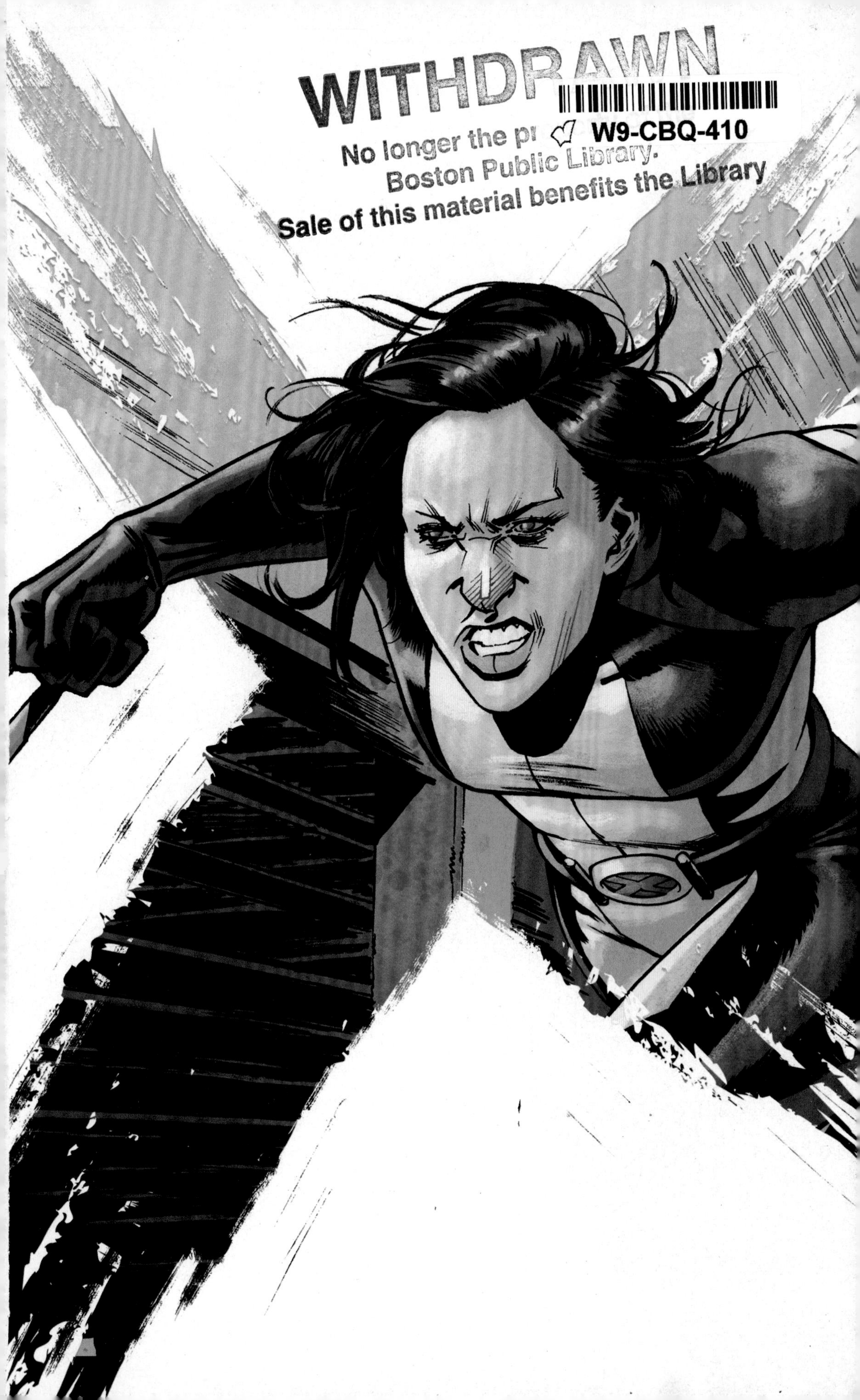

collection editor JENNIFER GRÜNWALD
assistant editor CAITLIN O'CONNELL
associate managing editor KATERI WOODY
editor, special projects MARK D. BEAZLEY
vp production & special projects JEFF YOUNGQUIST
svp print, sales & marketing DAVID GABRIEL
book designer ADAM DEL RE

editor in chief AXEL ALONSO
chief creative officer JOE QUESADA
president DAN BUCKLEY
executive producer ALAN FINE

ALL-NEW WOLVERINE VOL. 3: ENEMY OF THE STATE II. Contains material originally published in magazine form as ALL-NEW WOLVERINE #13-18. First printing 2017. ISBN# 978-1-302-90290-2. Published by MARVEL WORLDWIDE, INC., a subsidiary of MARVEL ENTERTAINMENT, LLC. OFFICE OF PUBLICATION: 135 West 50th Street, New York, NY 10020. Copyright © 2017 MARVEL No similarity between any of the names, characters, persons, and/or institutions in this magazine with those of any living or dead person or institution is intended, and any such similarity which may exist is purely coincidental. Printed in Canada. DAN BUCKLEY, President, Marvel Entertainment; JOE QUESADA, Chief Creative Officer; TOM BREVOORT, SVP of Publishing; DAVID BOGART, SVP of Business Affairs & Operations, Publishing & Partnership; C.B. CEBULSKI, VP of Brand Management & Development, Asia; DAVID GABRIEL, SVP of Sales & Marketing, Publishing; JEFF YOUNGQUIST, VP of Production & Special Projects; DAN CARR, Executive Director of Publishing Technology; ALEX MORALES, Director of Publishing Operations; SUSAN CRESPI, Production Manager; STAN LEE, Chairman Emeritus. For information regarding advertising in Marvel Comics or on Marvel.com, please contact Vit DeBellis, Integrated Sales Manager, at vdebellis@marvel.com. For Marvel subscription inquiries, please call 888-511-5480. Manufactured between 3/10/2017 and 4/11/2017 by SOLISCO PRINTERS, SCOTT, QC, CANADA.

10 9 8 7 6 5 4 3 2 1

X-23 WAS CREATED TO BE A WEAPON.
For a time, that's all she was. But Laura Kinney escaped that life
with the help of the man she was cloned from, the man who became her
mentor: THE WOLVERINE. Tragically, the original Wolverine has fallen,
but Laura will live as his legacy, and fight for her better future. She is the...

ALL-NEW WOLVERINE

Lately, life's been no bowl of cherries for Laura. Death threats, assassination attempts, killer
clones, berserker alternate-reality versions of her "father," Logan. Being sent to an alternate
reality. Switching bodies with someone from an alternate reality. Dang. Does this girl need a
break or what?

writer
TOM TAYLOR

ISSUES #13-14
penciler   inker
NIC VIRELLA   SCOTT HANNA

ISSUES #15 & #17
artist
DJIBRIL MORISSETTE-PHAN

ISSUES #16 & #18
artist
NIC VIRELLA

color artists   letterer
MICHAEL GARLAND   VC's CORY PETIT
WITH JESUS ABURTOV (#14)

cover art   assistant editor   editor
DAVID   CHRISTINA   MARK
LOPEZ   HARRINGTON   PANICCIA

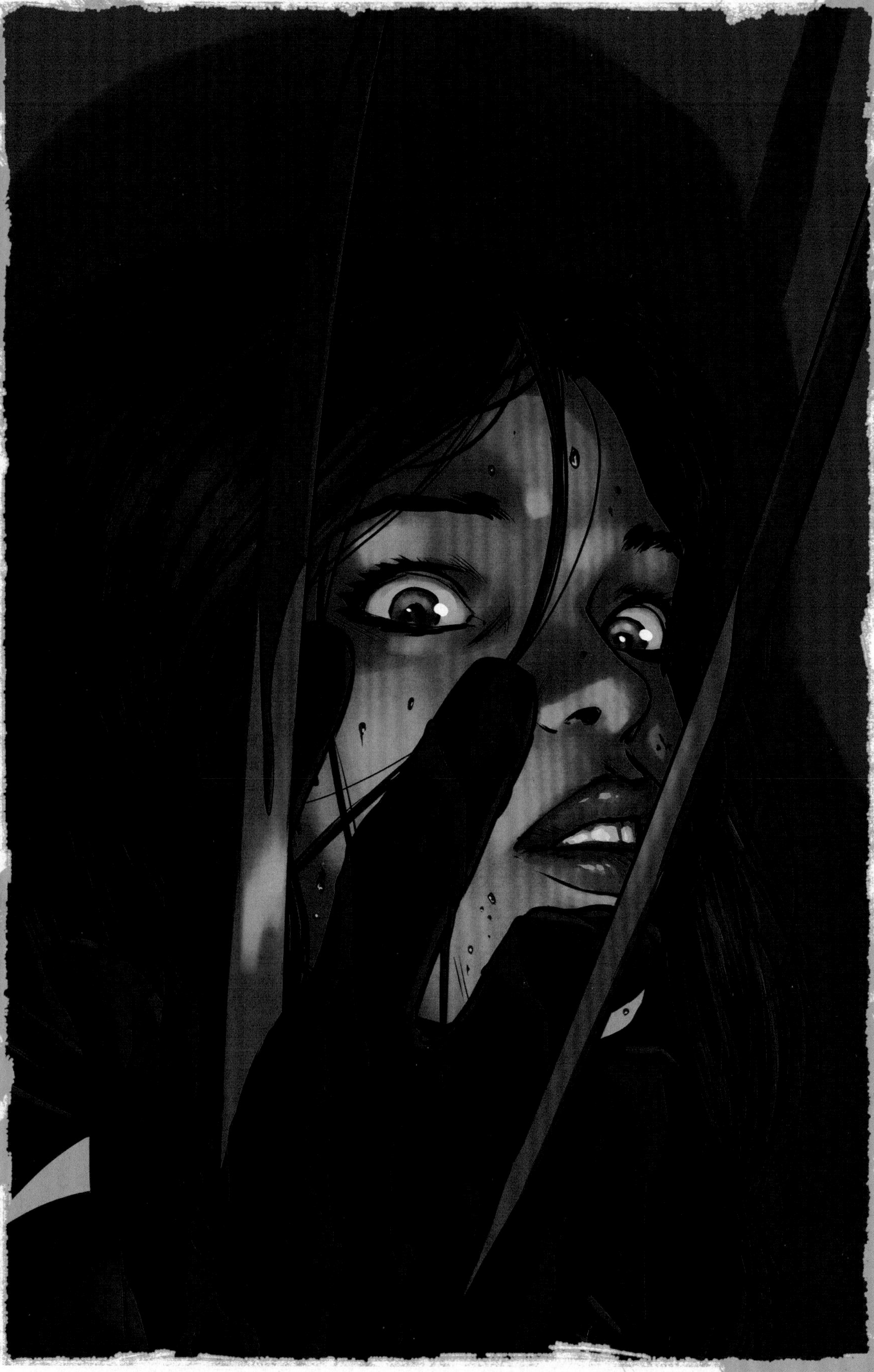

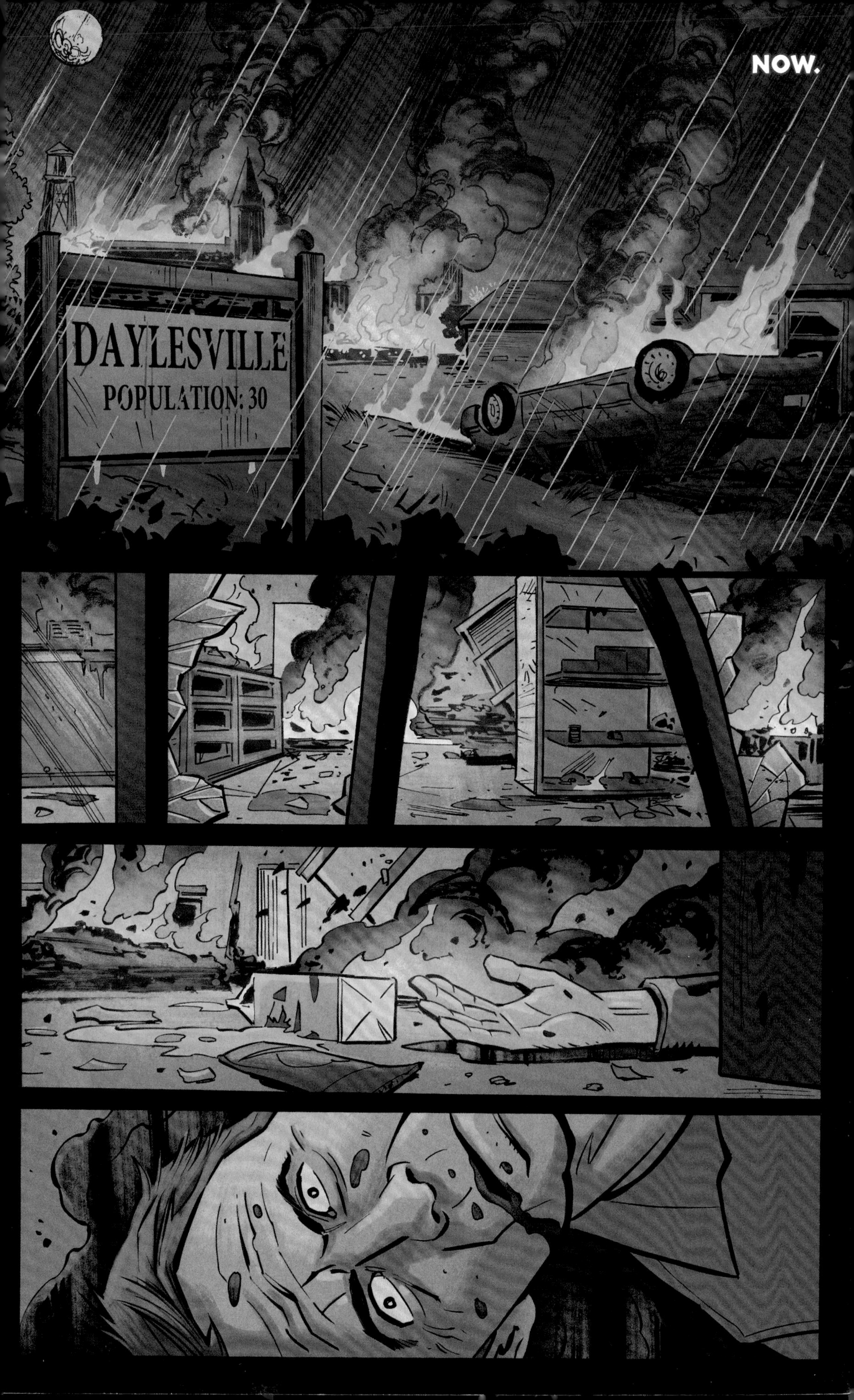
NOW.
DAYLESVILLE
POPULATION: 30

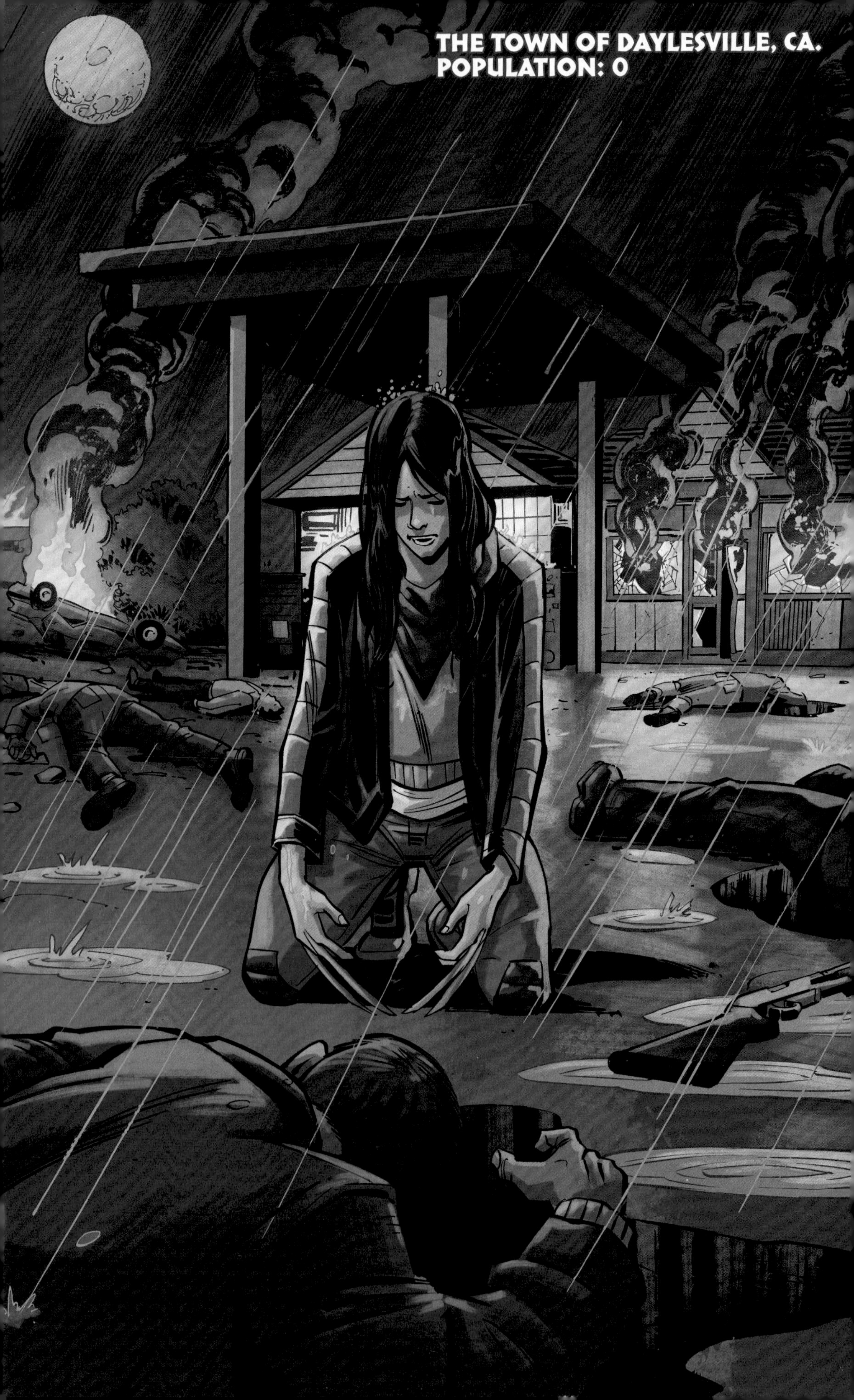
THE TOWN OF DAYLESVILLE, CA.
POPULATION: 0

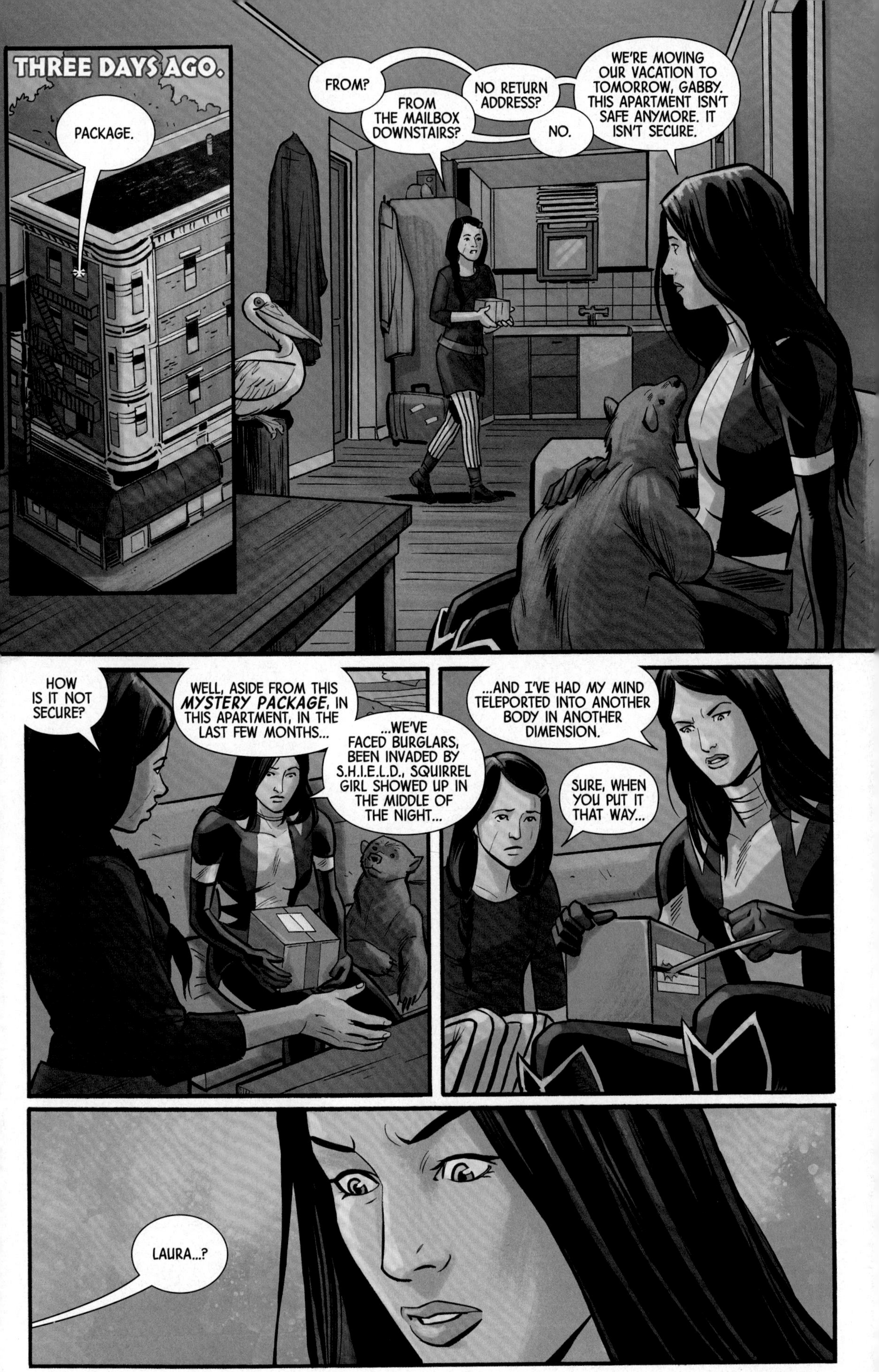
THREE DAYS AGO.
PACKAGE.
FROM?
FROM THE MAILBOX DOWNSTAIRS?
NO RETURN ADDRESS?
NO.
WE'RE MOVING OUR VACATION TO TOMORROW, GABBY. THIS APARTMENT ISN'T SAFE ANYMORE. IT ISN'T SECURE.
HOW IS IT NOT SECURE?
WELL, ASIDE FROM THIS MYSTERY PACKAGE, IN THIS APARTMENT, IN THE LAST FEW MONTHS...
...WE'VE FACED BURGLARS, BEEN INVADED BY S.H.I.E.L.D., SQUIRREL GIRL SHOWED UP IN THE MIDDLE OF THE NIGHT...
...AND I'VE HAD MY MIND TELEPORTED INTO ANOTHER BODY IN ANOTHER DIMENSION.
SURE, WHEN YOU PUT IT THAT WAY...
LAURA...?

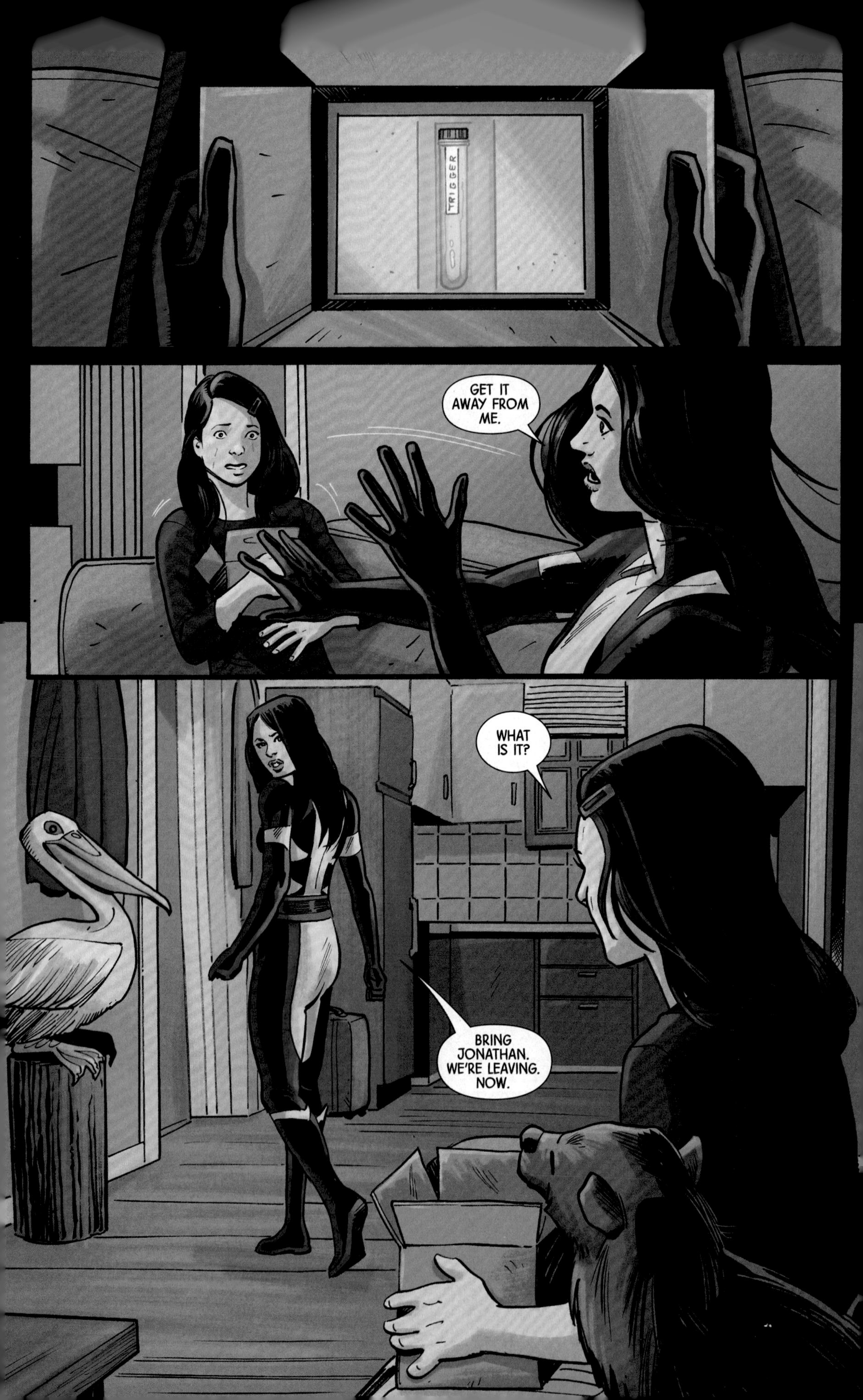
TRIGGER
GET IT AWAY FROM ME.
WHAT IS IT?
BRING JONATHAN. WE'RE LEAVING. NOW.

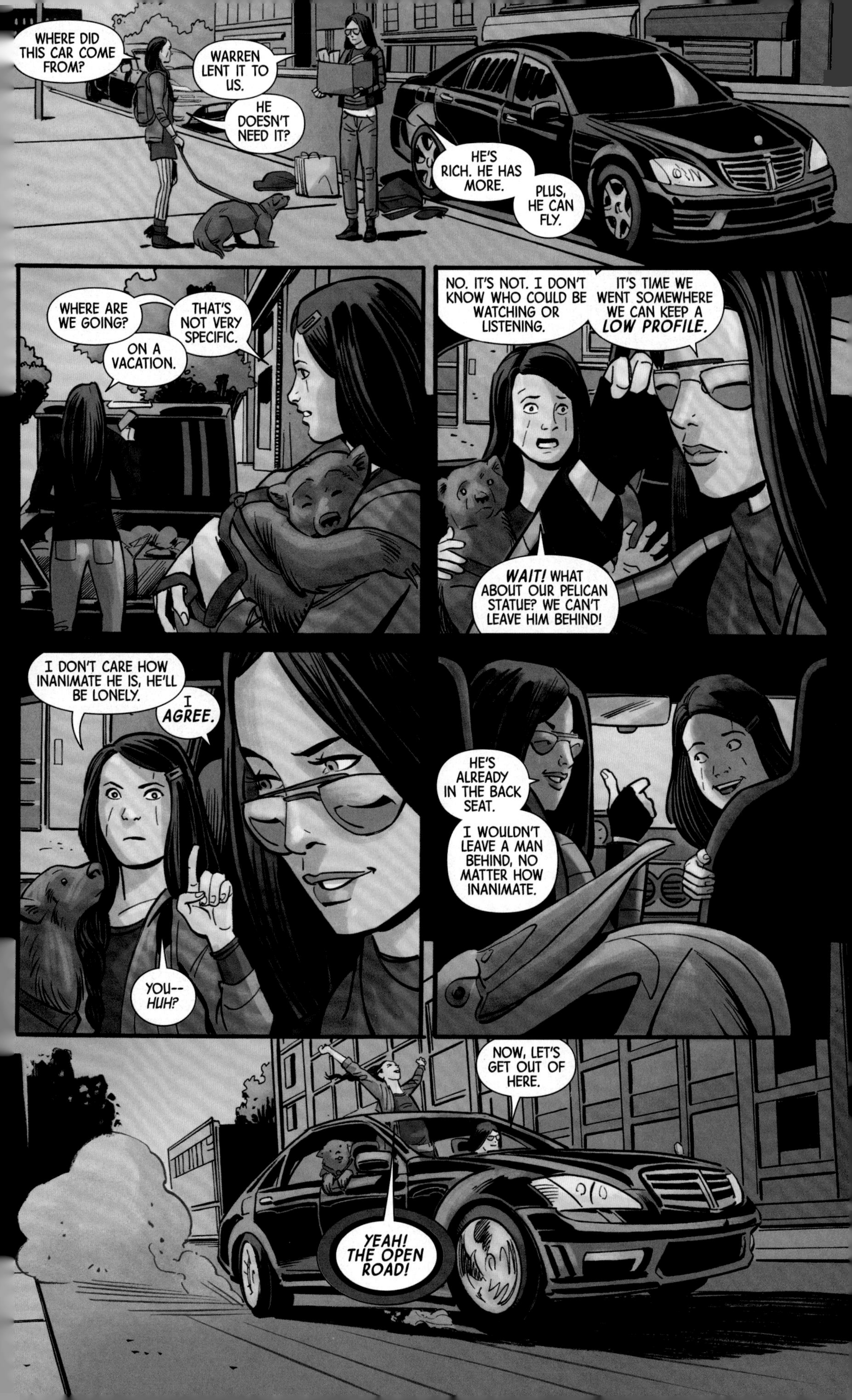
WHERE DID THIS CAR COME FROM?
WARREN LENT IT TO US.
HE DOESN'T NEED IT?
HE'S RICH. HE HAS MORE.
PLUS, HE CAN FLY.
WHERE ARE WE GOING?
ON A VACATION.
THAT'S NOT VERY SPECIFIC.
NO. IT'S NOT. I DON'T KNOW WHO COULD BE WATCHING OR LISTENING.
IT'S TIME WE WENT SOMEWHERE WE CAN KEEP A *LOW PROFILE.*
WAIT! WHAT ABOUT OUR PELICAN STATUE? WE CAN'T LEAVE HIM BEHIND!
I DON'T CARE HOW INANIMATE HE IS, HE'LL BE LONELY.
I *AGREE.*
YOU-- HUH?
HE'S ALREADY IN THE BACK SEAT.
I WOULDN'T LEAVE A MAN BEHIND, NO MATTER HOW INANIMATE.
NOW, LET'S GET OUT OF HERE.
YEAH! THE OPEN ROAD!

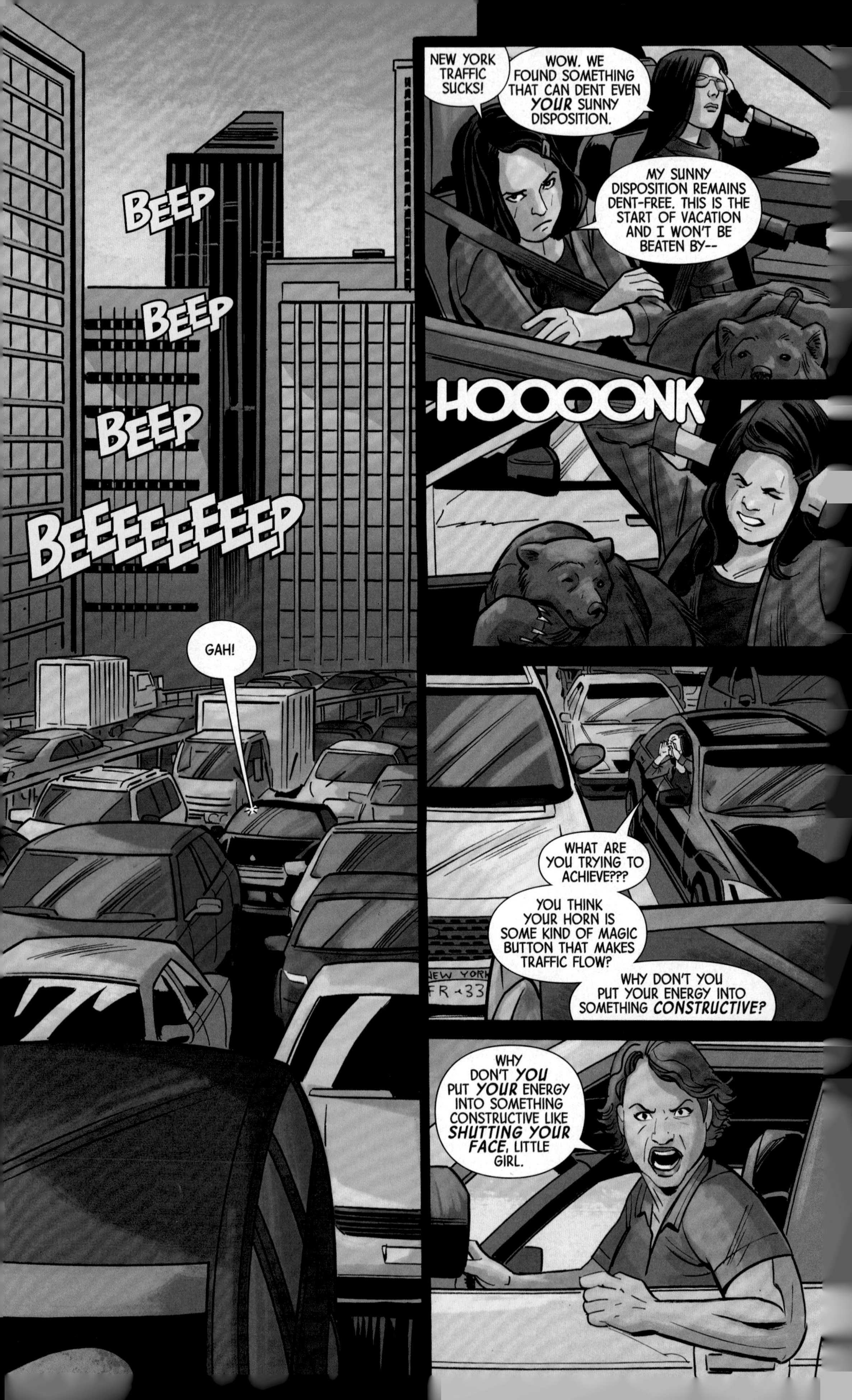
BEEP
BEEP
BEEP
BEEEEEEEEP
GAH!
NEW YORK TRAFFIC SUCKS!
WOW. WE FOUND SOMETHING THAT CAN DENT EVEN YOUR SUNNY DISPOSITION.
MY SUNNY DISPOSITION REMAINS DENT-FREE. THIS IS THE START OF VACATION AND I WON'T BE BEATEN BY--
HOOOONK
WHAT ARE YOU TRYING TO ACHIEVE???
YOU THINK YOUR HORN IS SOME KIND OF MAGIC BUTTON THAT MAKES TRAFFIC FLOW?
WHY DON'T YOU PUT YOUR ENERGY INTO SOMETHING CONSTRUCTIVE?
WHY DON'T YOU PUT YOUR ENERGY INTO SOMETHING CONSTRUCTIVE LIKE SHUTTING YOUR FACE, LITTLE GIRL.

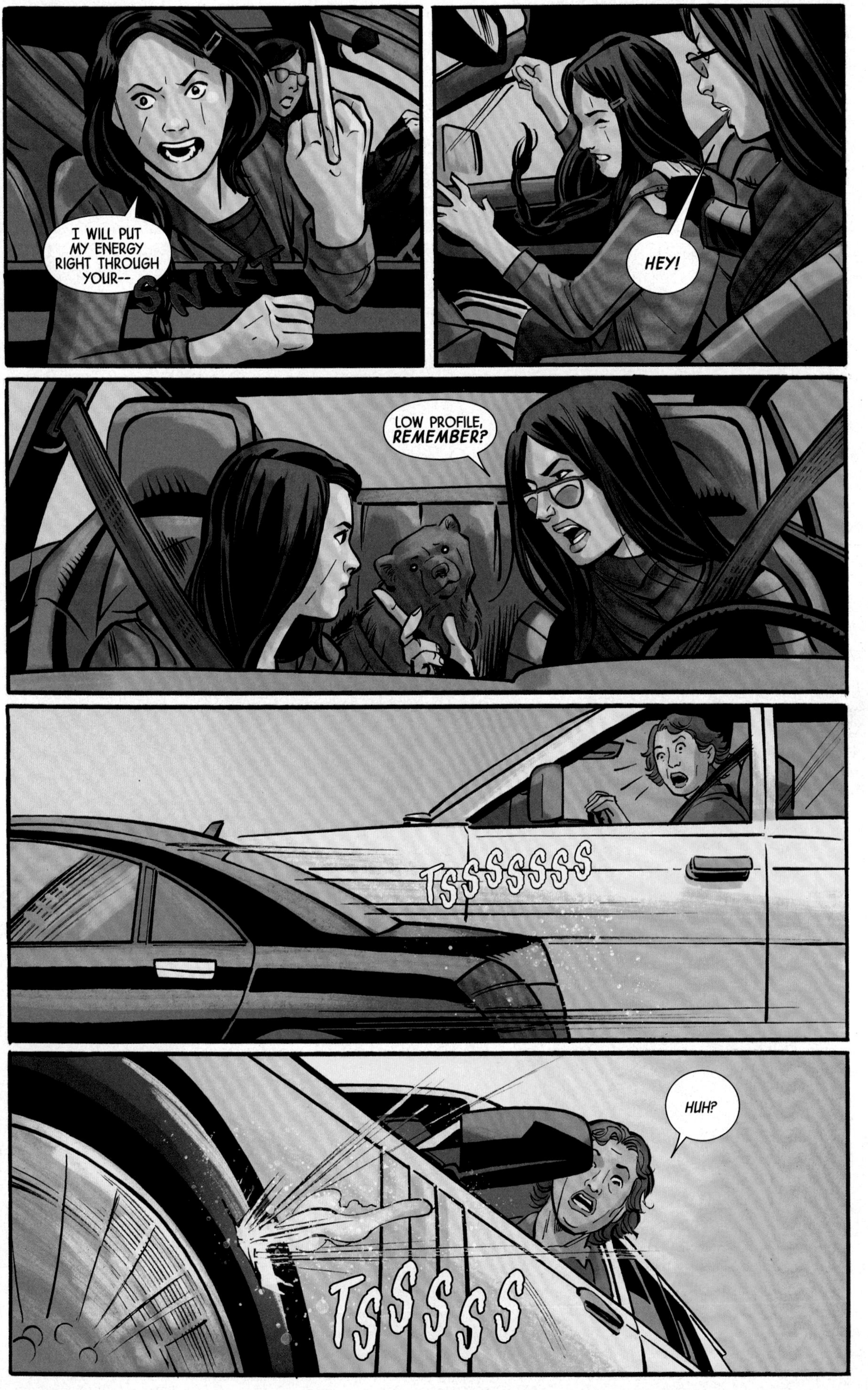

I WILL PUT MY ENERGY RIGHT THROUGH YOUR--
SNIKT
HEY!
LOW PROFILE, REMEMBER?
TSSSSSSSS
HUH?
TSSSSS

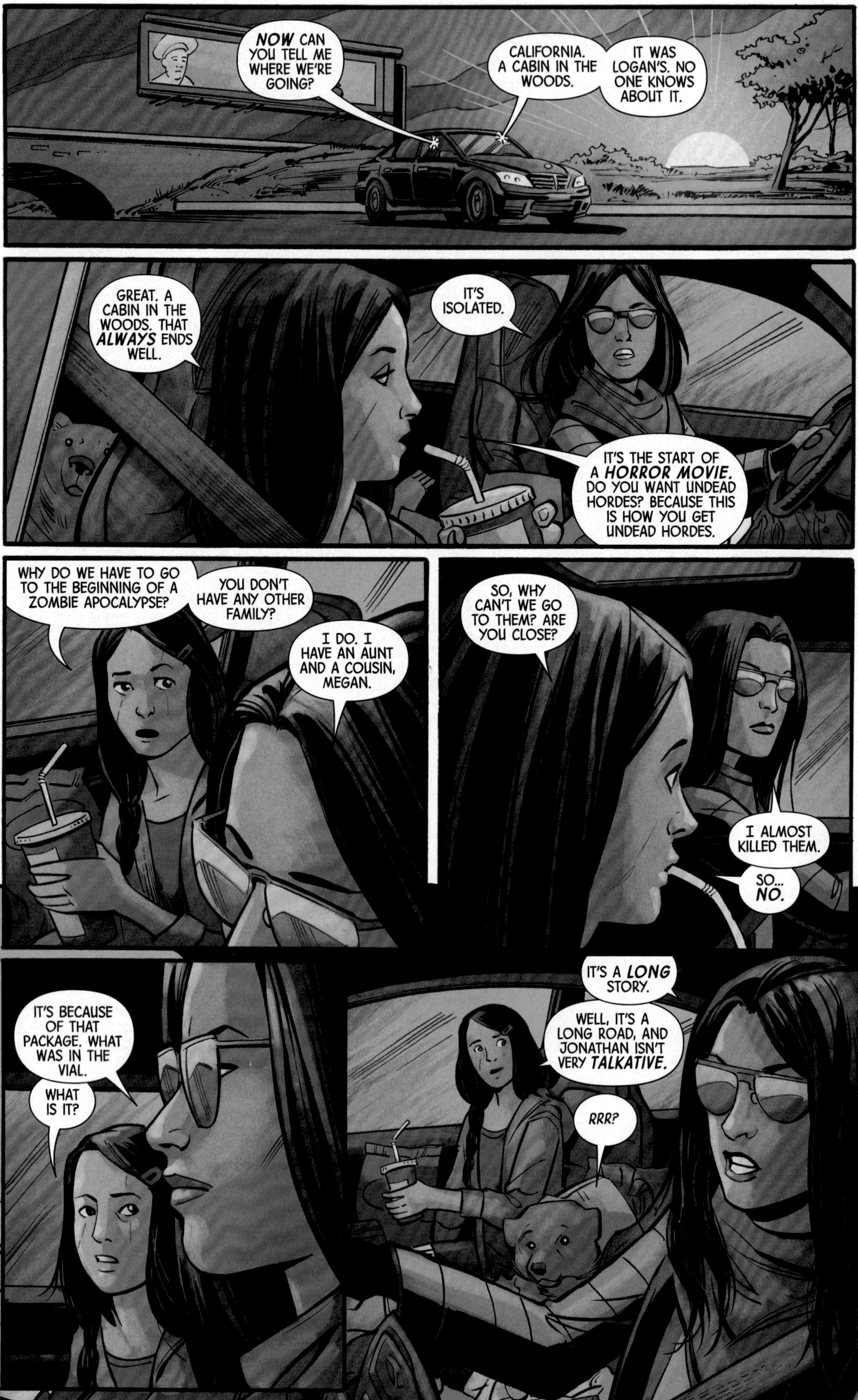
NOW CAN YOU TELL ME WHERE WE'RE GOING?
CALIFORNIA. A CABIN IN THE WOODS.
IT WAS LOGAN'S. NO ONE KNOWS ABOUT IT.
GREAT. A CABIN IN THE WOODS. THAT ALWAYS ENDS WELL.
IT'S ISOLATED.
IT'S THE START OF A HORROR MOVIE. DO YOU WANT UNDEAD HORDES? BECAUSE THIS IS HOW YOU GET UNDEAD HORDES.
WHY DO WE HAVE TO GO TO THE BEGINNING OF A ZOMBIE APOCALYPSE?
YOU DON'T HAVE ANY OTHER FAMILY?
I DO. I HAVE AN AUNT AND A COUSIN, MEGAN.
SO, WHY CAN'T WE GO TO THEM? ARE YOU CLOSE?
I ALMOST KILLED THEM.
SO... NO.
IT'S BECAUSE OF THAT PACKAGE. WHAT WAS IN THE VIAL.
WHAT IS IT?
IT'S A LONG STORY.
WELL, IT'S A LONG ROAD, AND JONATHAN ISN'T VERY TALKATIVE.
RRR?

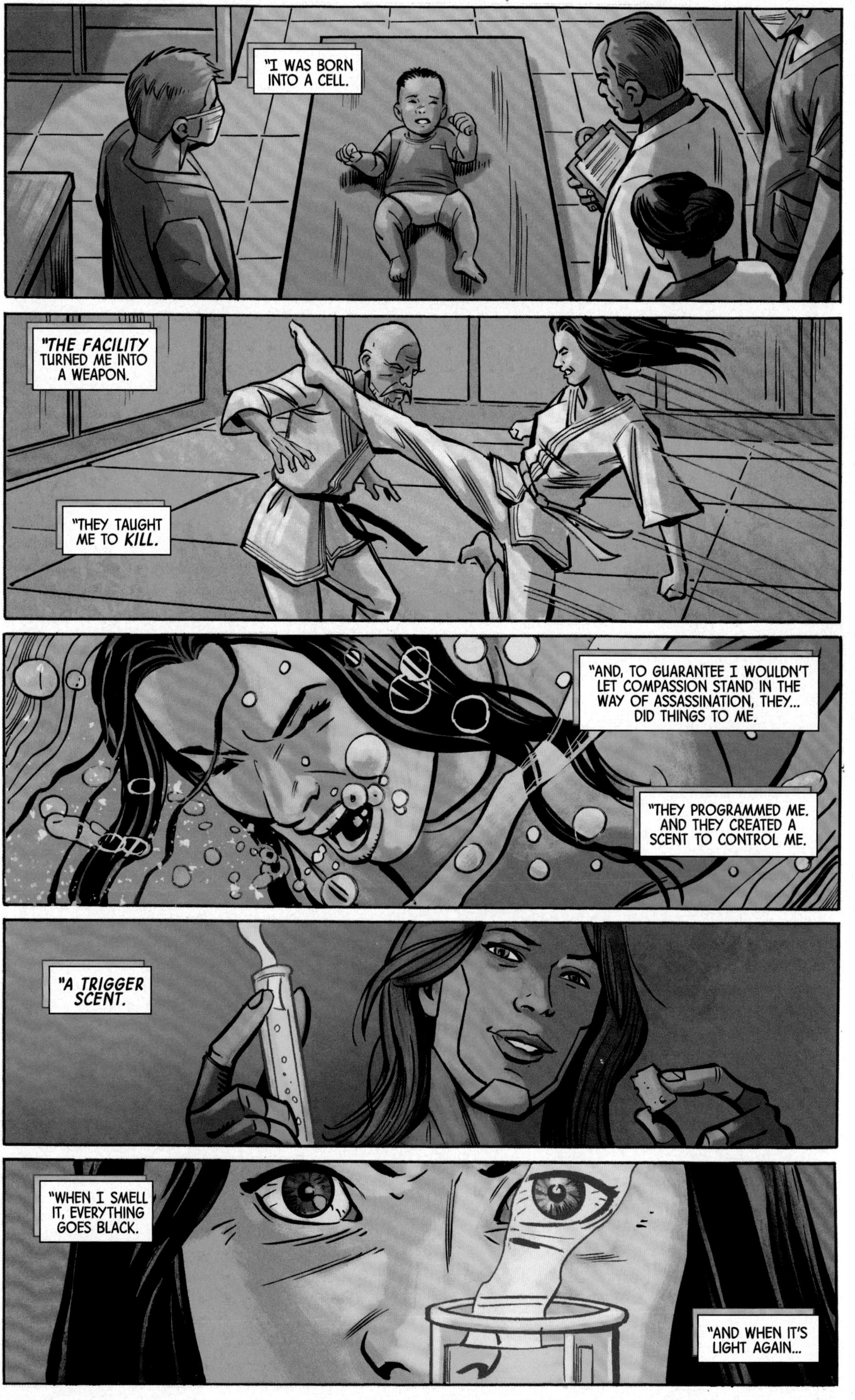
"I WAS BORN INTO A CELL.
"THE FACILITY TURNED ME INTO A WEAPON.
"THEY TAUGHT ME TO KILL.
"AND, TO GUARANTEE I WOULDN'T LET COMPASSION STAND IN THE WAY OF ASSASSINATION, THEY... DID THINGS TO ME.
"THEY PROGRAMMED ME. AND THEY CREATED A SCENT TO CONTROL ME.
"A TRIGGER SCENT.
"WHEN I SMELL IT, EVERYTHING GOES BLACK.
"AND WHEN IT'S LIGHT AGAIN...

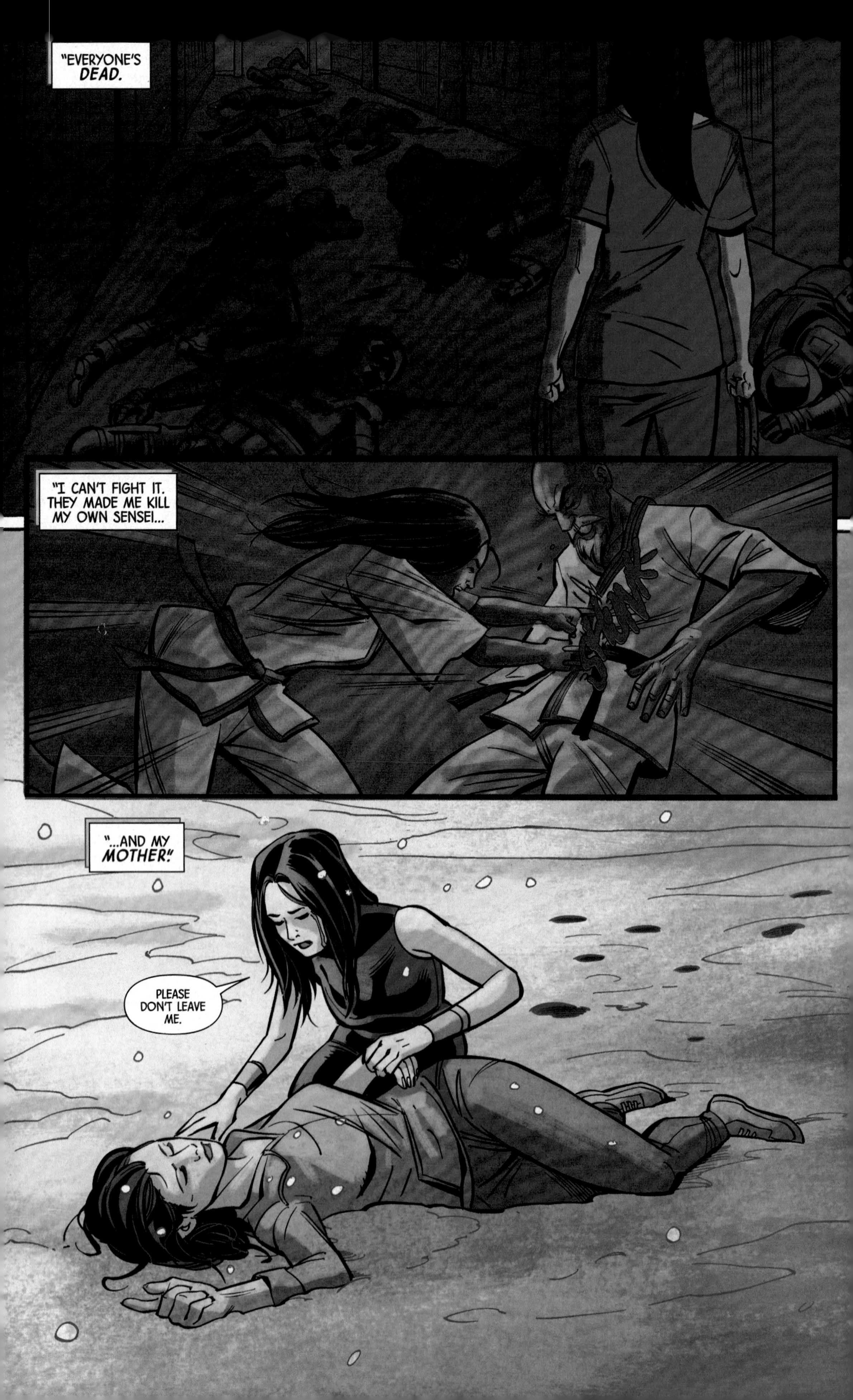
"EVERYONE'S DEAD.
"I CAN'T FIGHT IT. THEY MADE ME KILL MY OWN SENSEI...
"...AND MY MOTHER!"
PLEASE DON'T LEAVE ME.

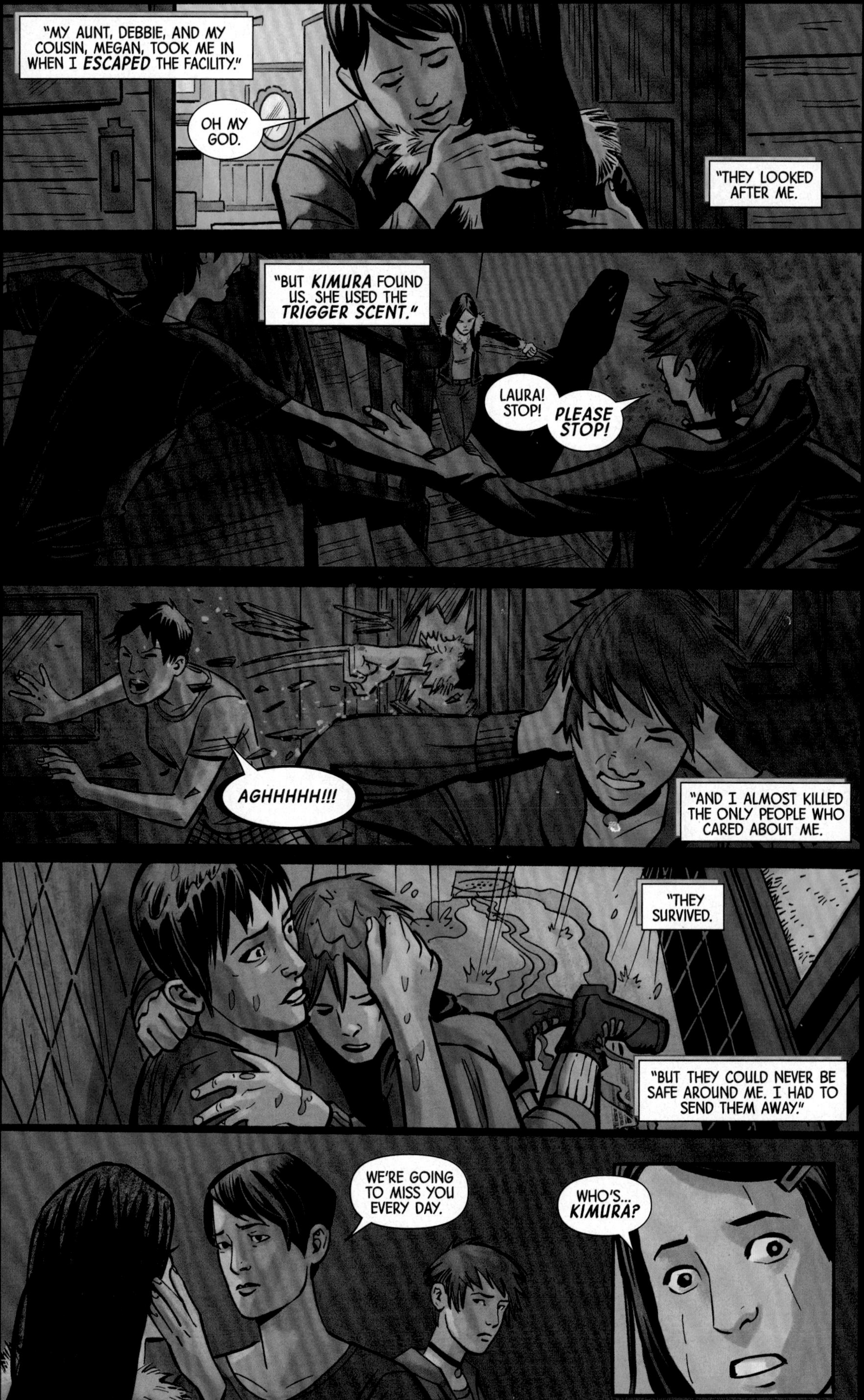
"MY AUNT, DEBBIE, AND MY COUSIN, MEGAN, TOOK ME IN WHEN I ESCAPED THE FACILITY."
OH MY GOD.
"THEY LOOKED AFTER ME.
"BUT KIMURA FOUND US. SHE USED THE TRIGGER SCENT."
LAURA! STOP!
PLEASE STOP!
AGHHHHH!!!
"AND I ALMOST KILLED THE ONLY PEOPLE WHO CARED ABOUT ME.
"THEY SURVIVED.
"BUT THEY COULD NEVER BE SAFE AROUND ME. I HAD TO SEND THEM AWAY."
WE'RE GOING TO MISS YOU EVERY DAY.
WHO'S... KIMURA?

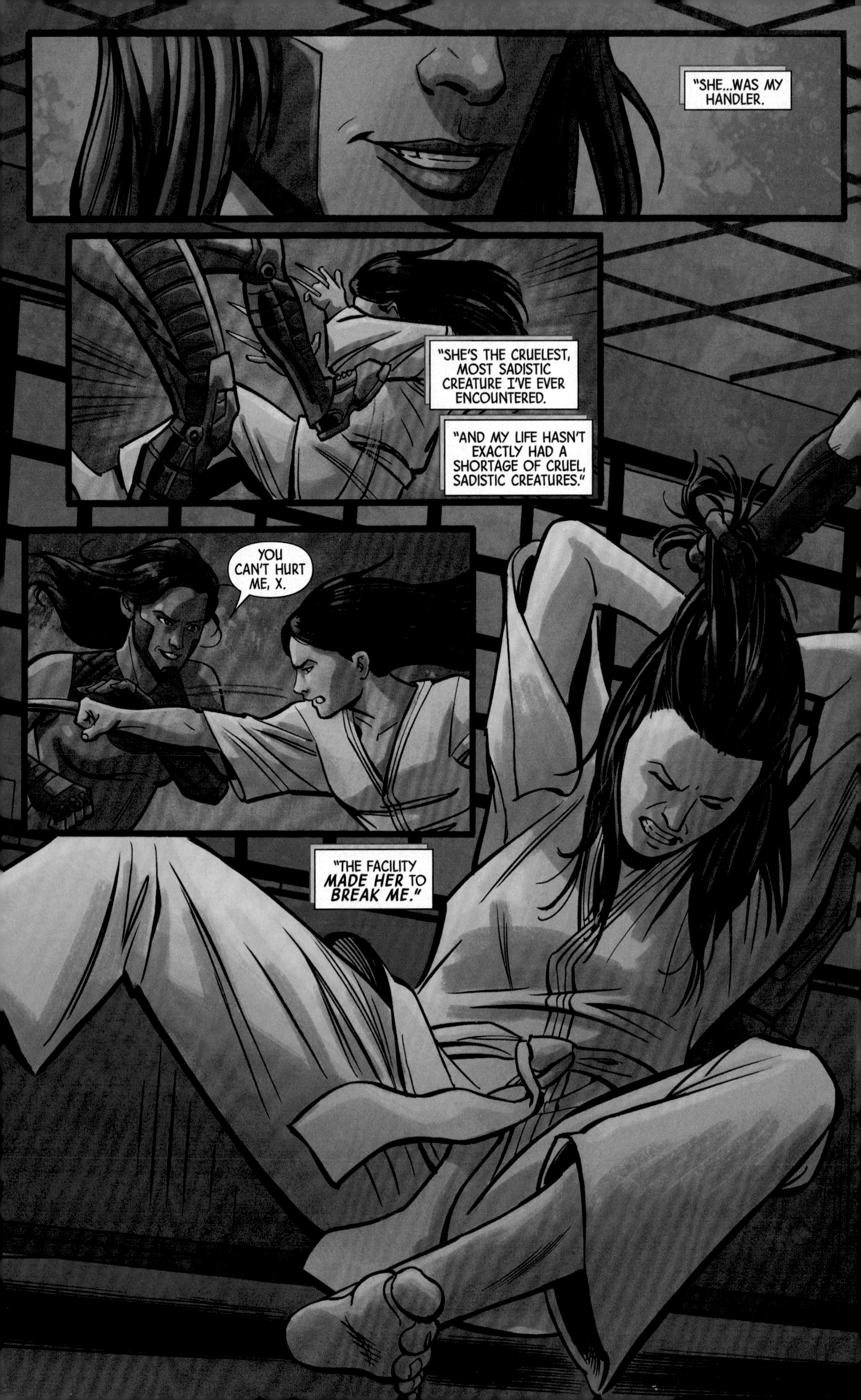
"SHE...WAS MY HANDLER.
"SHE'S THE CRUELEST, MOST SADISTIC CREATURE I'VE EVER ENCOUNTERED.
"AND MY LIFE HASN'T EXACTLY HAD A SHORTAGE OF CRUEL, SADISTIC CREATURES."
YOU CAN'T HURT ME, X.
"THE FACILITY *MADE HER* TO *BREAK ME.*"

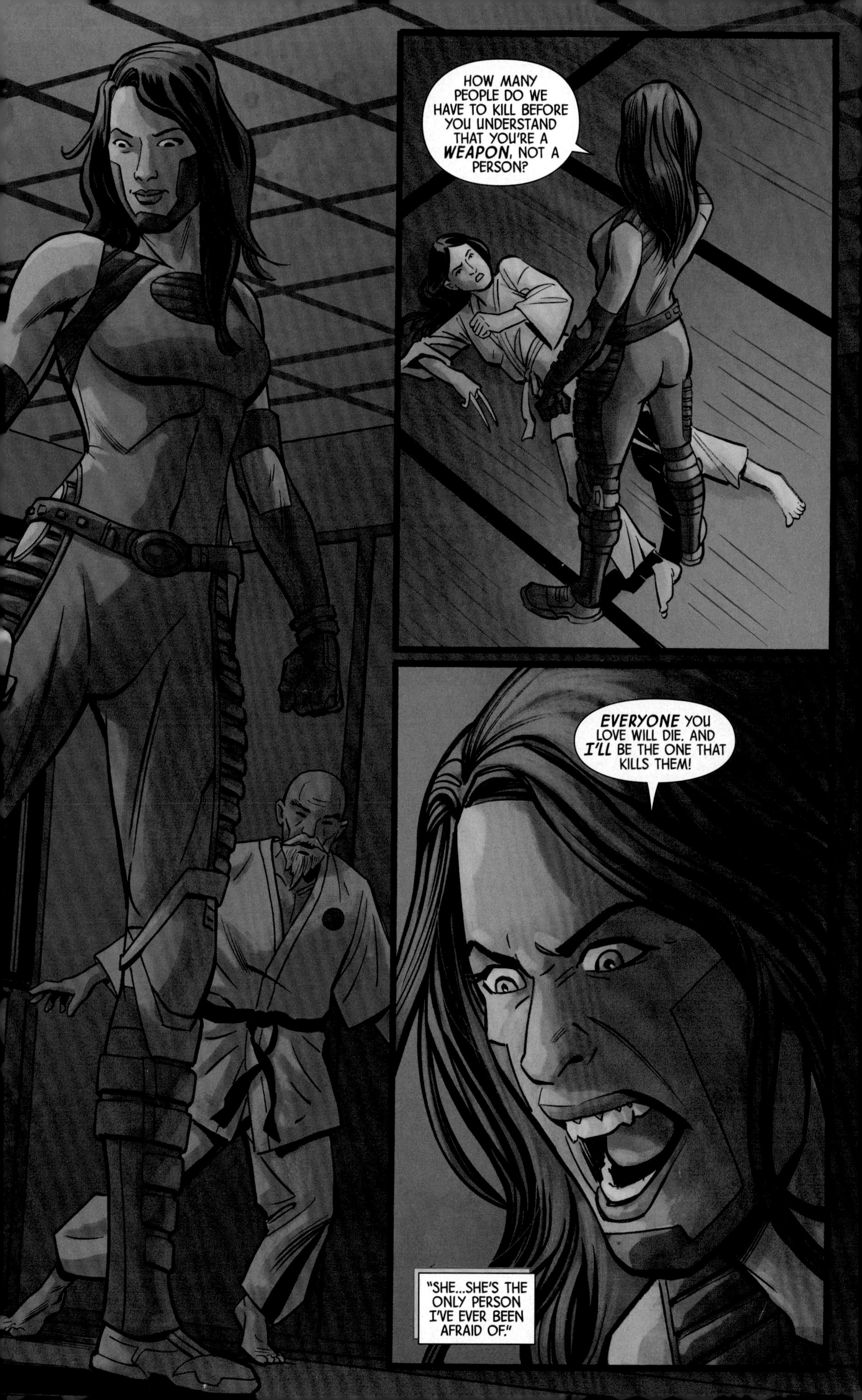
HOW MANY PEOPLE DO WE HAVE TO KILL BEFORE YOU UNDERSTAND THAT YOU'RE A WEAPON, NOT A PERSON?
EVERYONE YOU LOVE WILL DIE. AND I'LL BE THE ONE THAT KILLS THEM!
"SHE...SHE'S THE ONLY PERSON I'VE EVER BEEN AFRAID OF."

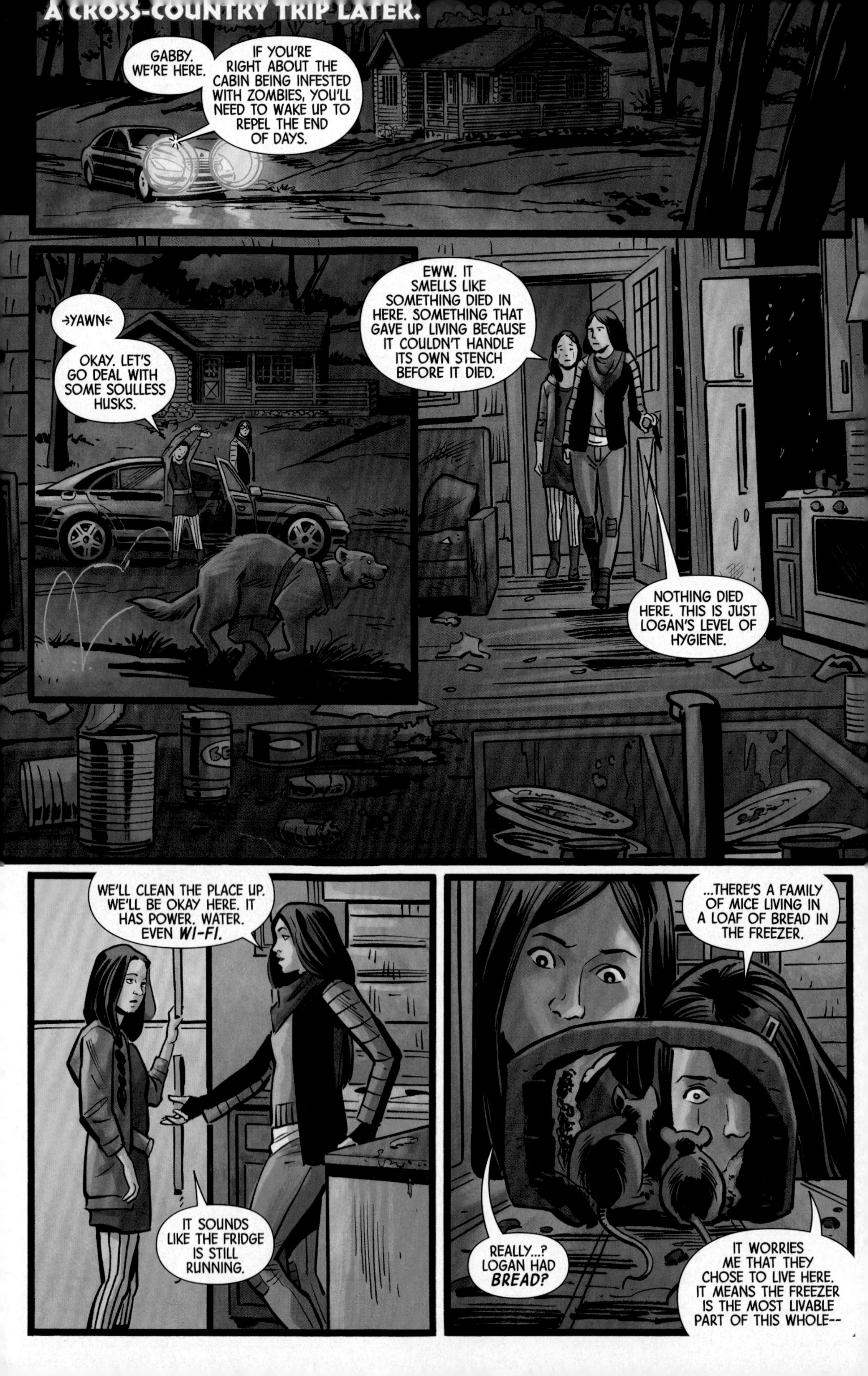
A CROSS-COUNTRY TRIP LATER.
GABBY. WE'RE HERE.
IF YOU'RE RIGHT ABOUT THE CABIN BEING INFESTED WITH ZOMBIES, YOU'LL NEED TO WAKE UP TO REPEL THE END OF DAYS.
>YAWN<
OKAY. LET'S GO DEAL WITH SOME SOULLESS HUSKS.
EWW. IT SMELLS LIKE SOMETHING DIED IN HERE. SOMETHING THAT GAVE UP LIVING BECAUSE IT COULDN'T HANDLE ITS OWN STENCH BEFORE IT DIED.
NOTHING DIED HERE. THIS IS JUST LOGAN'S LEVEL OF HYGIENE.
WE'LL CLEAN THE PLACE UP. WE'LL BE OKAY HERE. IT HAS POWER. WATER. EVEN *WI-FI.*
IT SOUNDS LIKE THE FRIDGE IS STILL RUNNING.
...THERE'S A FAMILY OF MICE LIVING IN A LOAF OF BREAD IN THE FREEZER.
REALLY...? LOGAN HAD *BREAD?*
IT WORRIES ME THAT THEY CHOSE TO LIVE HERE. IT MEANS THE FREEZER IS THE MOST LIVABLE PART OF THIS WHOLE--

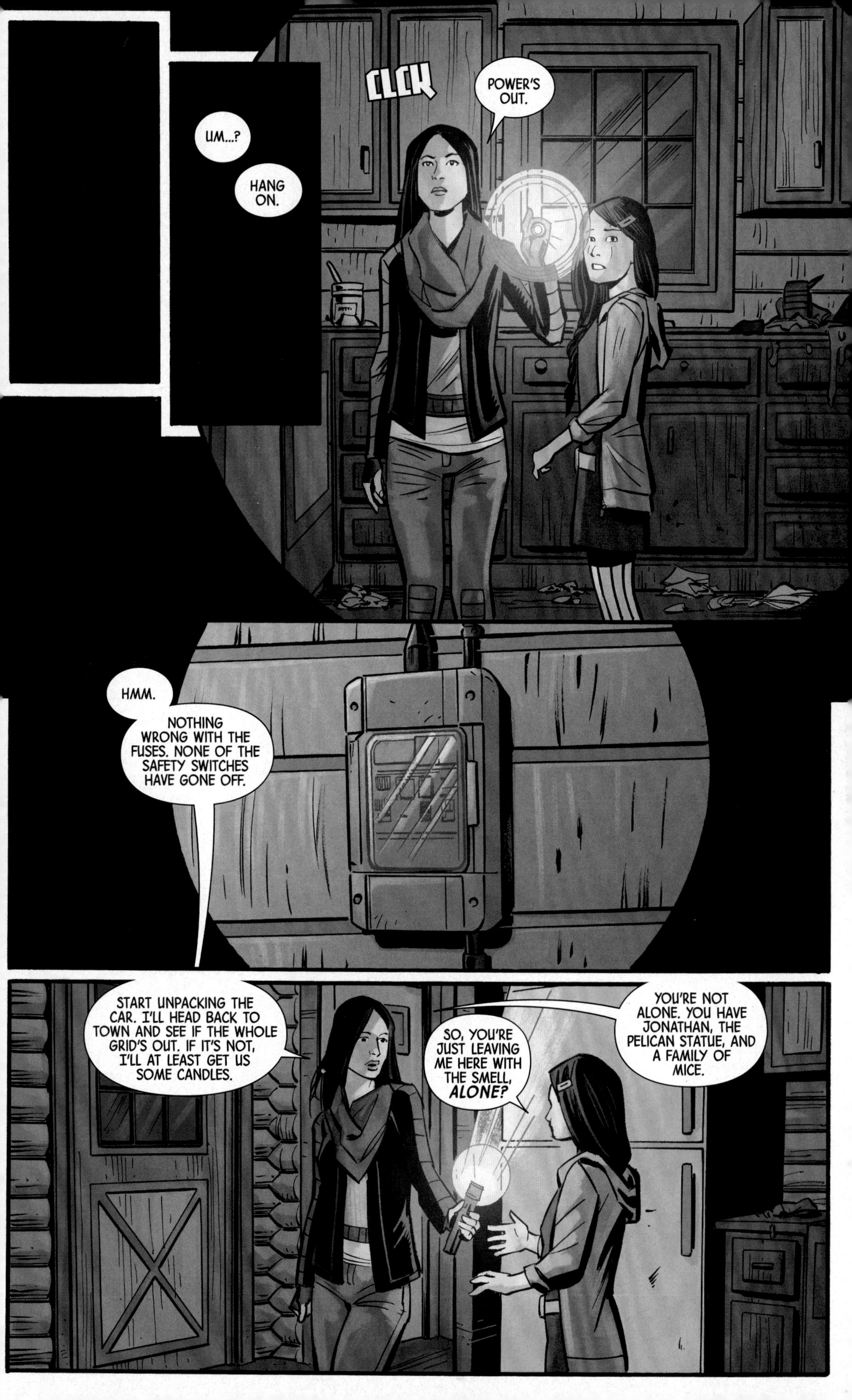
CLCK
POWER'S OUT.
UM...?
HANG ON.
HMM.
NOTHING WRONG WITH THE FUSES. NONE OF THE SAFETY SWITCHES HAVE GONE OFF.
START UNPACKING THE CAR. I'LL HEAD BACK TO TOWN AND SEE IF THE WHOLE GRID'S OUT. IF IT'S NOT, I'LL AT LEAST GET US SOME CANDLES.
SO, YOU'RE JUST LEAVING ME HERE WITH THE SMELL, *ALONE?*
YOU'RE NOT ALONE. YOU HAVE JONATHAN, THE PELICAN STATUE, AND A FAMILY OF MICE.

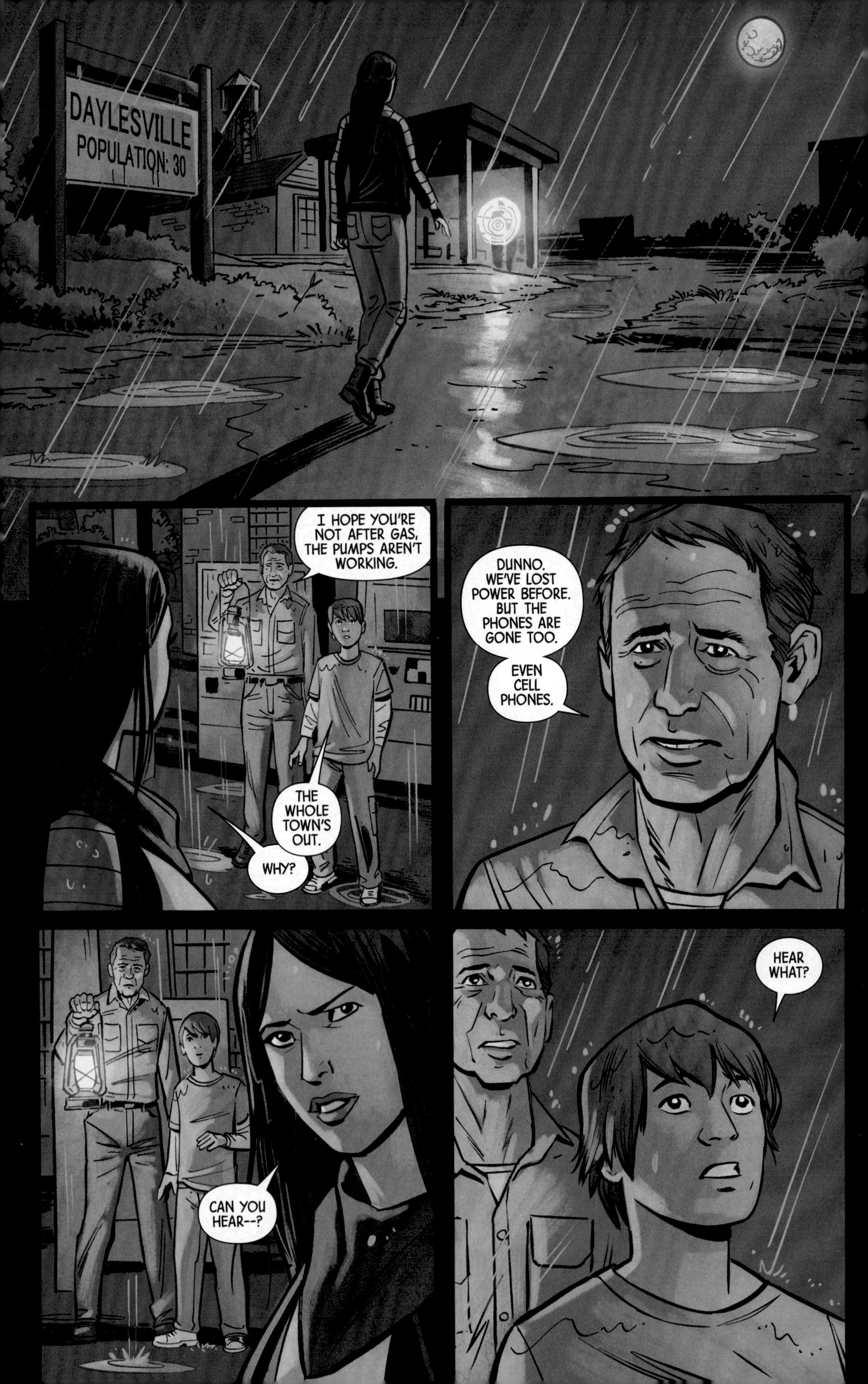
DAYLESVILLE
POPULATION: 30
I HOPE YOU'RE NOT AFTER GAS, THE PUMPS AREN'T WORKING.
THE WHOLE TOWN'S OUT.
WHY?
DUNNO. WE'VE LOST POWER BEFORE. BUT THE PHONES ARE GONE TOO.
EVEN CELL PHONES.
CAN YOU HEAR--?
HEAR WHAT?

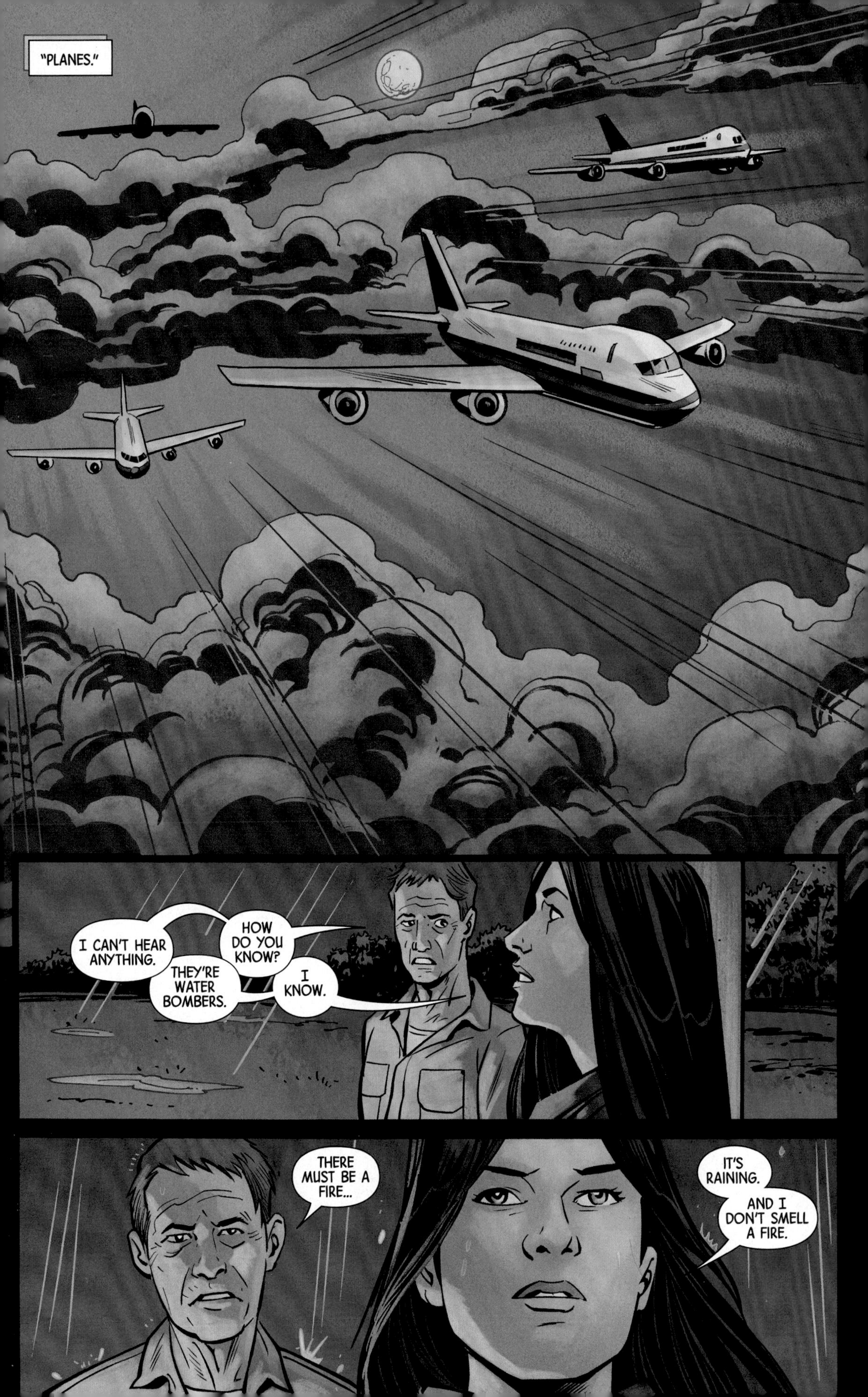
"PLANES."
I CAN'T HEAR ANYTHING.
HOW DO YOU KNOW?
THEY'RE WATER BOMBERS.
I KNOW.
THERE MUST BE A FIRE...
IT'S RAINING.
AND I DON'T SMELL A FIRE.

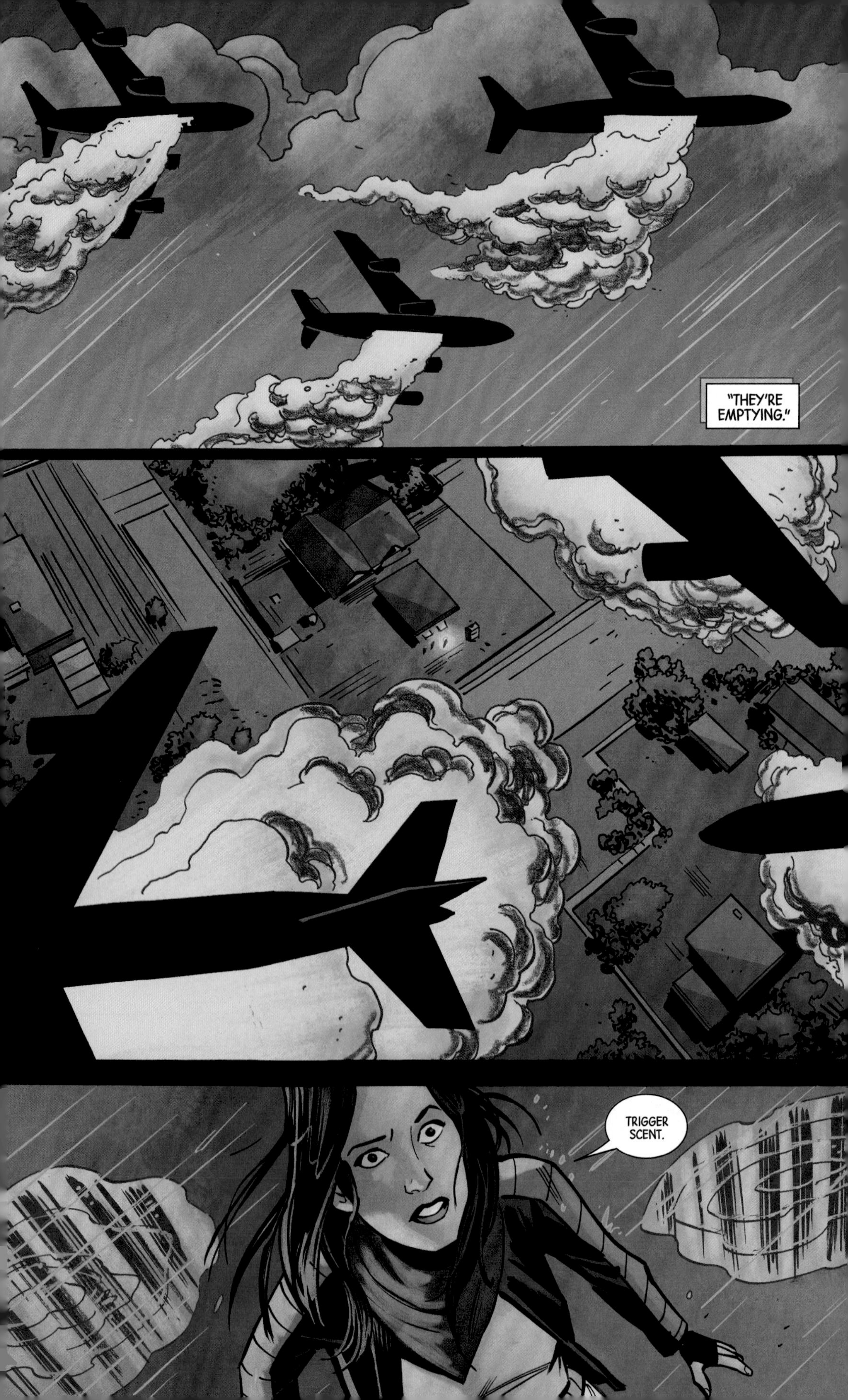
"THEY'RE EMPTYING."
TRIGGER SCENT.

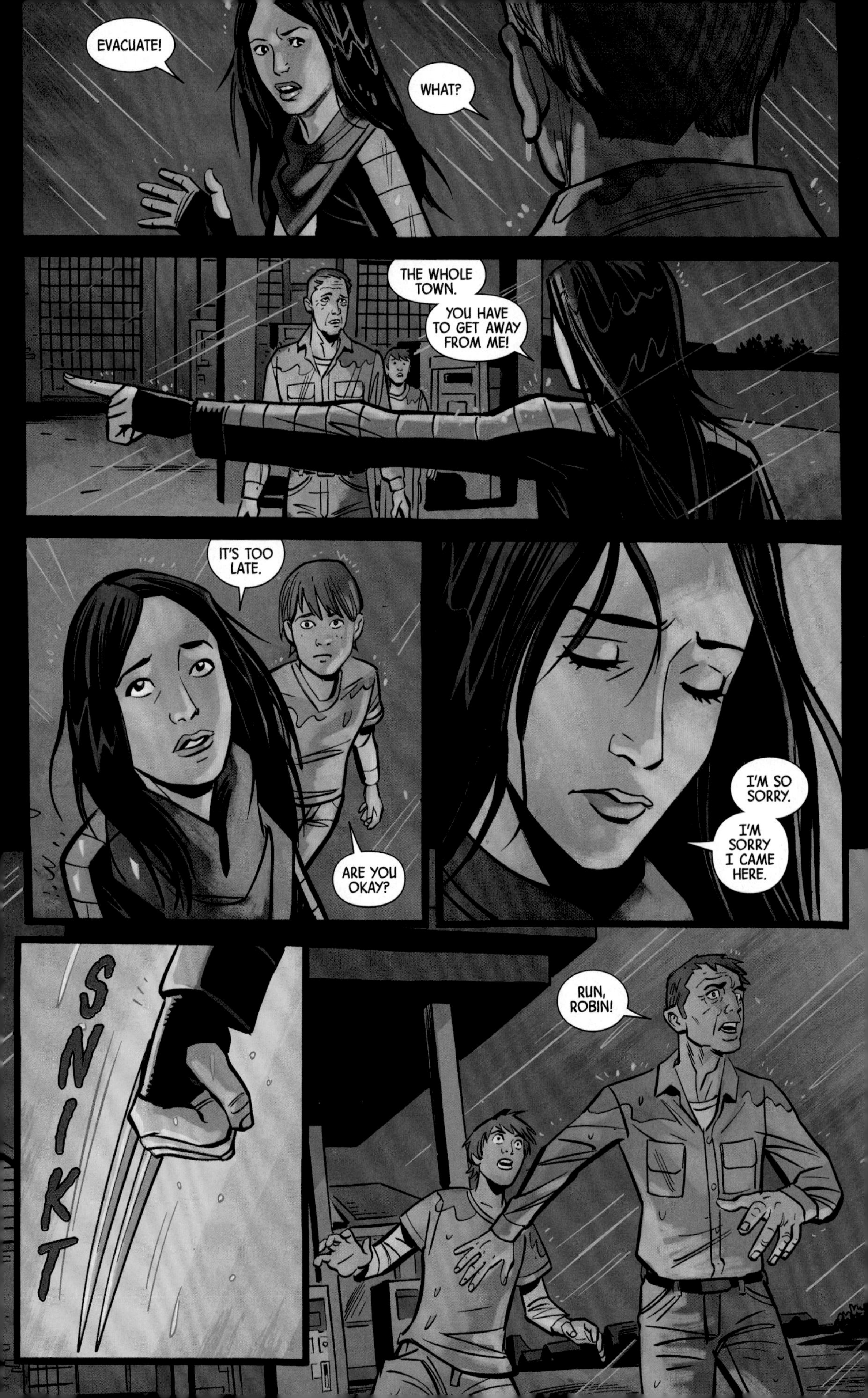
EVACUATE!
WHAT?
THE WHOLE TOWN.
YOU HAVE TO GET AWAY FROM ME!
IT'S TOO LATE.
ARE YOU OKAY?
I'M SO SORRY.
I'M SORRY I CAME HERE.
SNIKT
RUN, ROBIN!

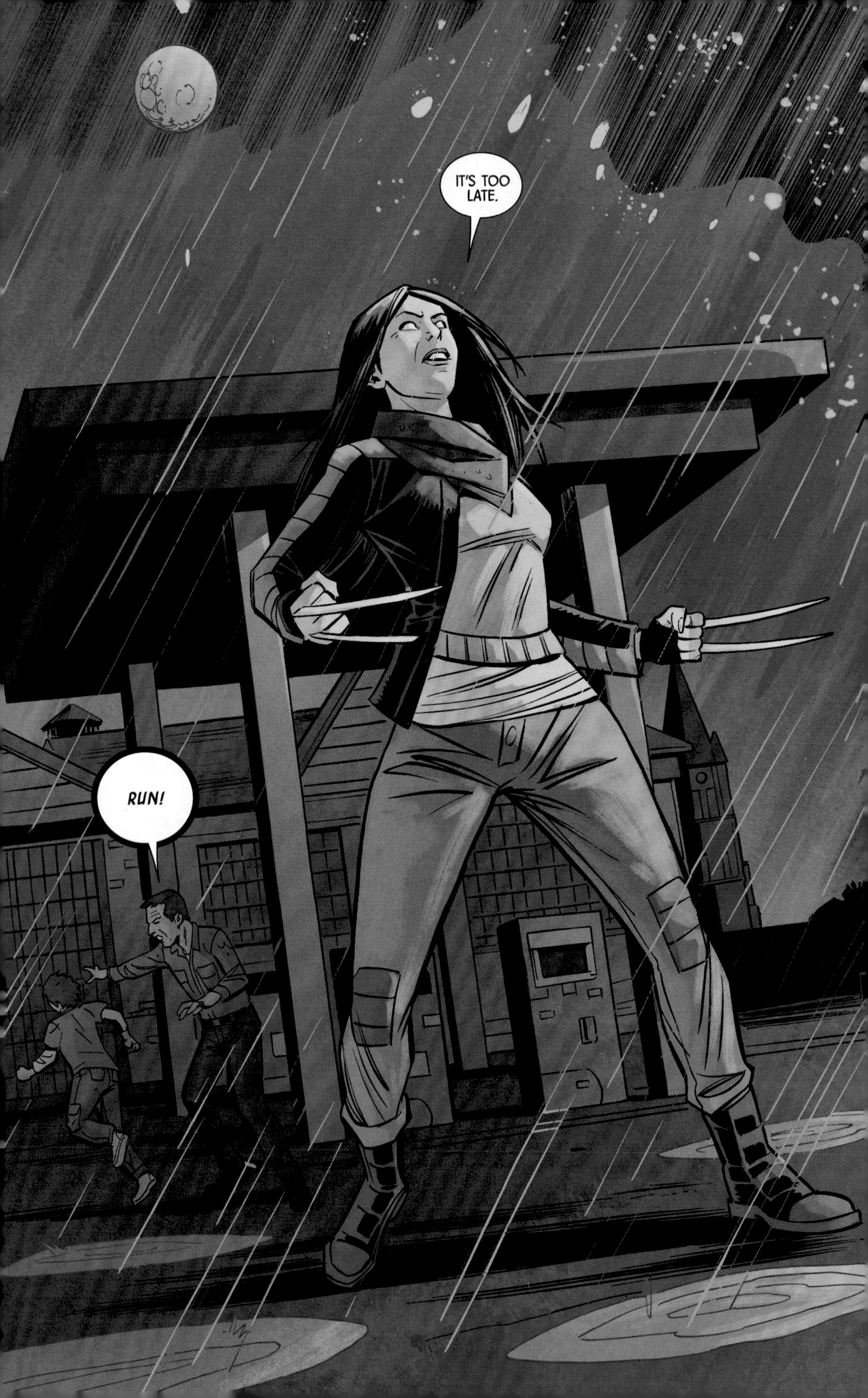
IT'S TOO LATE.
RUN!

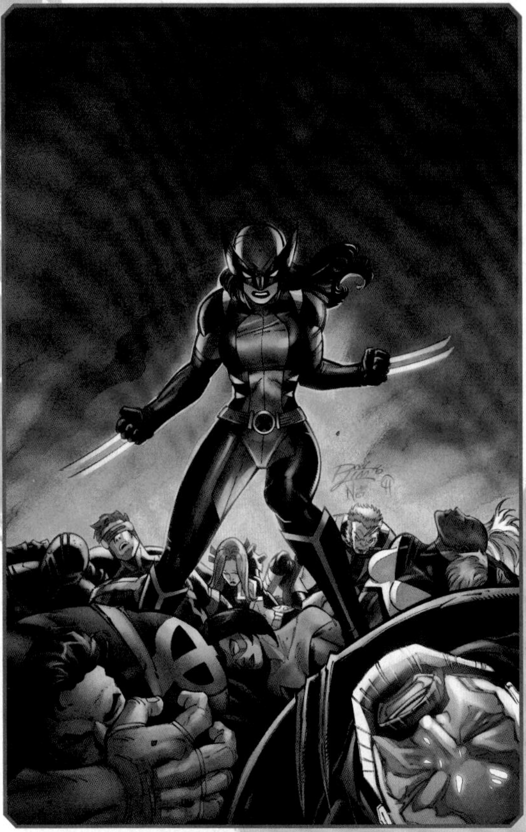

#13 variant by
RON LIM, CORY HAMSCHER & NEI RUFFINO

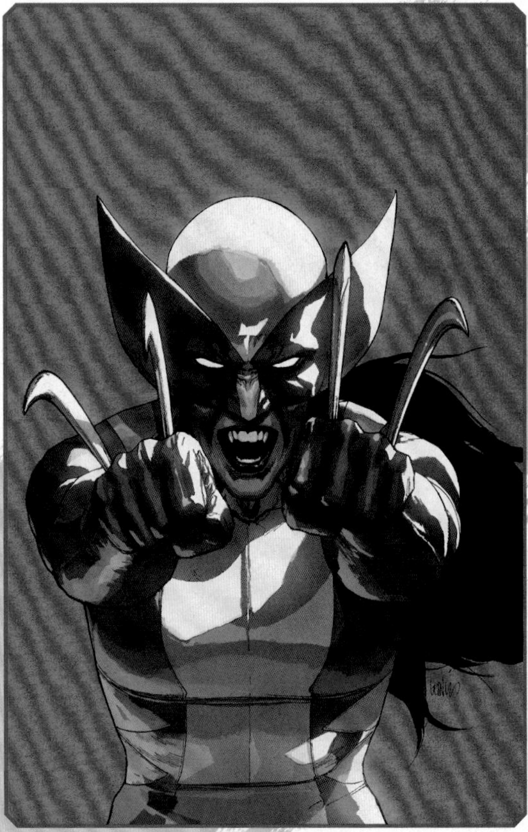

#14 variant by
LEINIL FRANCIS YU

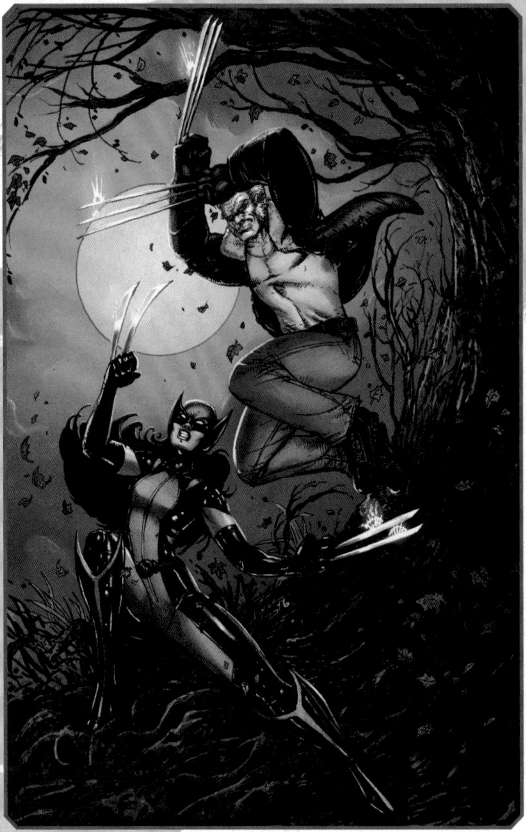

#14 variant by
JOYCE CHIN & CHRIS SOTOMAYOR

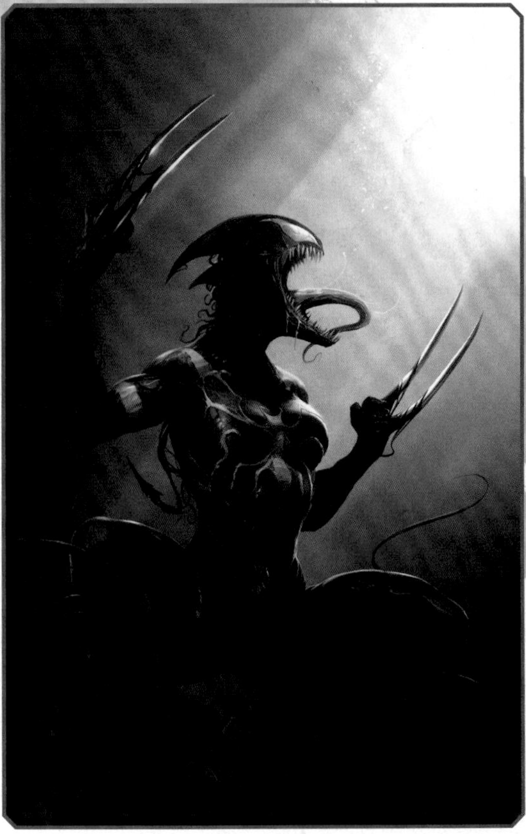

#18 Venomized variant by
FRANCESCO MATTINA

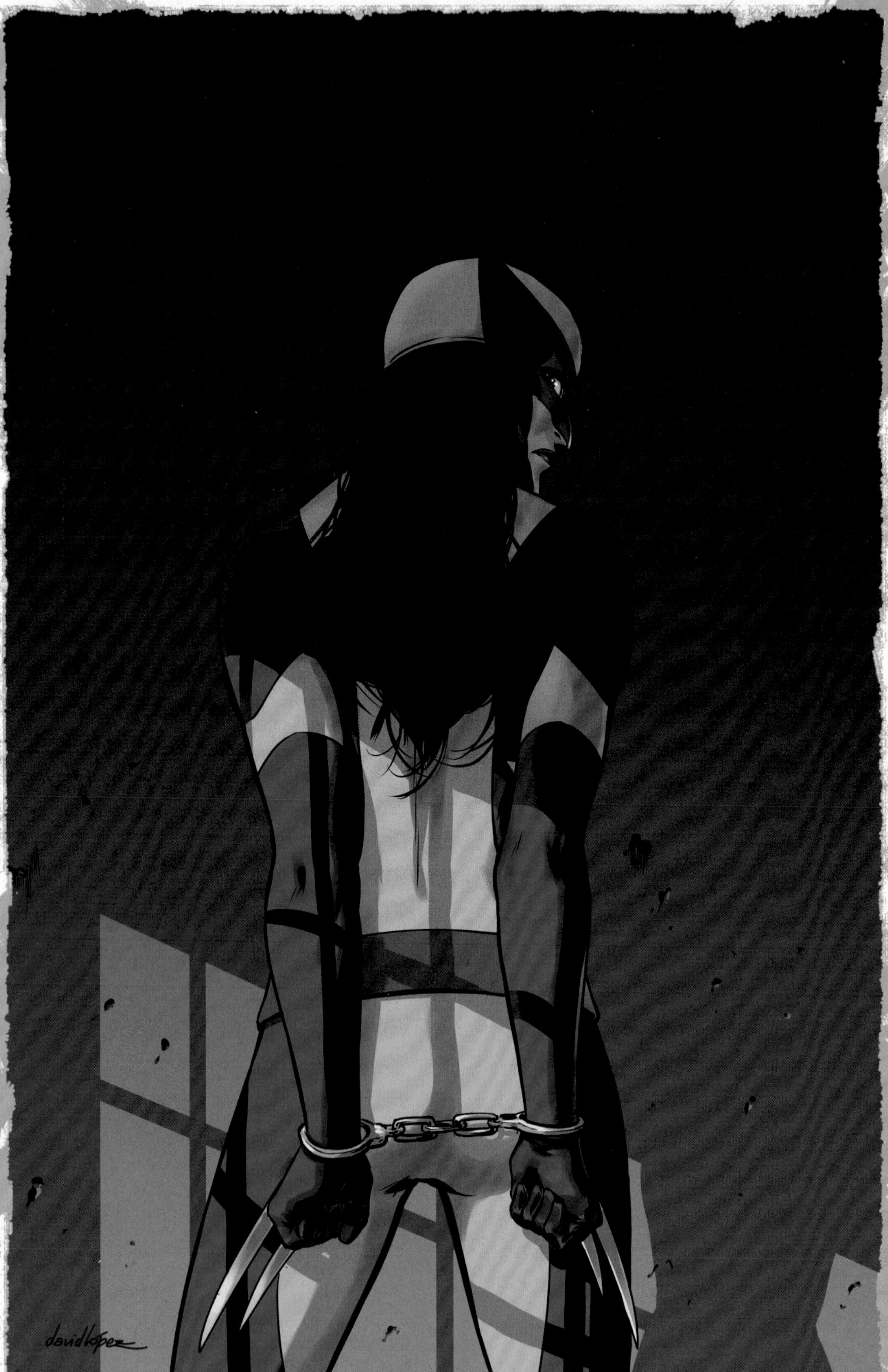

14

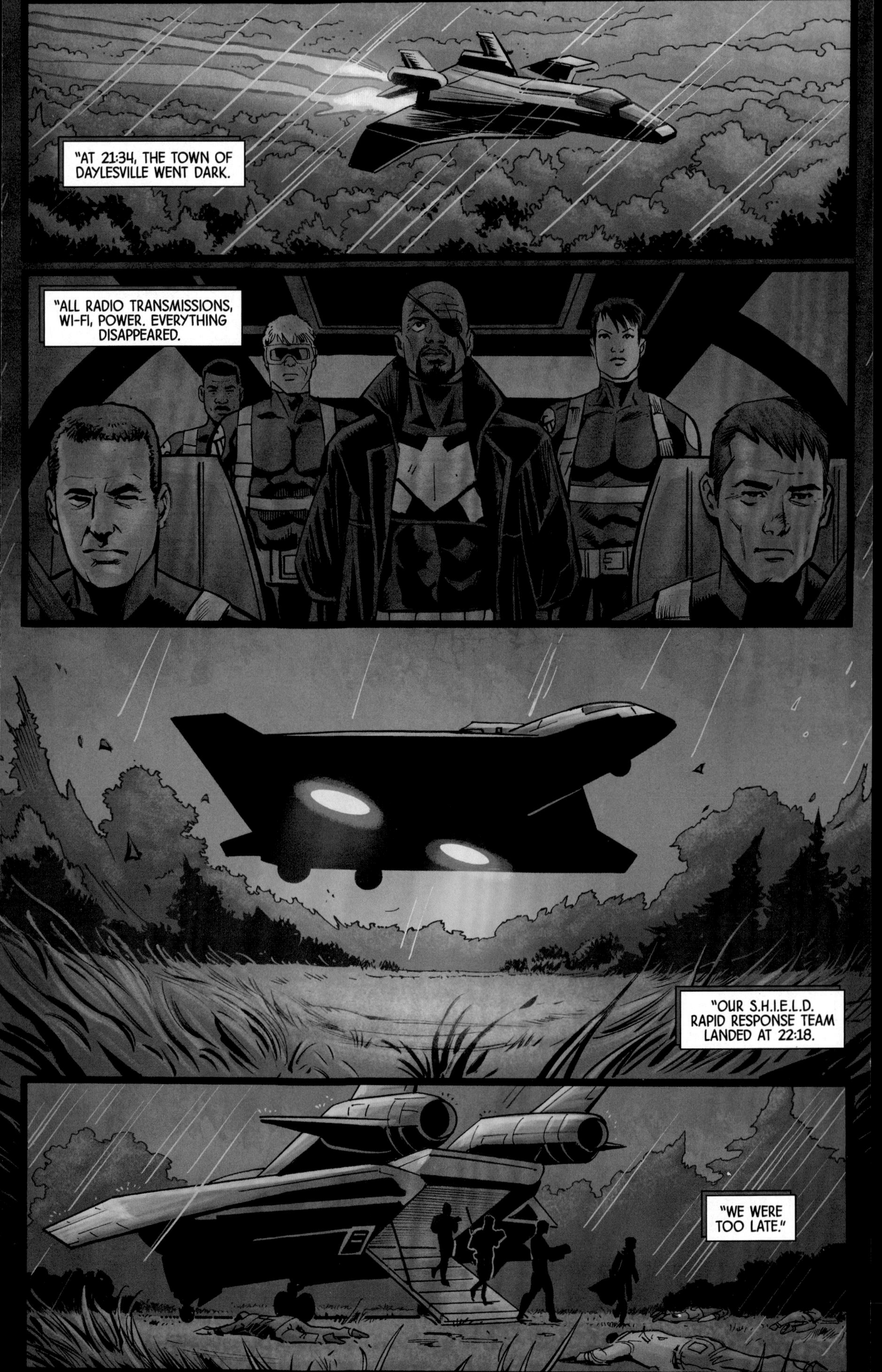
"AT 21:34, THE TOWN OF DAYLESVILLE WENT DARK.
"ALL RADIO TRANSMISSIONS, WI-FI, POWER. EVERYTHING DISAPPEARED.
"OUR S.H.I.E.L.D. RAPID RESPONSE TEAM LANDED AT 22:18.
"WE WERE TOO LATE."

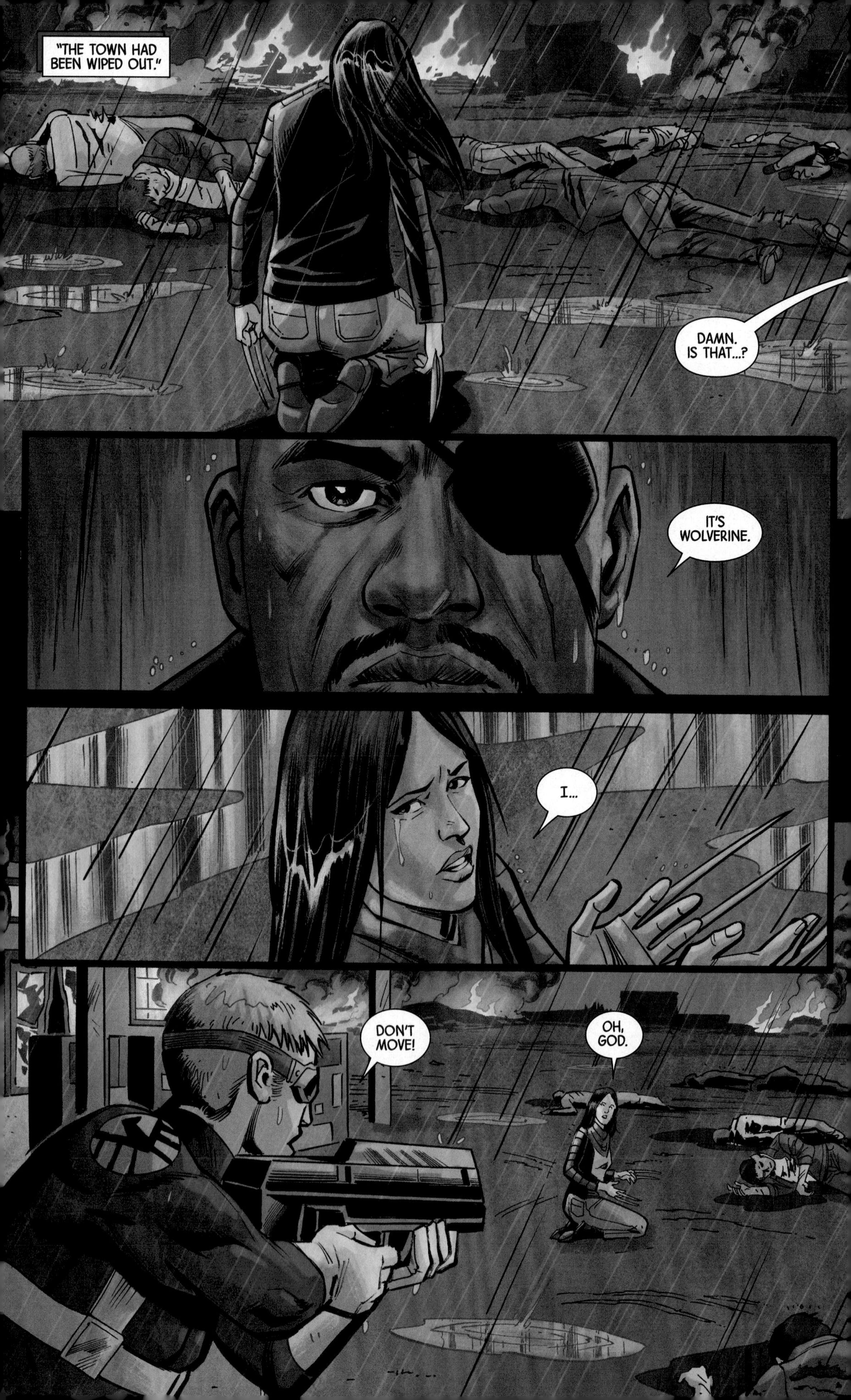
"THE TOWN HAD BEEN WIPED OUT."
DAMN. IS THAT...?
IT'S WOLVERINE.
I...
DON'T MOVE!
OH, GOD.

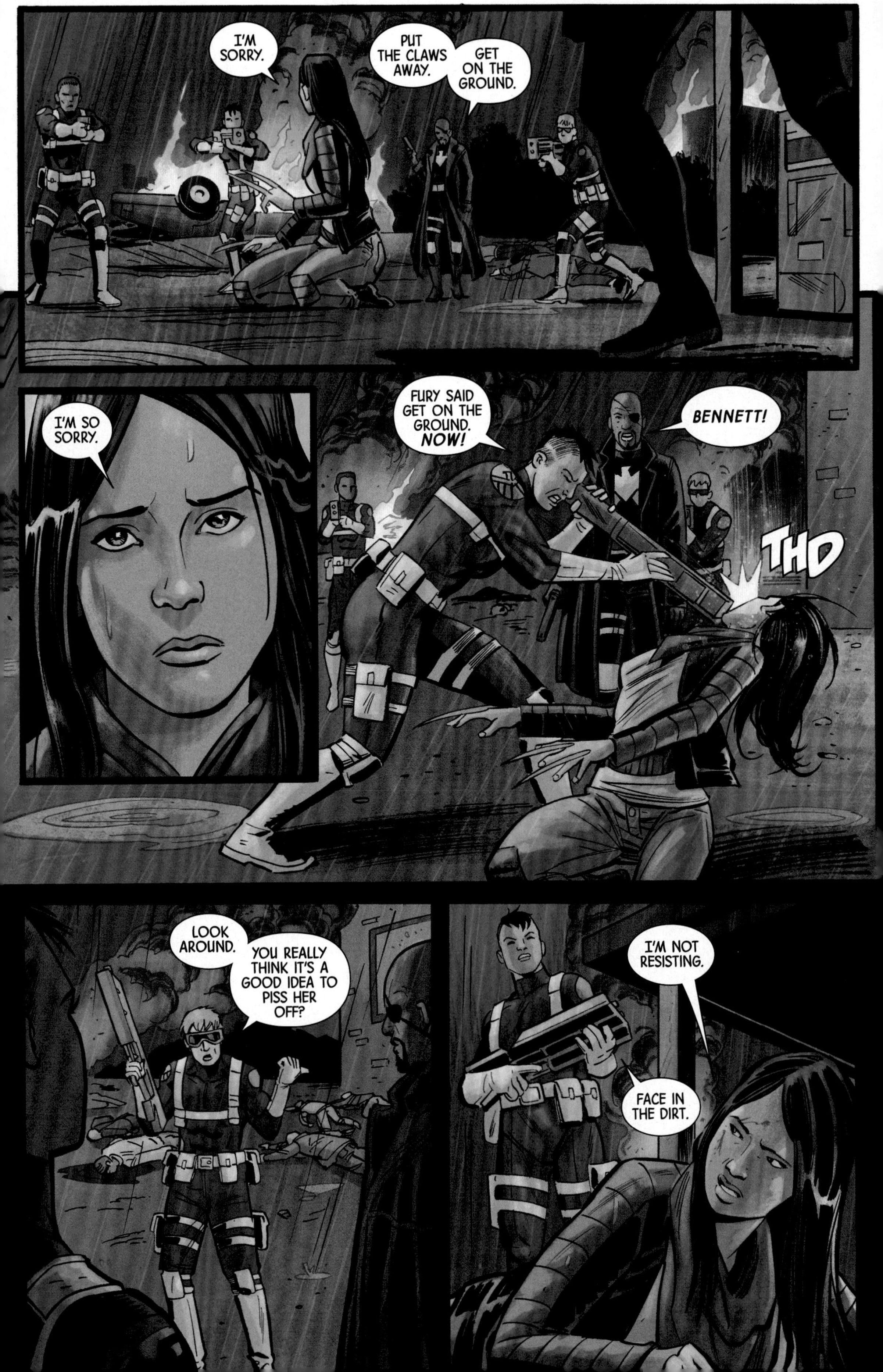
I'M SORRY.
PUT THE CLAWS AWAY.
GET ON THE GROUND.
I'M SO SORRY.
FURY SAID GET ON THE GROUND. NOW!
BENNETT!
THD
LOOK AROUND.
YOU REALLY THINK IT'S A GOOD IDEA TO PISS HER OFF?
I'M NOT RESISTING.
FACE IN THE DIRT.

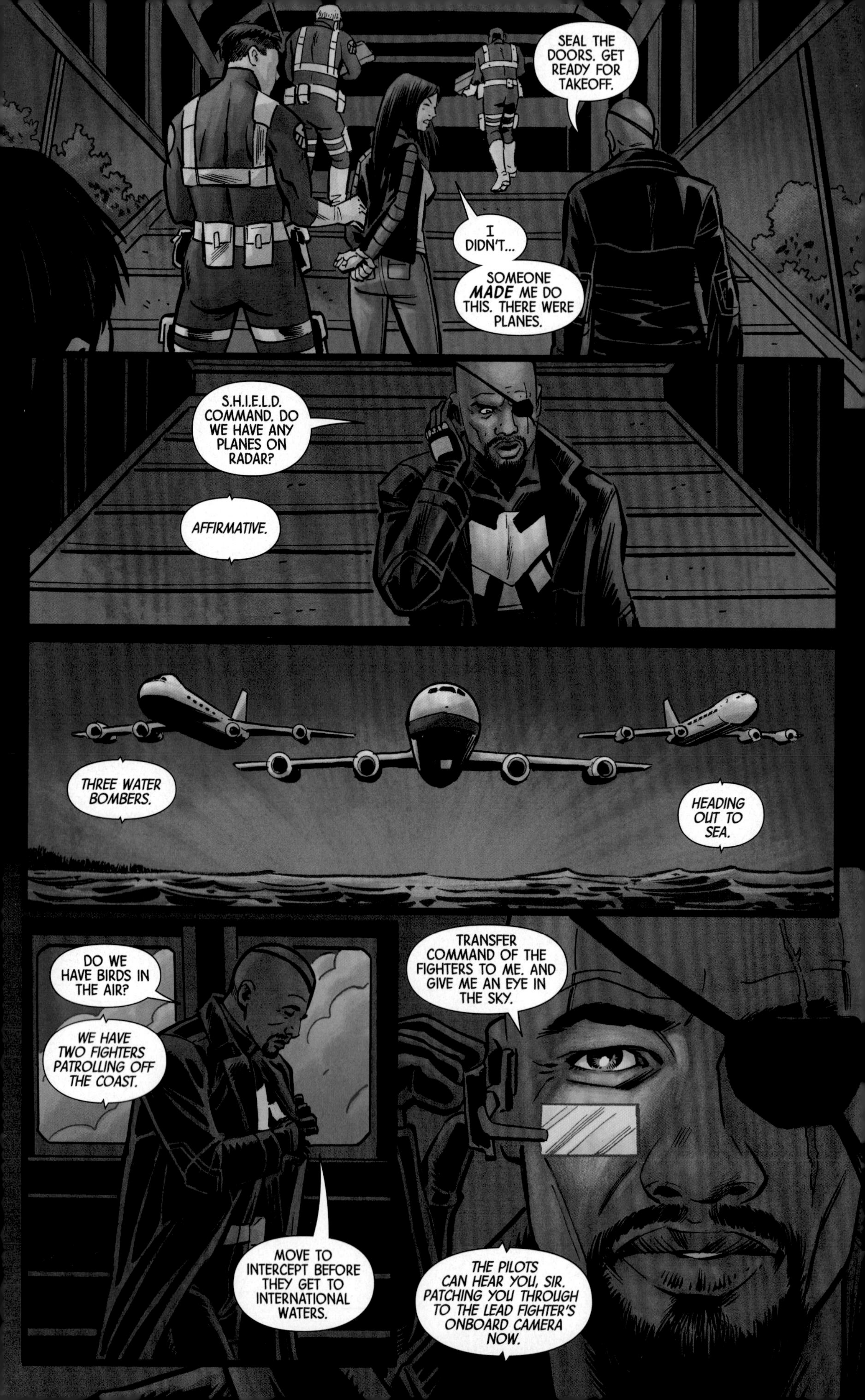
SEAL THE DOORS. GET READY FOR TAKEOFF.
I DIDN'T...
SOMEONE MADE ME DO THIS. THERE WERE PLANES.
S.H.I.E.L.D. COMMAND. DO WE HAVE ANY PLANES ON RADAR?
AFFIRMATIVE.
THREE WATER BOMBERS.
HEADING OUT TO SEA.
DO WE HAVE BIRDS IN THE AIR?
WE HAVE TWO FIGHTERS PATROLLING OFF THE COAST.
MOVE TO INTERCEPT BEFORE THEY GET TO INTERNATIONAL WATERS.
TRANSFER COMMAND OF THE FIGHTERS TO ME. AND GIVE ME AN EYE IN THE SKY.
THE PILOTS CAN HEAR YOU, SIR. PATCHING YOU THROUGH TO THE LEAD FIGHTER'S ONBOARD CAMERA NOW.

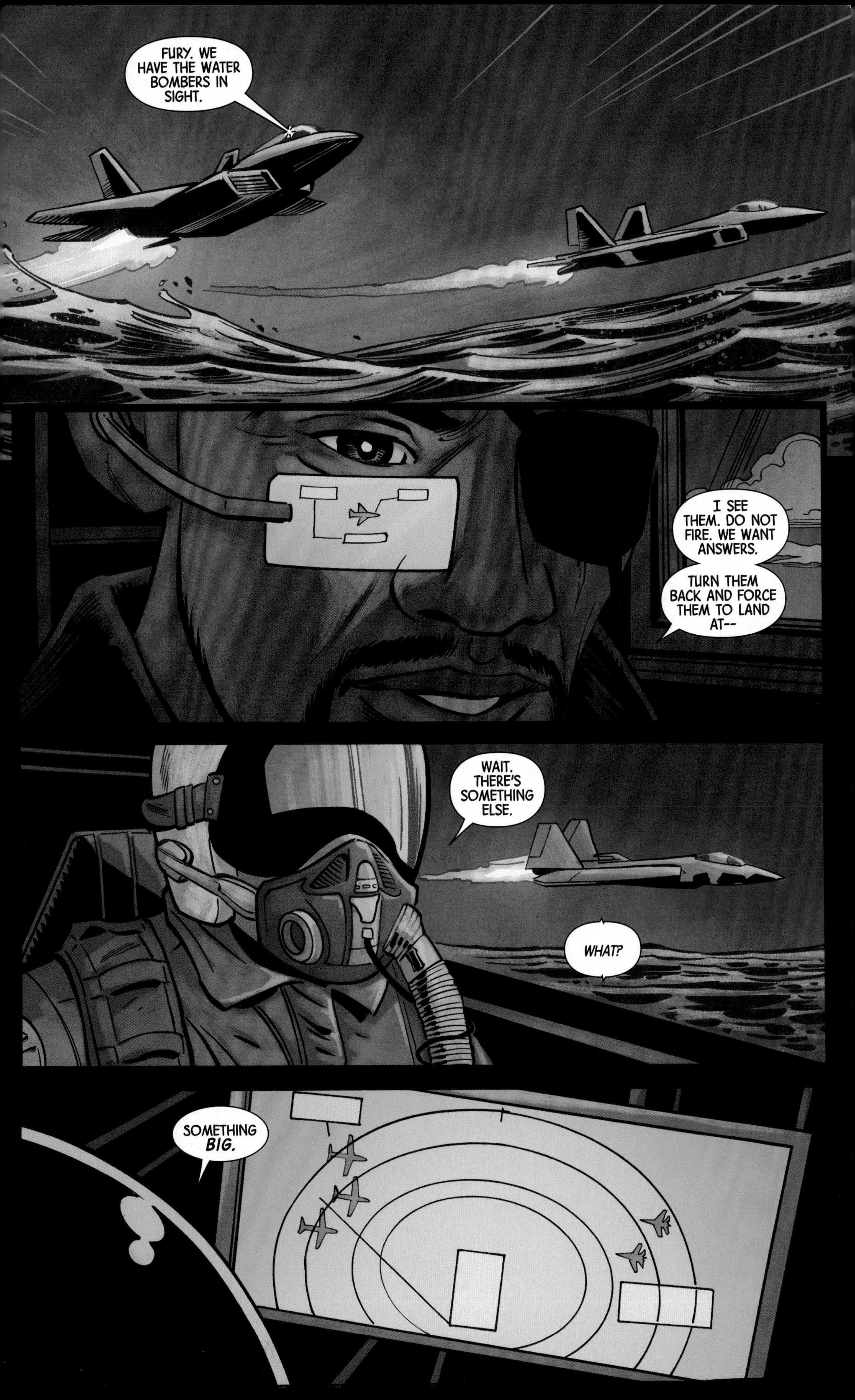
FURY. WE HAVE THE WATER BOMBERS IN SIGHT.
I SEE THEM. DO NOT FIRE. WE WANT ANSWERS.
TURN THEM BACK AND FORCE THEM TO LAND AT--
WAIT. THERE'S SOMETHING ELSE.
WHAT?
SOMETHING BIG.

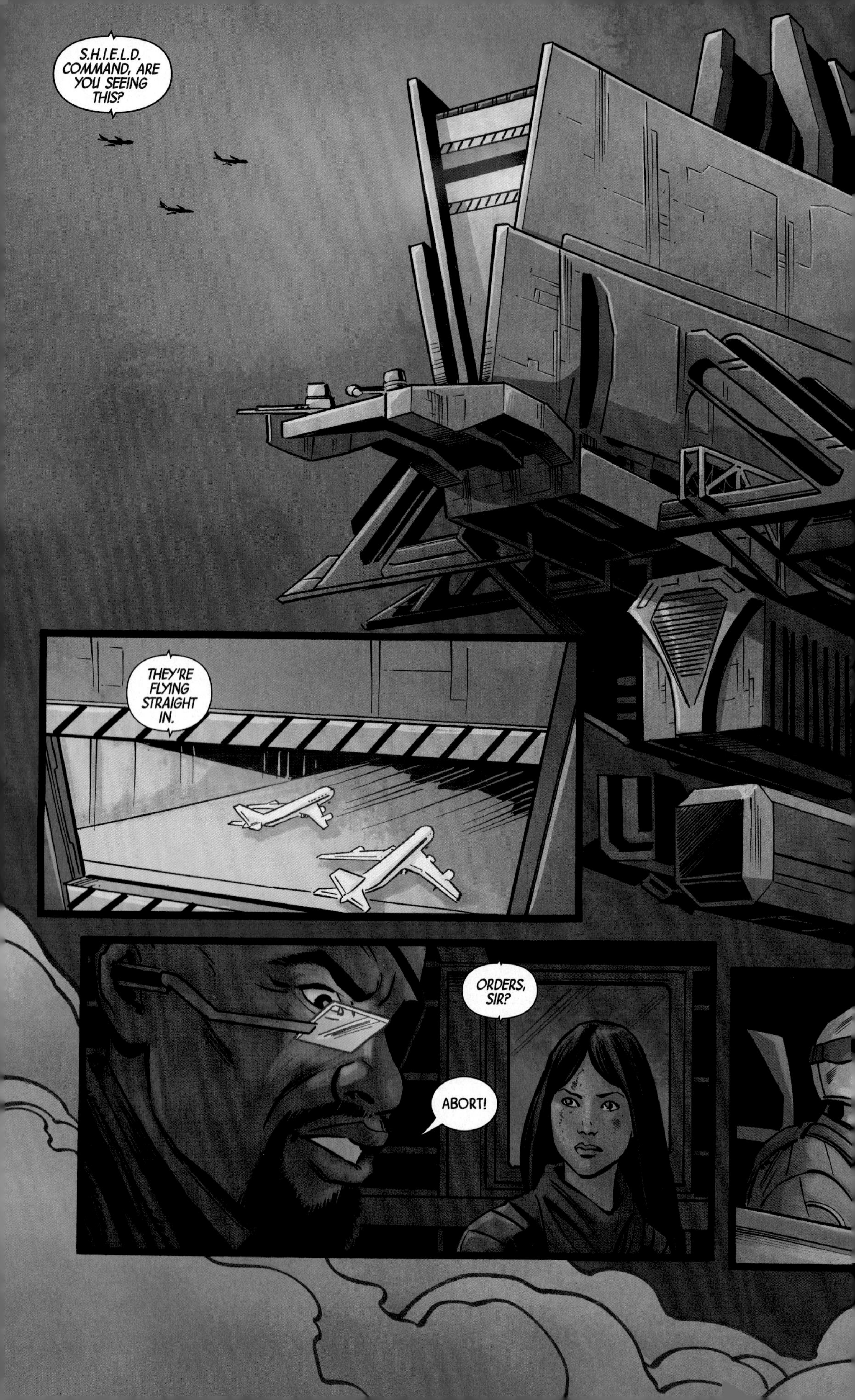
S.H.I.E.L.D. COMMAND, ARE YOU SEEING THIS?
THEY'RE FLYING STRAIGHT IN.
ORDERS, SIR?
ABORT!

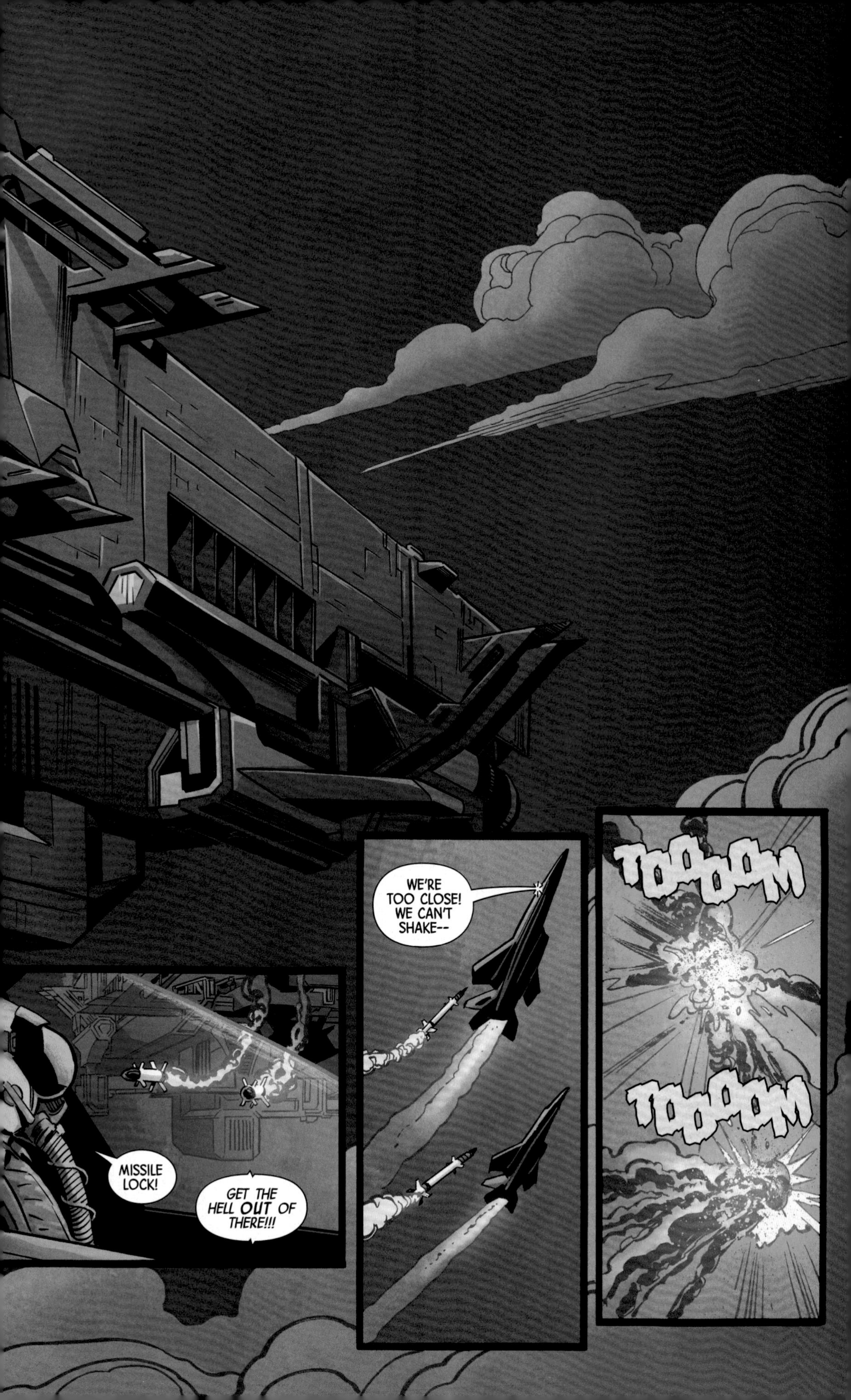
MISSILE LOCK!
GET THE HELL OUT OF THERE!!!
WE'RE TOO CLOSE! WE CAN'T SHAKE--
TOOOOM
TOOOOM

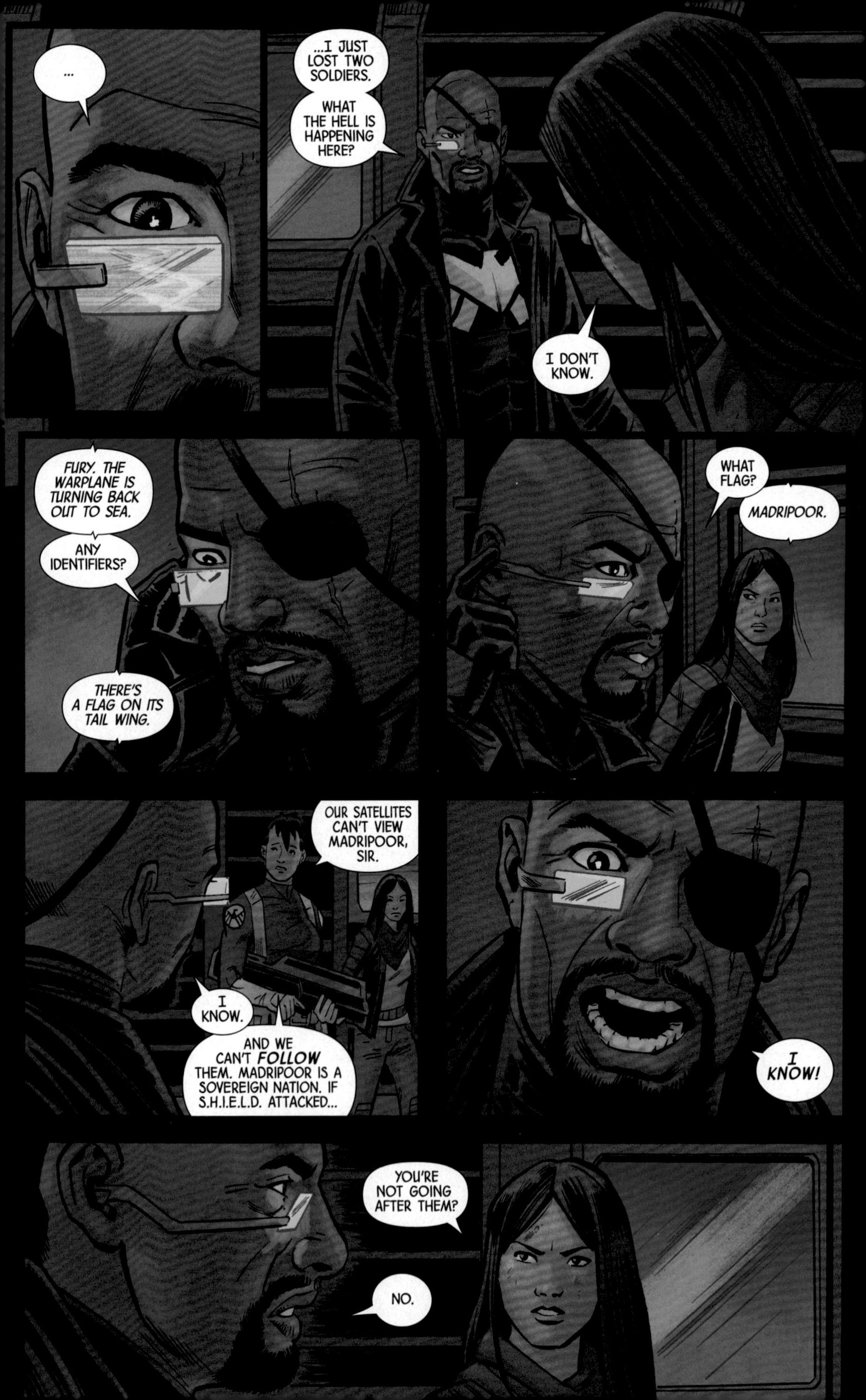
...
...I JUST LOST TWO SOLDIERS.
WHAT THE HELL IS HAPPENING HERE?
I DON'T KNOW.
FURY. THE WARPLANE IS TURNING BACK OUT TO SEA.
ANY IDENTIFIERS?
THERE'S A FLAG ON ITS TAIL WING.
WHAT FLAG?
MADRIPOOR.
OUR SATELLITES CAN'T VIEW MADRIPOOR, SIR.
I KNOW.
AND WE CAN'T FOLLOW THEM. MADRIPOOR IS A SOVEREIGN NATION. IF S.H.I.E.L.D. ATTACKED...
I KNOW!
YOU'RE NOT GOING AFTER THEM?
NO.

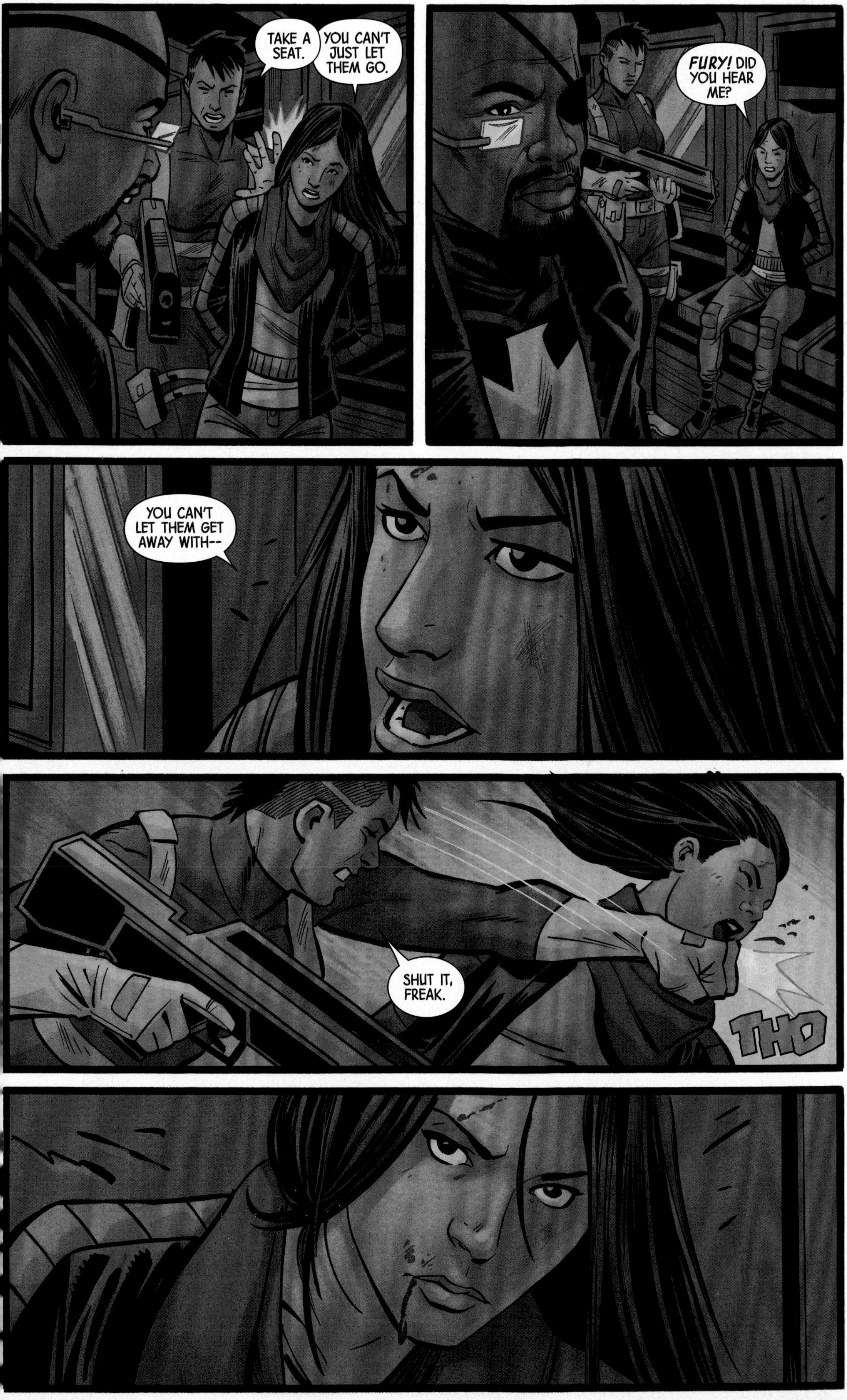
TAKE A SEAT.
YOU CAN'T JUST LET THEM GO.
FURY! DID YOU HEAR ME?
YOU CAN'T LET THEM GET AWAY WITH--
SHUT IT, FREAK.
THD

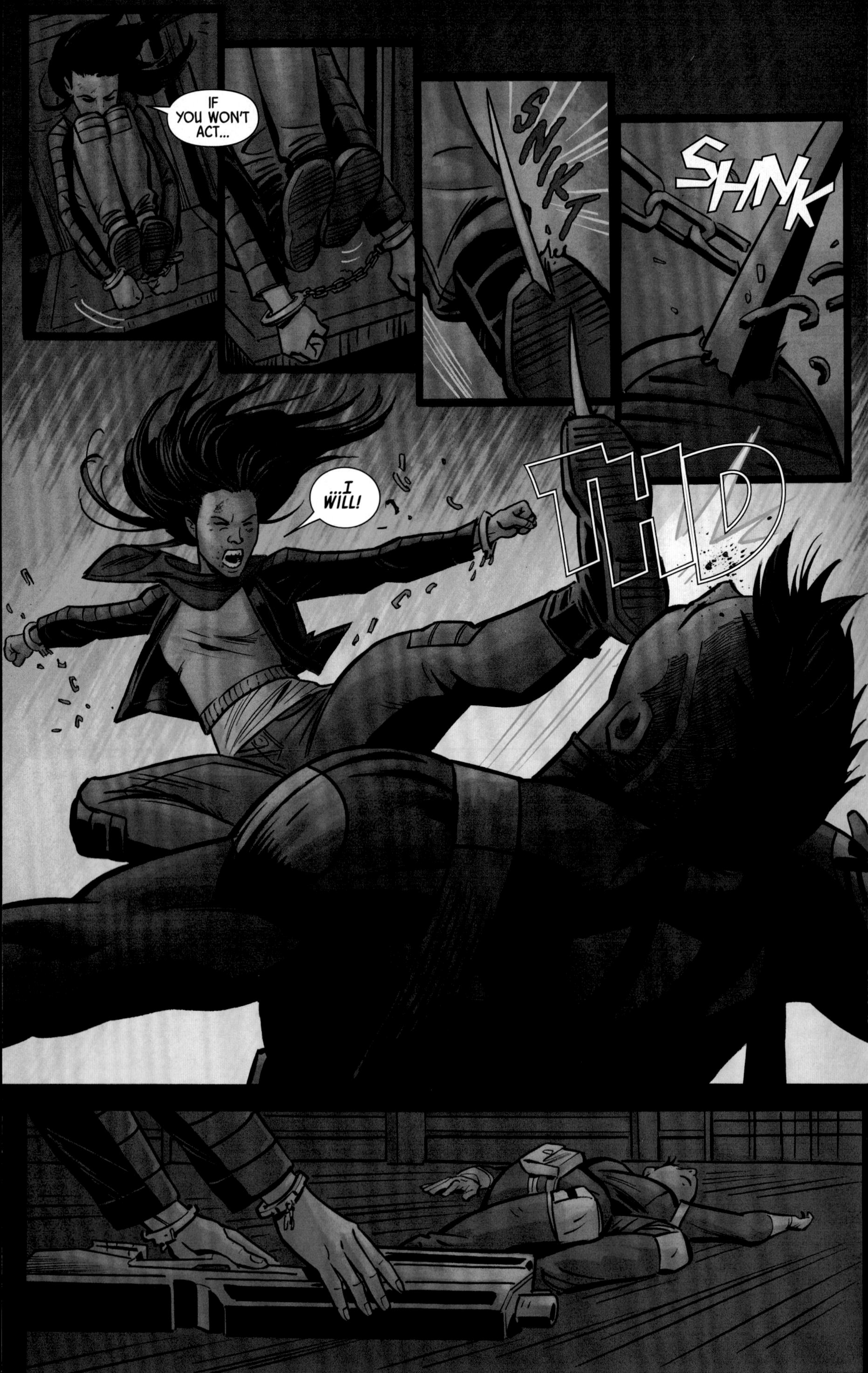
IF YOU WON'T ACT...
SNIKT
SHNK
...I WILL!
THD

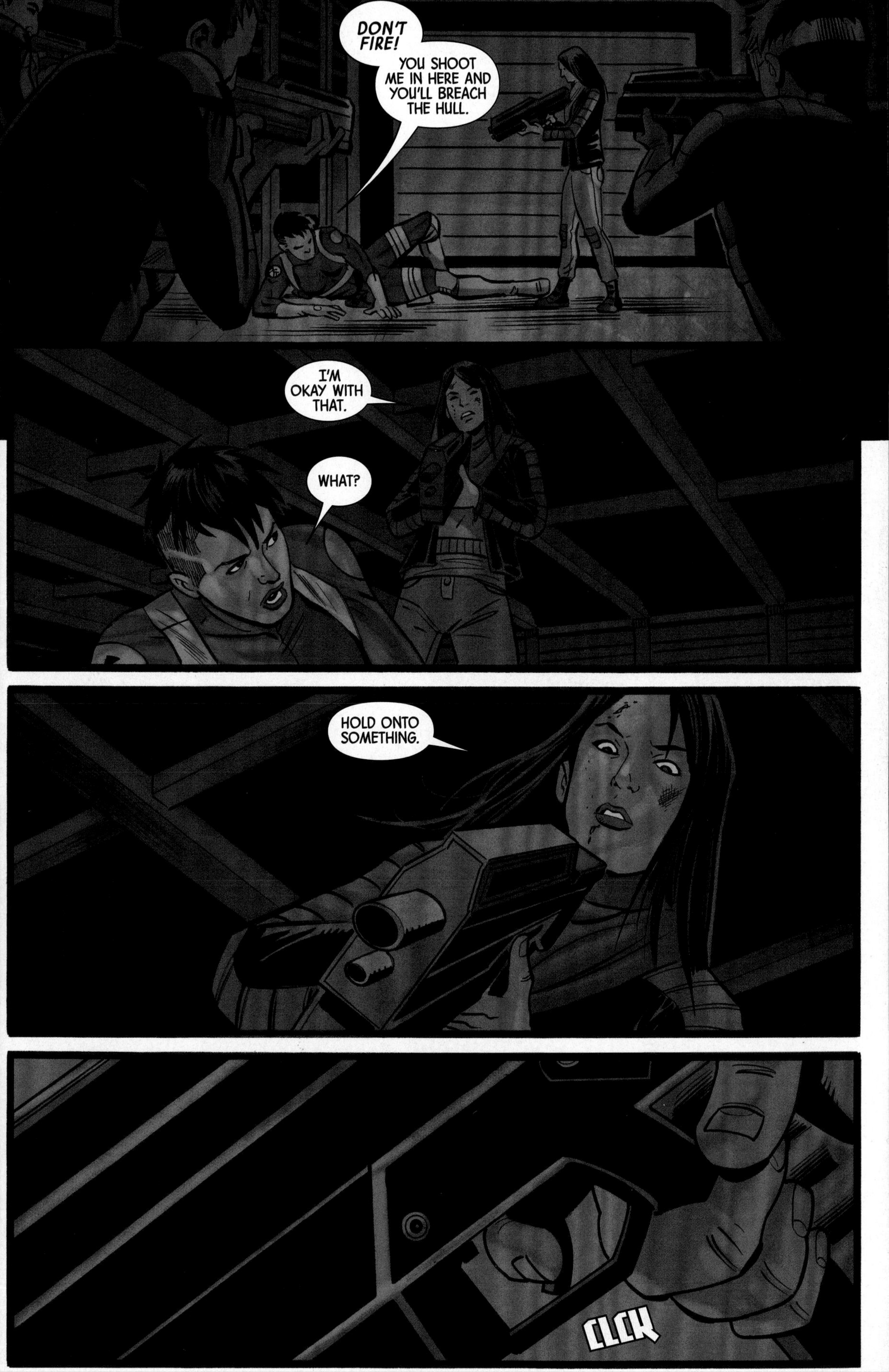
DON'T FIRE!
YOU SHOOT ME IN HERE AND YOU'LL BREACH THE HULL.
I'M OKAY WITH THAT.
WHAT?
HOLD ONTO SOMETHING.
CLCK

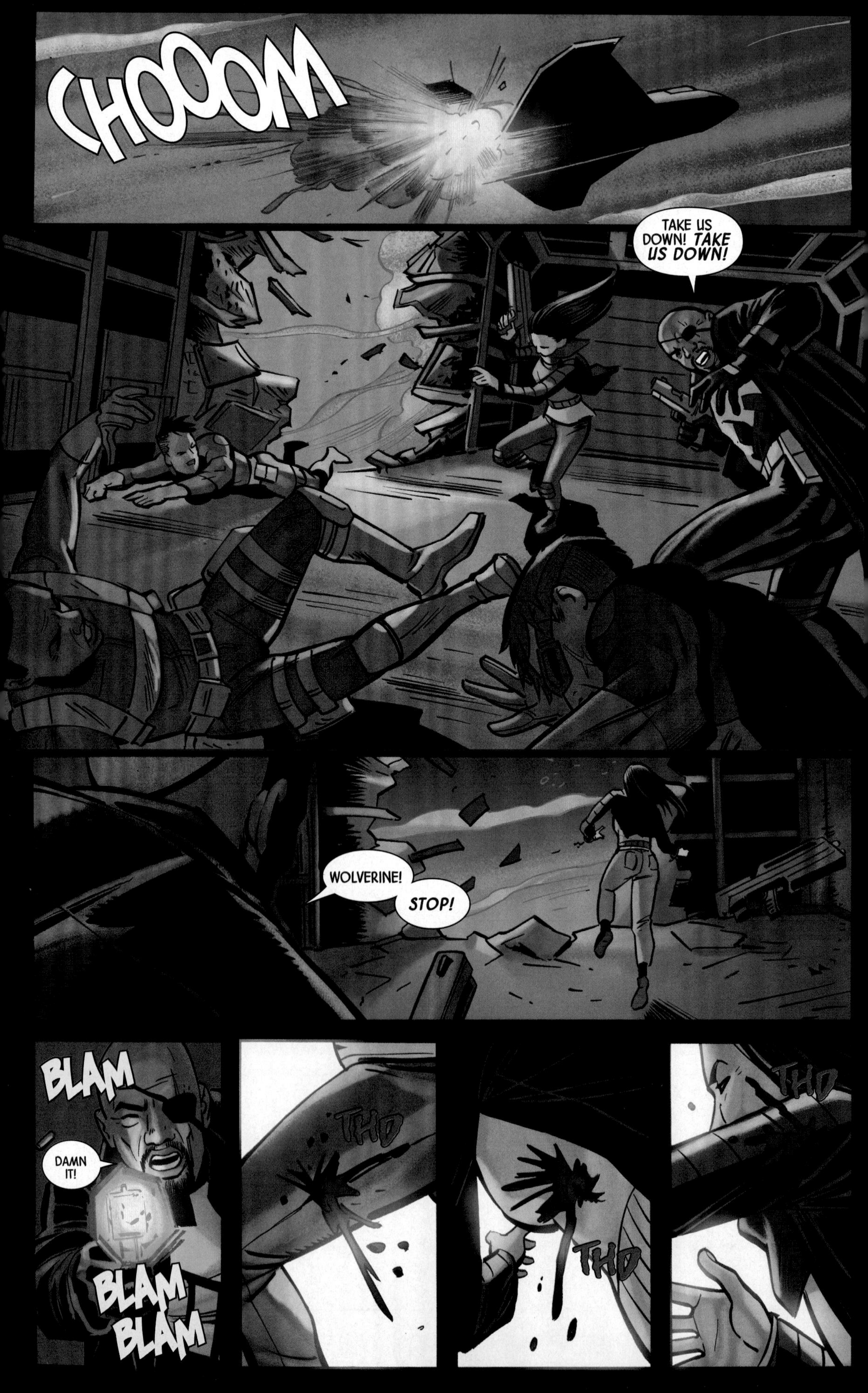
CHOOOM
TAKE US DOWN! TAKE US DOWN!
WOLVERINE!
STOP!
BLAM
DAMN IT!
BLAM BLAM
THD
THD
THD

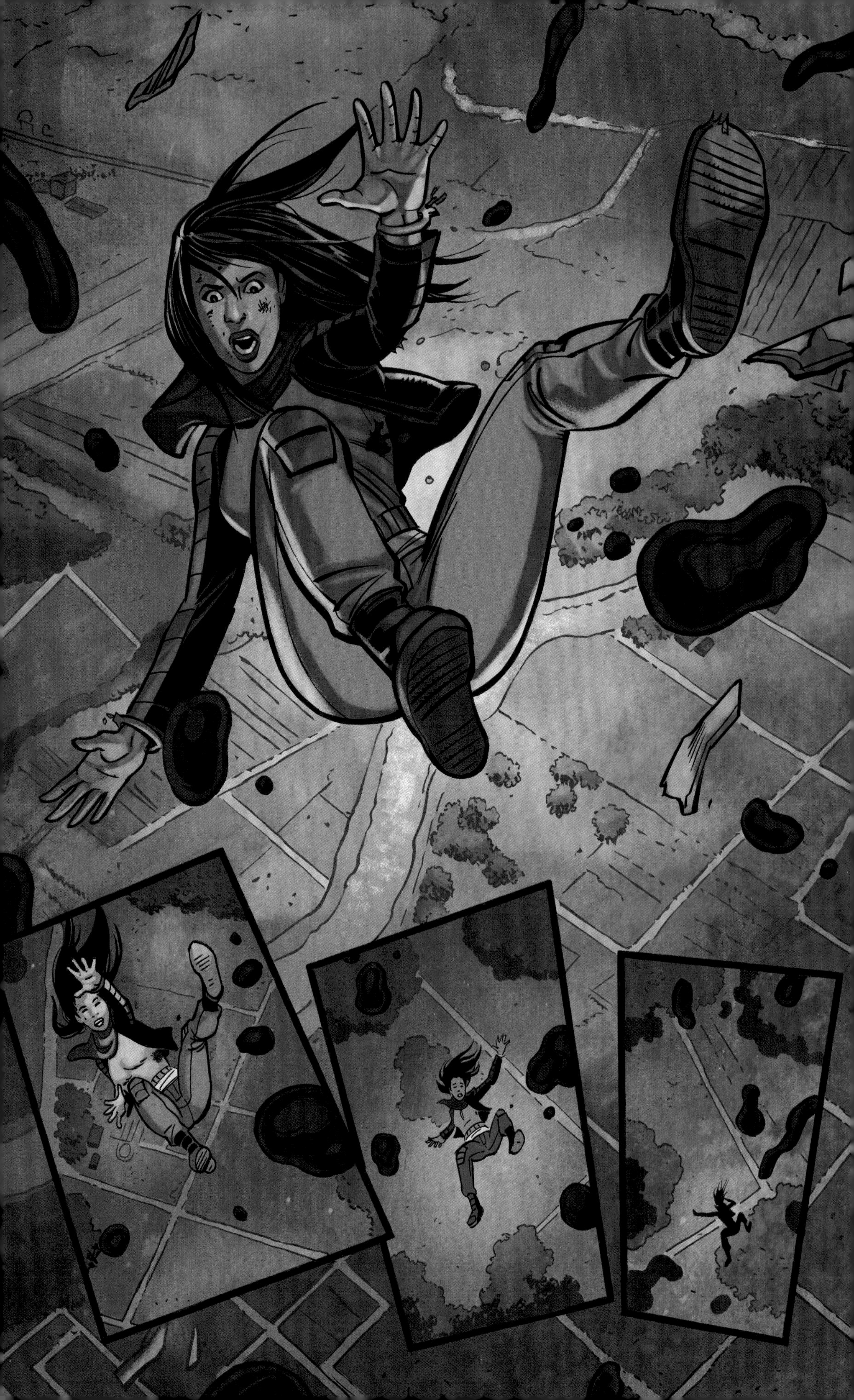

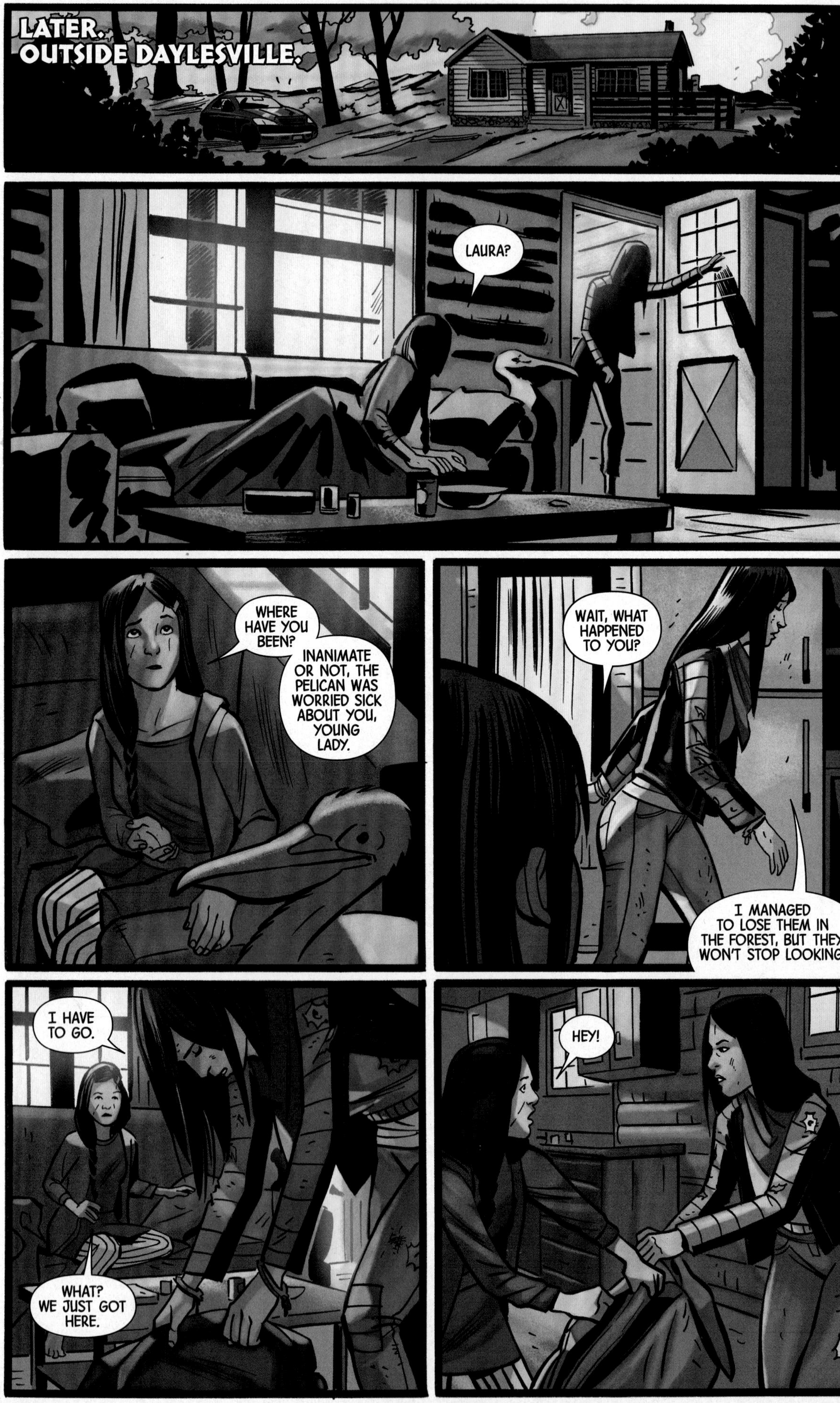
LATER.
OUTSIDE DAYLESVILLE.
LAURA?
WHERE HAVE YOU BEEN?
INANIMATE OR NOT, THE PELICAN WAS WORRIED SICK ABOUT YOU, YOUNG LADY.
WAIT, WHAT HAPPENED TO YOU?
I MANAGED TO LOSE THEM IN THE FOREST, BUT THEY WON'T STOP LOOKING.
I HAVE TO GO.
WHAT? WE JUST GOT HERE.
HEY!

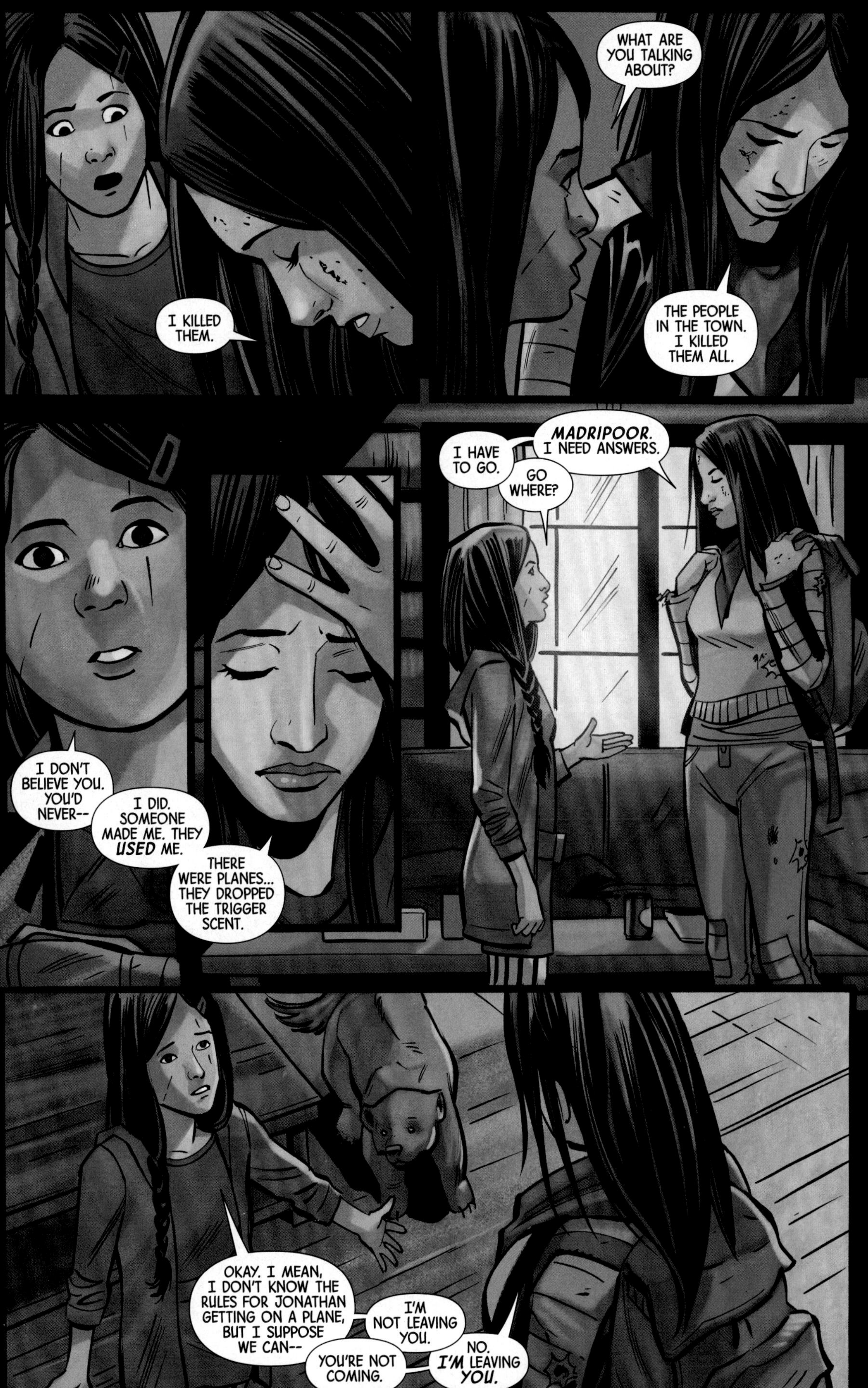
I KILLED THEM.
WHAT ARE YOU TALKING ABOUT?
THE PEOPLE IN THE TOWN. I KILLED THEM ALL.
I DON'T BELIEVE YOU. YOU'D NEVER--
I DID. SOMEONE MADE ME. THEY USED ME.
THERE WERE PLANES... THEY DROPPED THE TRIGGER SCENT.
I HAVE TO GO.
GO WHERE?
MADRIPOOR. I NEED ANSWERS.
OKAY. I MEAN, I DON'T KNOW THE RULES FOR JONATHAN GETTING ON A PLANE, BUT I SUPPOSE WE CAN--
YOU'RE NOT COMING.
I'M NOT LEAVING YOU.
NO. I'M LEAVING YOU.

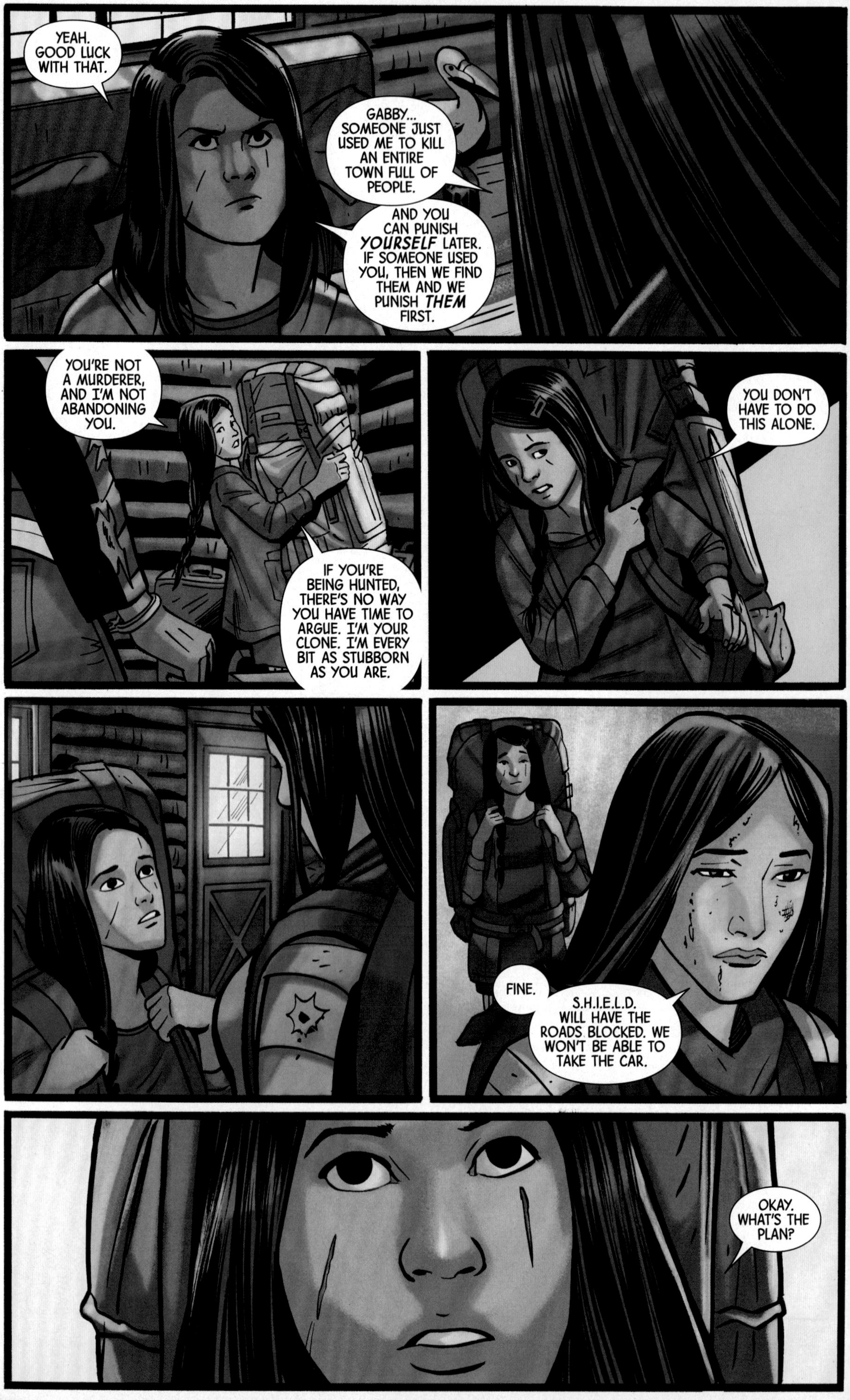
YEAH. GOOD LUCK WITH THAT.
GABBY... SOMEONE JUST USED ME TO KILL AN ENTIRE TOWN FULL OF PEOPLE.
AND YOU CAN PUNISH *YOURSELF* LATER. IF SOMEONE USED YOU, THEN WE FIND THEM AND WE PUNISH *THEM* FIRST.
YOU'RE NOT A MURDERER, AND I'M NOT ABANDONING YOU.
IF YOU'RE BEING HUNTED, THERE'S NO WAY YOU HAVE TIME TO ARGUE. I'M YOUR CLONE. I'M EVERY BIT AS STUBBORN AS YOU ARE.
YOU DON'T HAVE TO DO THIS ALONE.
FINE.
S.H.I.E.L.D. WILL HAVE THE ROADS BLOCKED. WE WON'T BE ABLE TO TAKE THE CAR.
OKAY. WHAT'S THE PLAN?

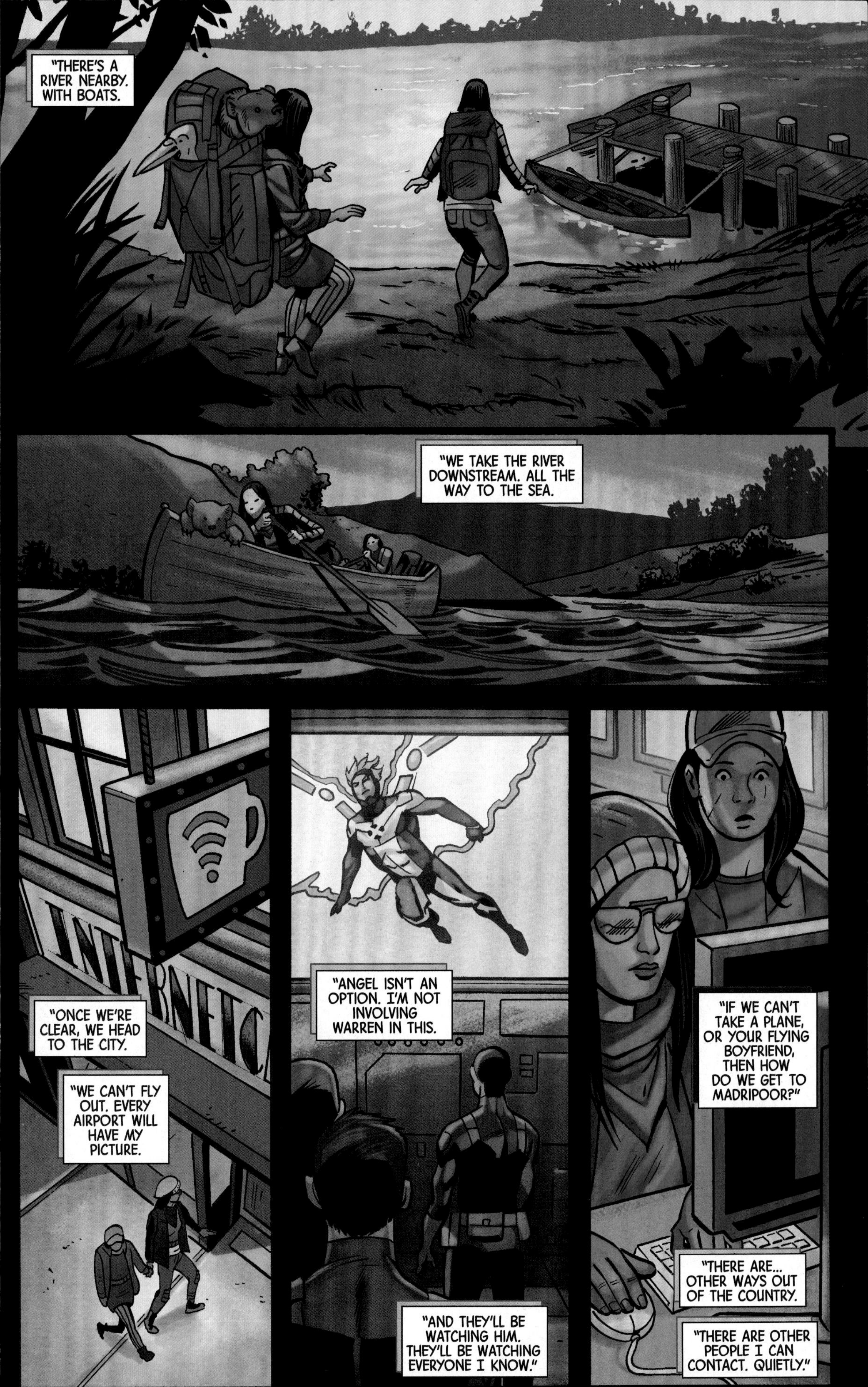
"THERE'S A RIVER NEARBY. WITH BOATS.
"WE TAKE THE RIVER DOWNSTREAM. ALL THE WAY TO THE SEA.
"ONCE WE'RE CLEAR, WE HEAD TO THE CITY.
"WE CAN'T FLY OUT. EVERY AIRPORT WILL HAVE MY PICTURE.
"ANGEL ISN'T AN OPTION. I'M NOT INVOLVING WARREN IN THIS.
"AND THEY'LL BE WATCHING HIM. THEY'LL BE WATCHING EVERYONE I KNOW."
"IF WE CAN'T TAKE A PLANE, OR YOUR FLYING BOYFRIEND, THEN HOW DO WE GET TO MADRIPOOR?"
"THERE ARE... OTHER WAYS OUT OF THE COUNTRY.
"THERE ARE OTHER PEOPLE I CAN CONTACT. QUIETLY."

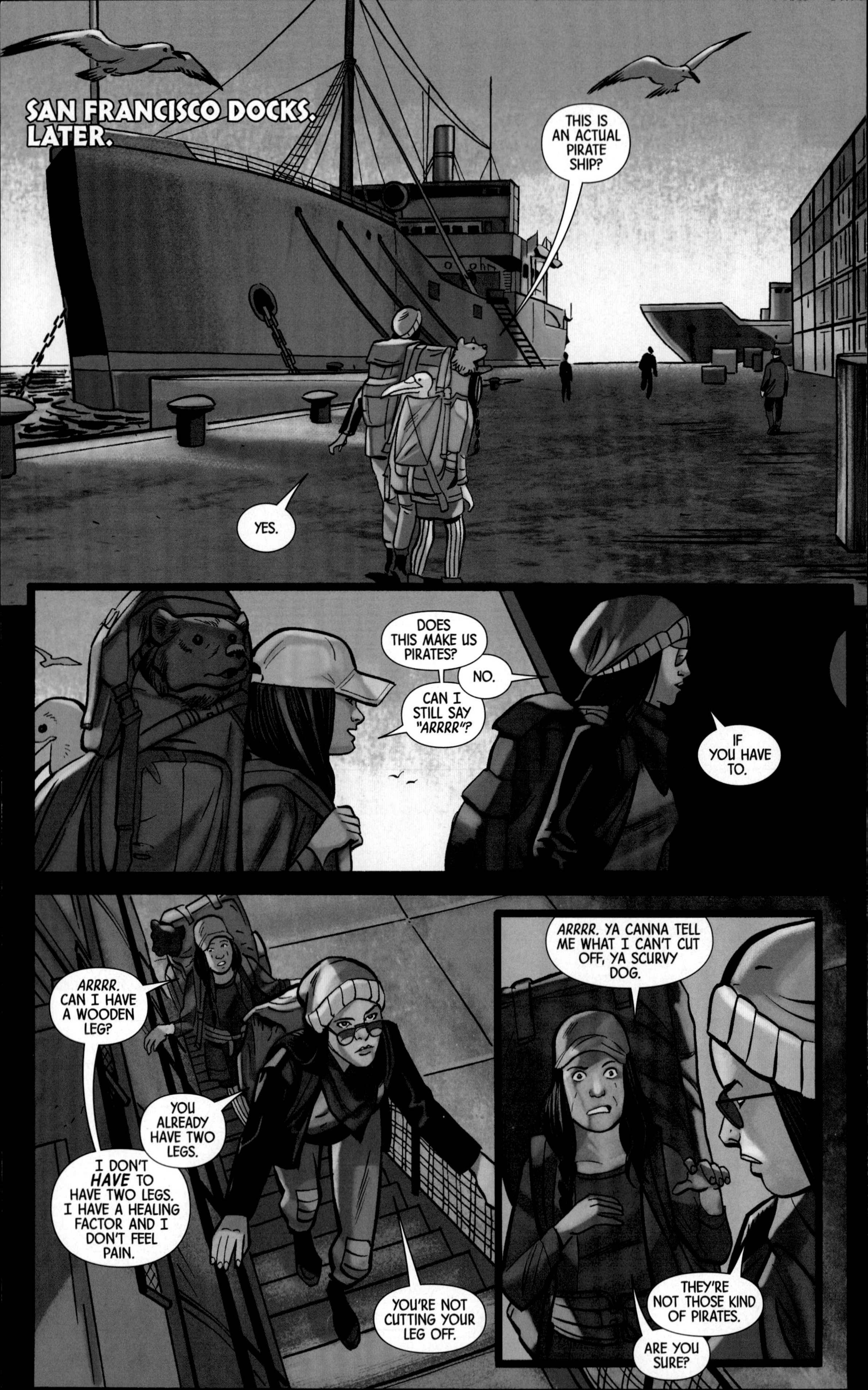
SAN FRANCISCO DOCKS. LATER.
THIS IS AN ACTUAL PIRATE SHIP?
YES.
DOES THIS MAKE US PIRATES?
NO.
CAN I STILL SAY "ARRRR"?
IF YOU HAVE TO.
ARRRR. CAN I HAVE A WOODEN LEG?
YOU ALREADY HAVE TWO LEGS.
I DON'T HAVE TO HAVE TWO LEGS. I HAVE A HEALING FACTOR AND I DON'T FEEL PAIN.
YOU'RE NOT CUTTING YOUR LEG OFF.
ARRRR. YA CANNA TELL ME WHAT I CAN'T CUT OFF, YA SCURVY DOG.
THEY'RE NOT THOSE KIND OF PIRATES.
ARE YOU SURE?

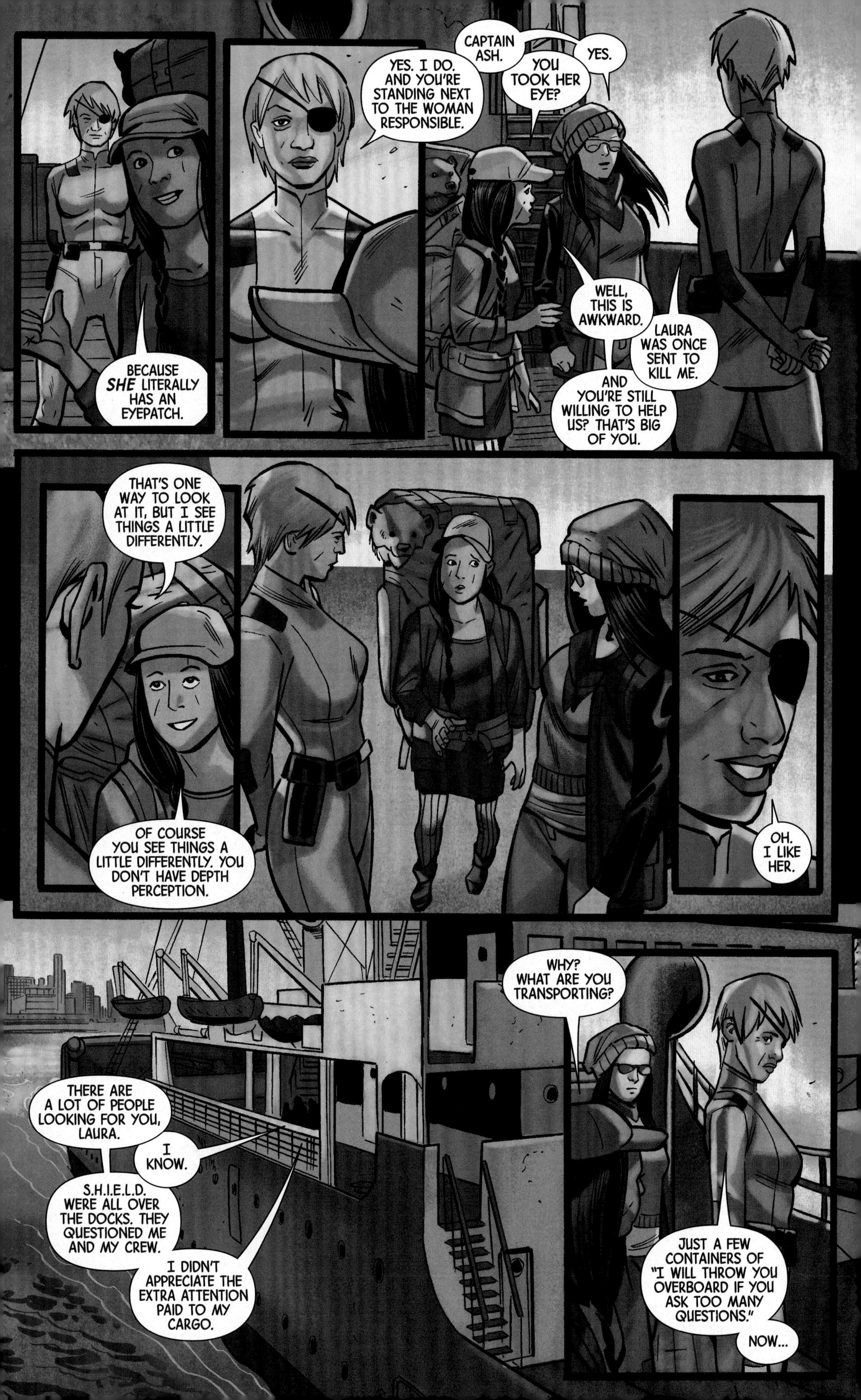
BECAUSE SHE LITERALLY HAS AN EYEPATCH.
YES. I DO. AND YOU'RE STANDING NEXT TO THE WOMAN RESPONSIBLE.
CAPTAIN ASH.
YOU TOOK HER EYE?
YES.
WELL, THIS IS AWKWARD.
LAURA WAS ONCE SENT TO KILL ME.
AND YOU'RE STILL WILLING TO HELP US? THAT'S BIG OF YOU.
THAT'S ONE WAY TO LOOK AT IT, BUT I SEE THINGS A LITTLE DIFFERENTLY.
OF COURSE YOU SEE THINGS A LITTLE DIFFERENTLY. YOU DON'T HAVE DEPTH PERCEPTION.
OH. I LIKE HER.
THERE ARE A LOT OF PEOPLE LOOKING FOR YOU, LAURA.
I KNOW.
S.H.I.E.L.D. WERE ALL OVER THE DOCKS. THEY QUESTIONED ME AND MY CREW.
I DIDN'T APPRECIATE THE EXTRA ATTENTION PAID TO MY CARGO.
WHY? WHAT ARE YOU TRANSPORTING?
JUST A FEW CONTAINERS OF "I WILL THROW YOU OVERBOARD IF YOU ASK TOO MANY QUESTIONS."
NOW...

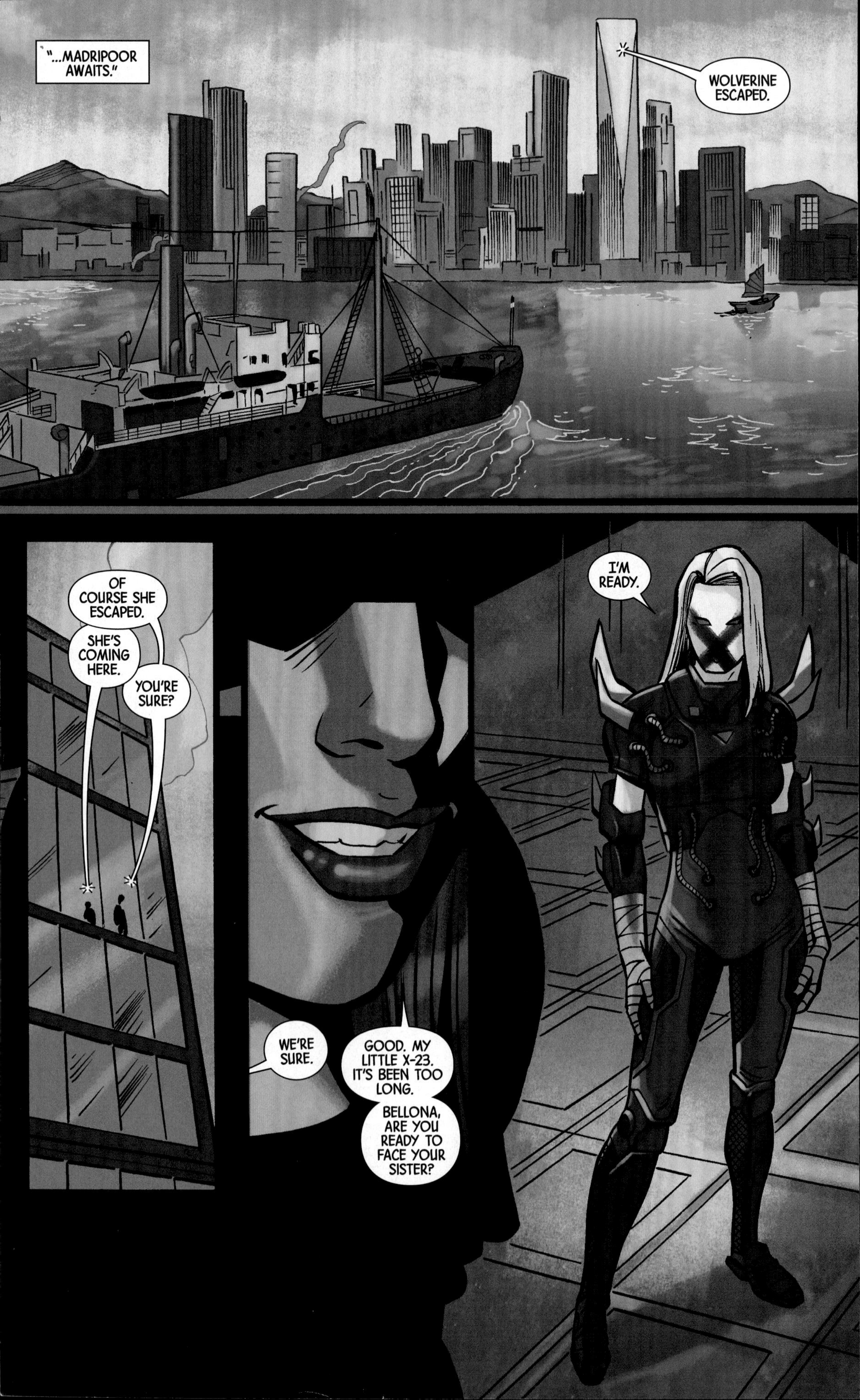
"...MADRIPOOR AWAITS."
WOLVERINE ESCAPED.
OF COURSE SHE ESCAPED.
SHE'S COMING HERE.
YOU'RE SURE?
WE'RE SURE.
GOOD. MY LITTLE X-23. IT'S BEEN TOO LONG.
BELLONA, ARE YOU READY TO FACE YOUR SISTER?
I'M READY.

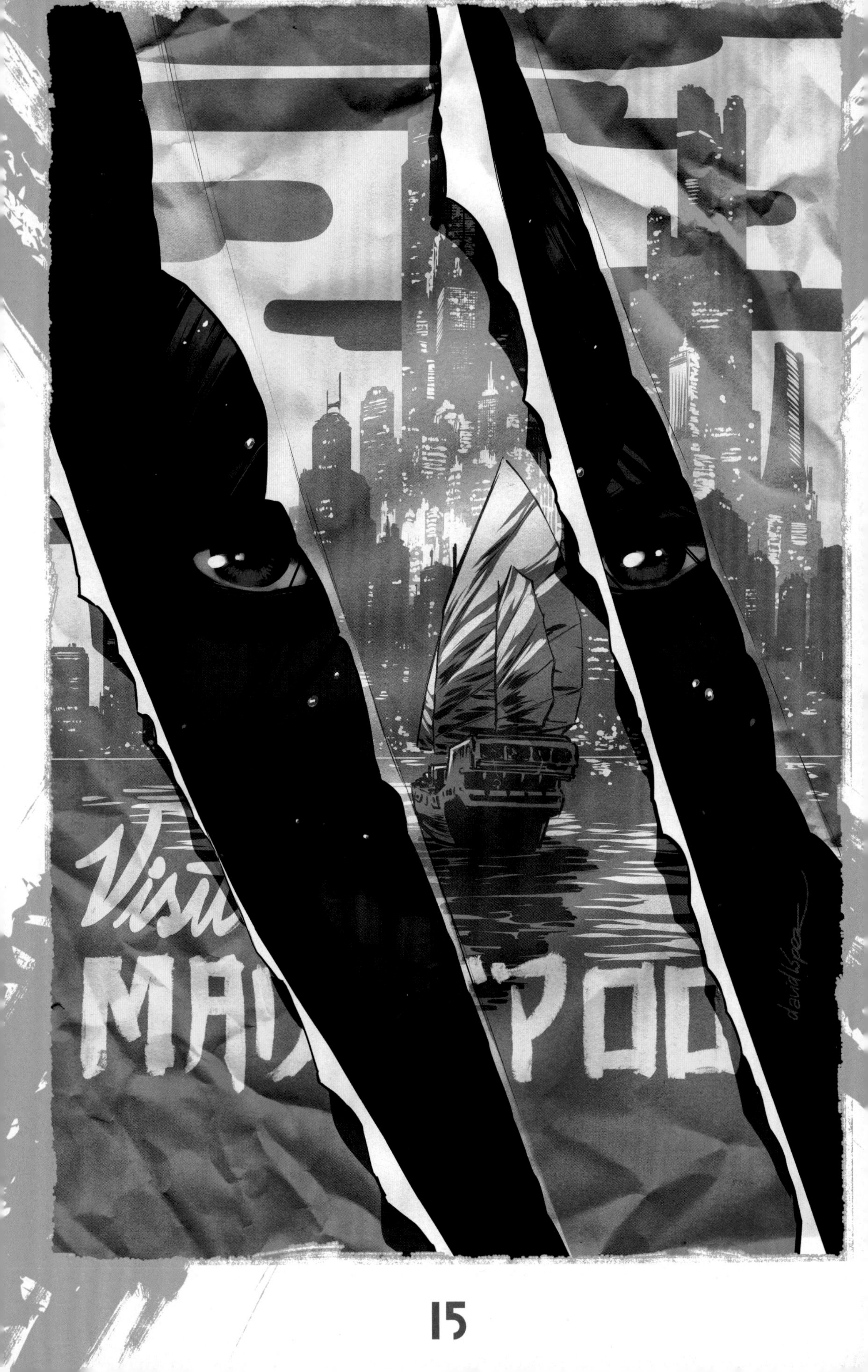

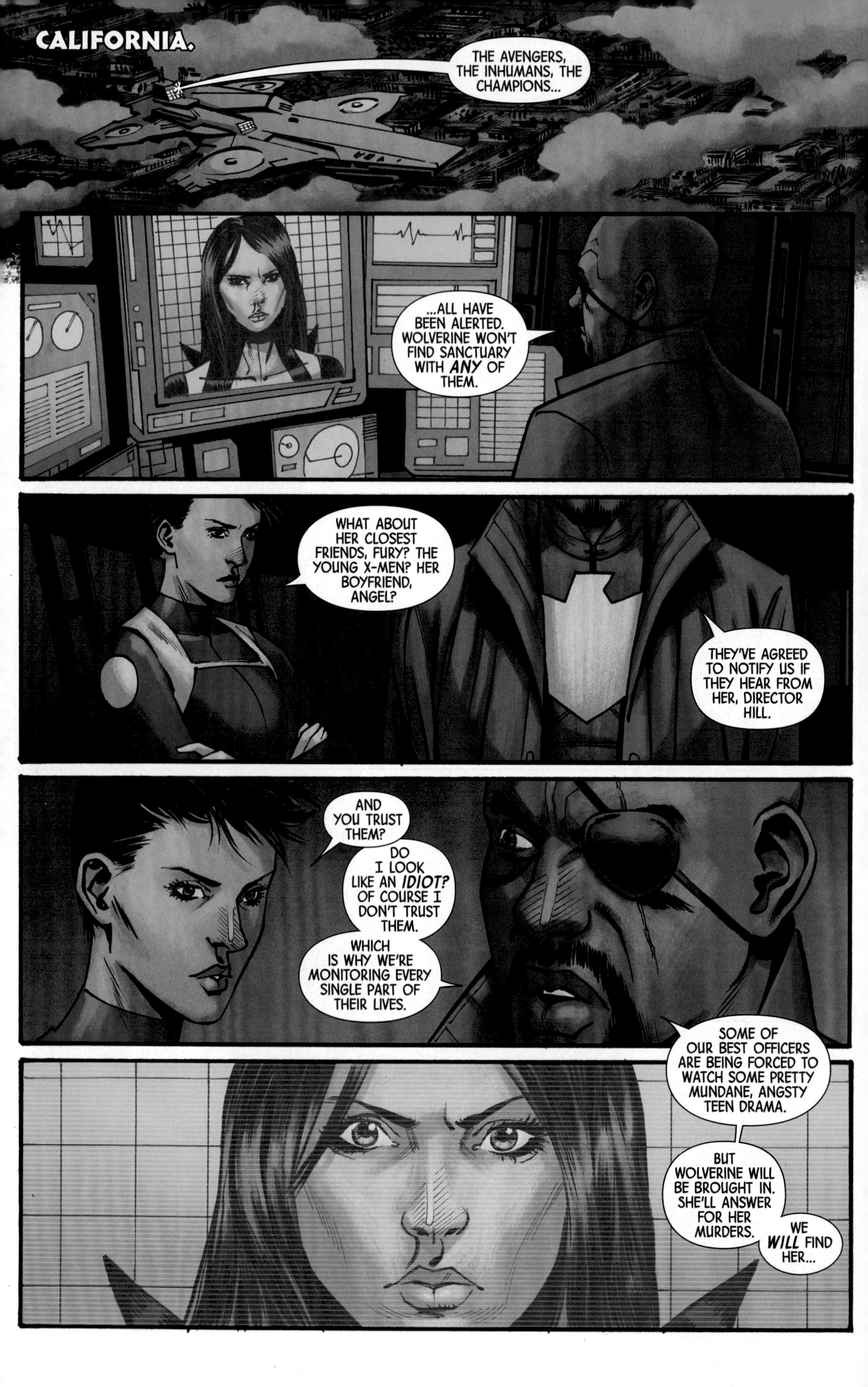
CALIFORNIA.
THE AVENGERS, THE INHUMANS, THE CHAMPIONS...
...ALL HAVE BEEN ALERTED. WOLVERINE WON'T FIND SANCTUARY WITH ANY OF THEM.
WHAT ABOUT HER CLOSEST FRIENDS, FURY? THE YOUNG X-MEN? HER BOYFRIEND, ANGEL?
THEY'VE AGREED TO NOTIFY US IF THEY HEAR FROM HER, DIRECTOR HILL.
AND YOU TRUST THEM?
DO I LOOK LIKE AN IDIOT? OF COURSE I DON'T TRUST THEM.
WHICH IS WHY WE'RE MONITORING EVERY SINGLE PART OF THEIR LIVES.
SOME OF OUR BEST OFFICERS ARE BEING FORCED TO WATCH SOME PRETTY MUNDANE, ANGSTY TEEN DRAMA.
BUT WOLVERINE WILL BE BROUGHT IN. SHE'LL ANSWER FOR HER MURDERS.
WE WILL FIND HER...

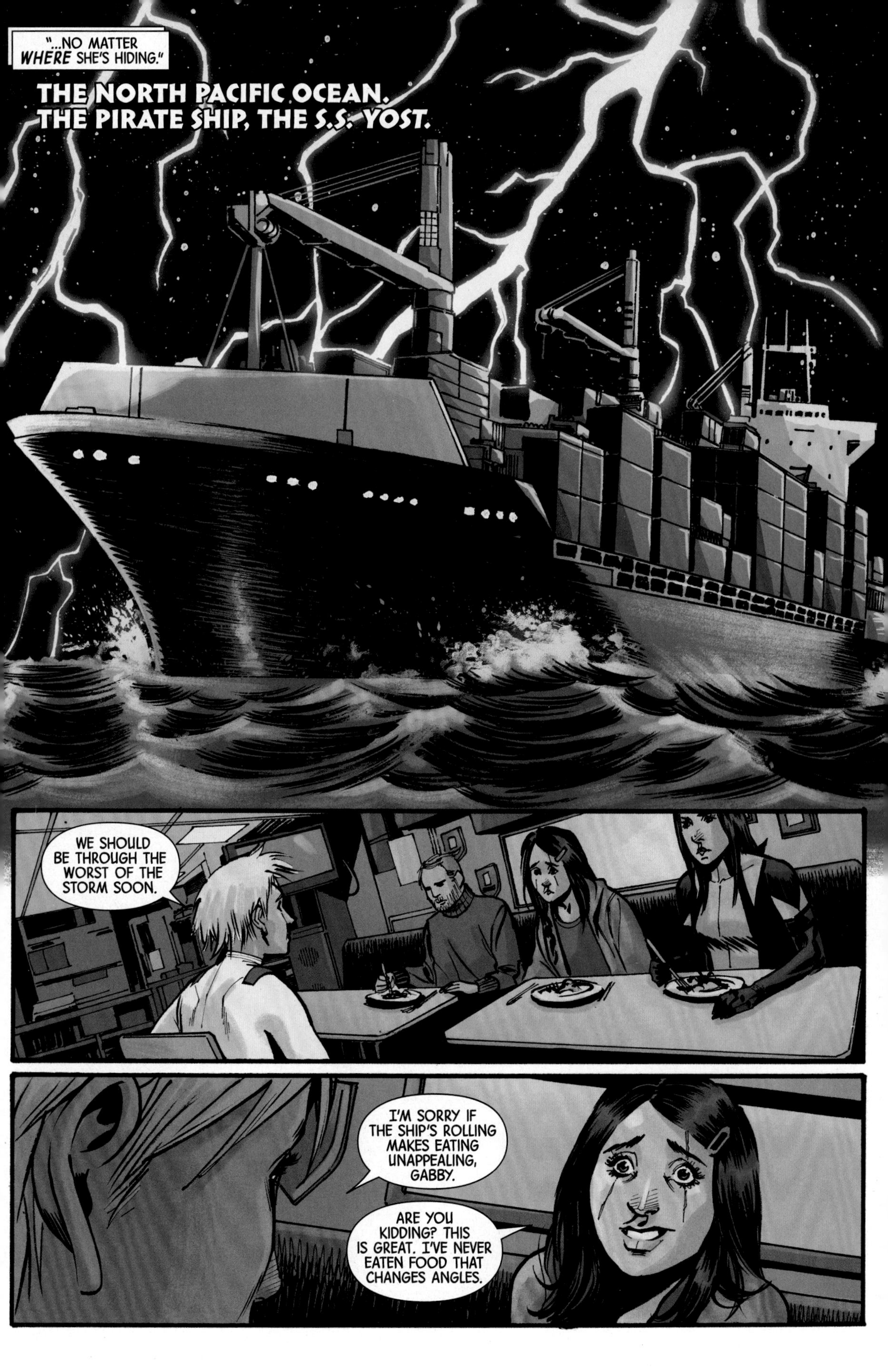
"...NO MATTER WHERE SHE'S HIDING."
THE NORTH PACIFIC OCEAN. THE PIRATE SHIP, THE S.S. YOST.
WE SHOULD BE THROUGH THE WORST OF THE STORM SOON.
I'M SORRY IF THE SHIP'S ROLLING MAKES EATING UNAPPEALING, GABBY.
ARE YOU KIDDING? THIS IS GREAT. I'VE NEVER EATEN FOOD THAT CHANGES ANGLES.

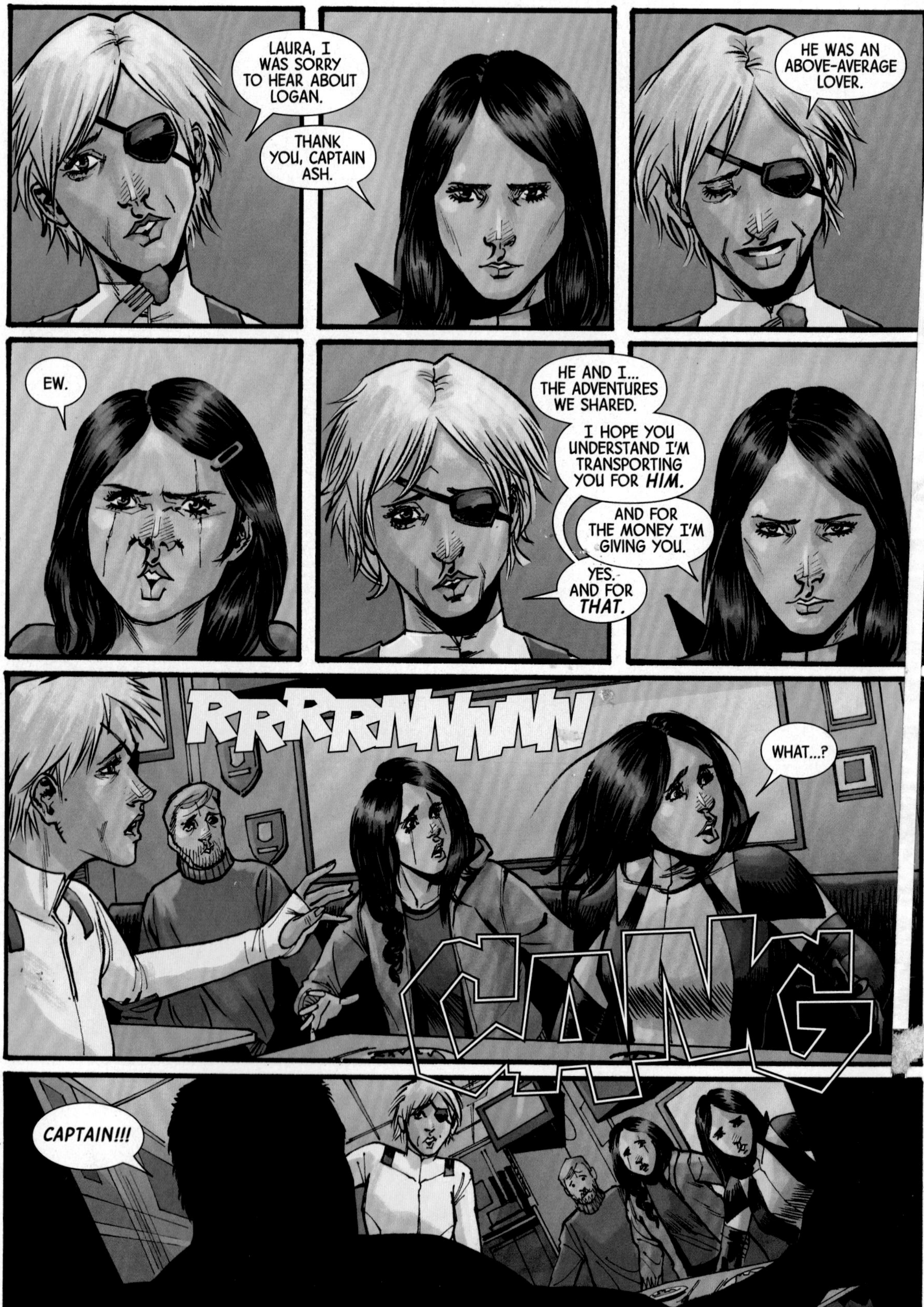
LAURA, I WAS SORRY TO HEAR ABOUT LOGAN.
THANK YOU, CAPTAIN ASH.
HE WAS AN ABOVE-AVERAGE LOVER.
EW.
HE AND I... THE ADVENTURES WE SHARED.
I HOPE YOU UNDERSTAND I'M TRANSPORTING YOU FOR HIM.
AND FOR THE MONEY I'M GIVING YOU.
YES. AND FOR THAT.
RRRRNNNNN
WHAT...?
CLANG
CAPTAIN!!!

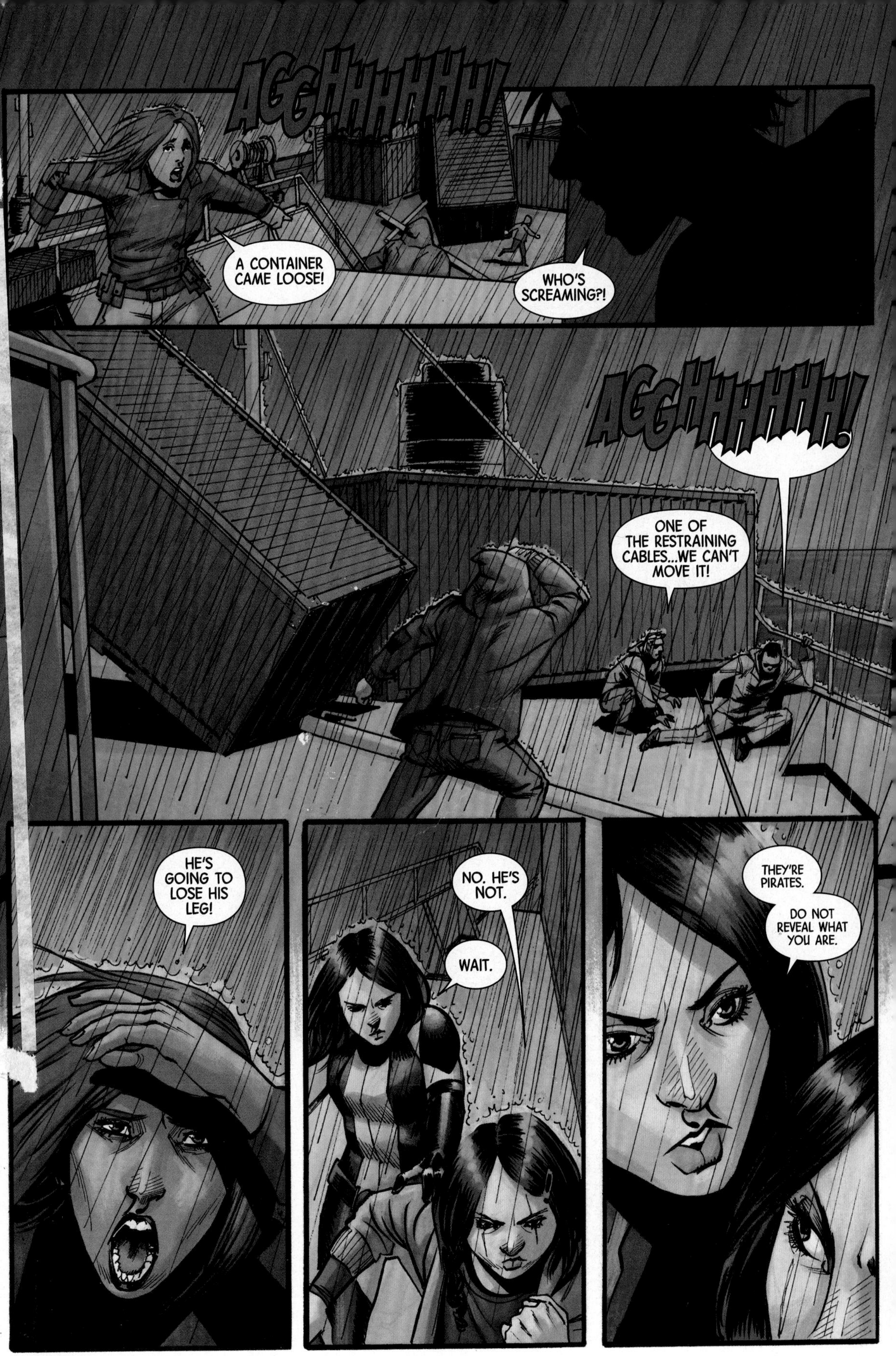
AGGHHHHHH!
A CONTAINER CAME LOOSE!
WHO'S SCREAMING?!
AGGHHHHHH!
ONE OF THE RESTRAINING CABLES...WE CAN'T MOVE IT!
HE'S GOING TO LOSE HIS LEG!
NO. HE'S NOT.
WAIT.
THEY'RE PIRATES.
DO NOT REVEAL WHAT YOU ARE.

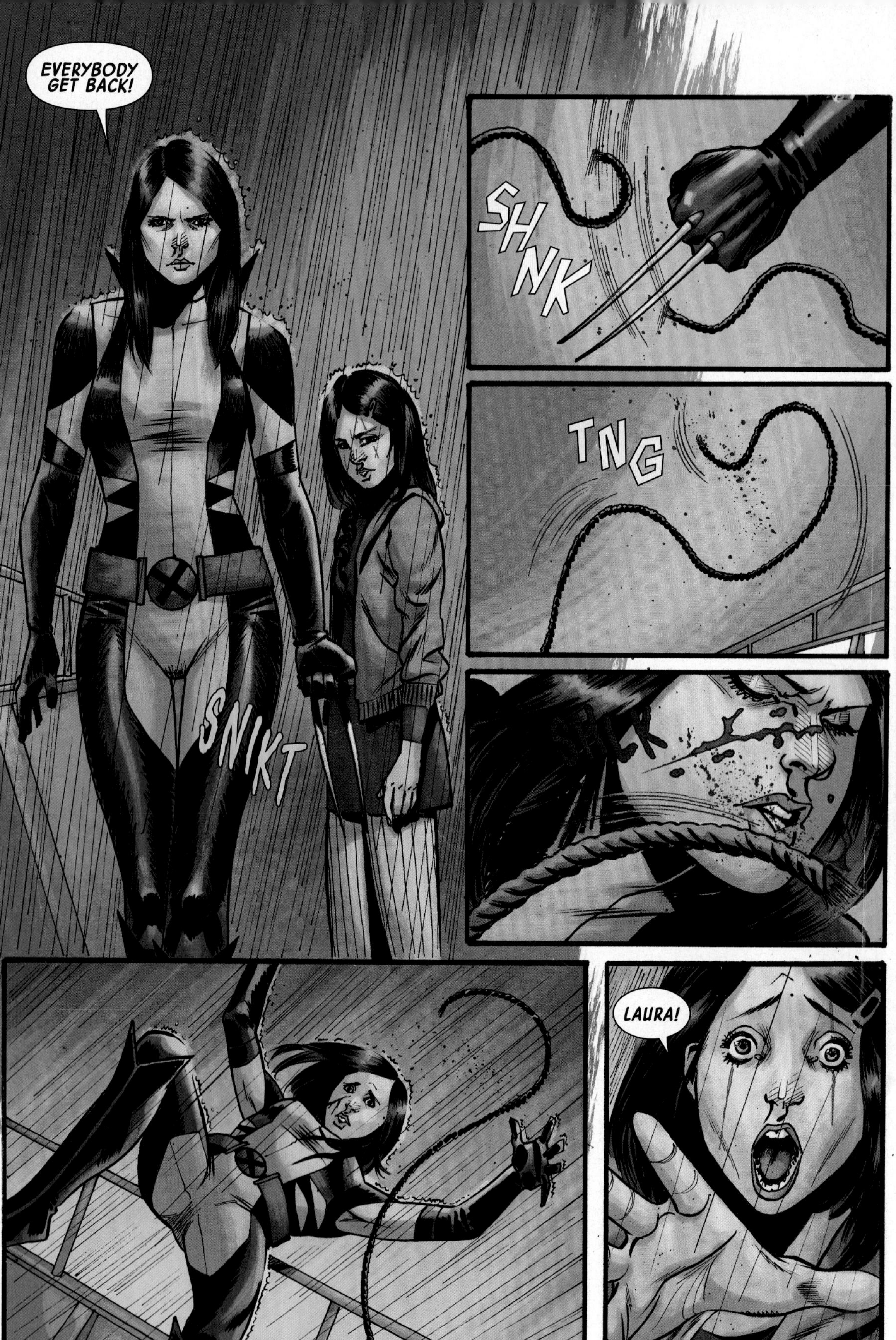
EVERYBODY GET BACK!
SNIKT
SHNK
TNG
LAURA!

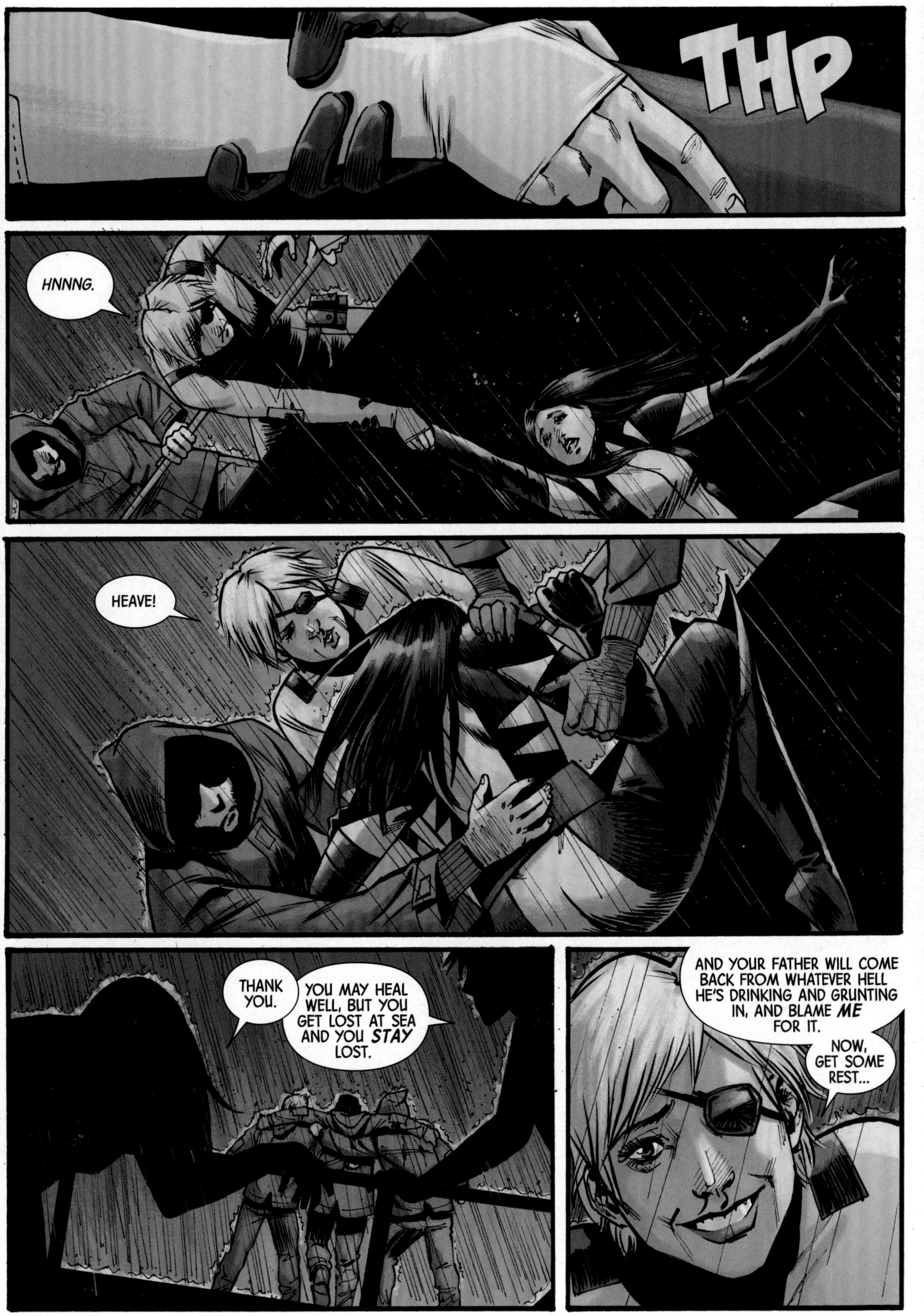
THP
HNNNG.
HEAVE!
THANK YOU.
YOU MAY HEAL WELL, BUT YOU GET LOST AT SEA AND YOU *STAY* LOST.
AND YOUR FATHER WILL COME BACK FROM WHATEVER HELL HE'S DRINKING AND GRUNTING IN, AND BLAME *ME* FOR IT.
NOW, GET SOME REST...

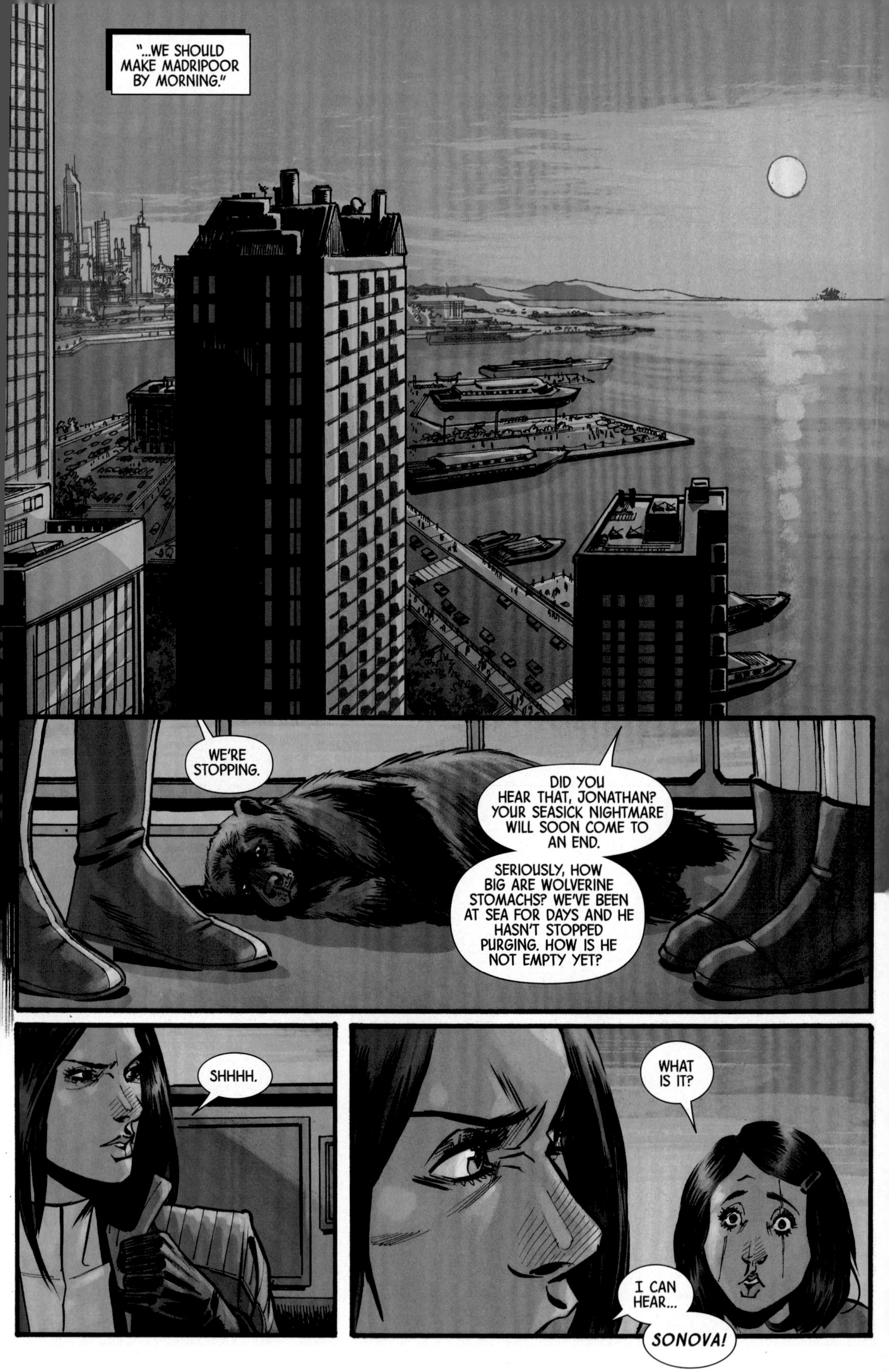
"...WE SHOULD MAKE MADRIPOOR BY MORNING."
WE'RE STOPPING.
DID YOU HEAR THAT, JONATHAN? YOUR SEASICK NIGHTMARE WILL SOON COME TO AN END.
SERIOUSLY, HOW BIG ARE WOLVERINE STOMACHS? WE'VE BEEN AT SEA FOR DAYS AND HE HASN'T STOPPED PURGING. HOW IS HE NOT EMPTY YET?
SHHHH.
WHAT IS IT?
I CAN HEAR...
SONOVA!

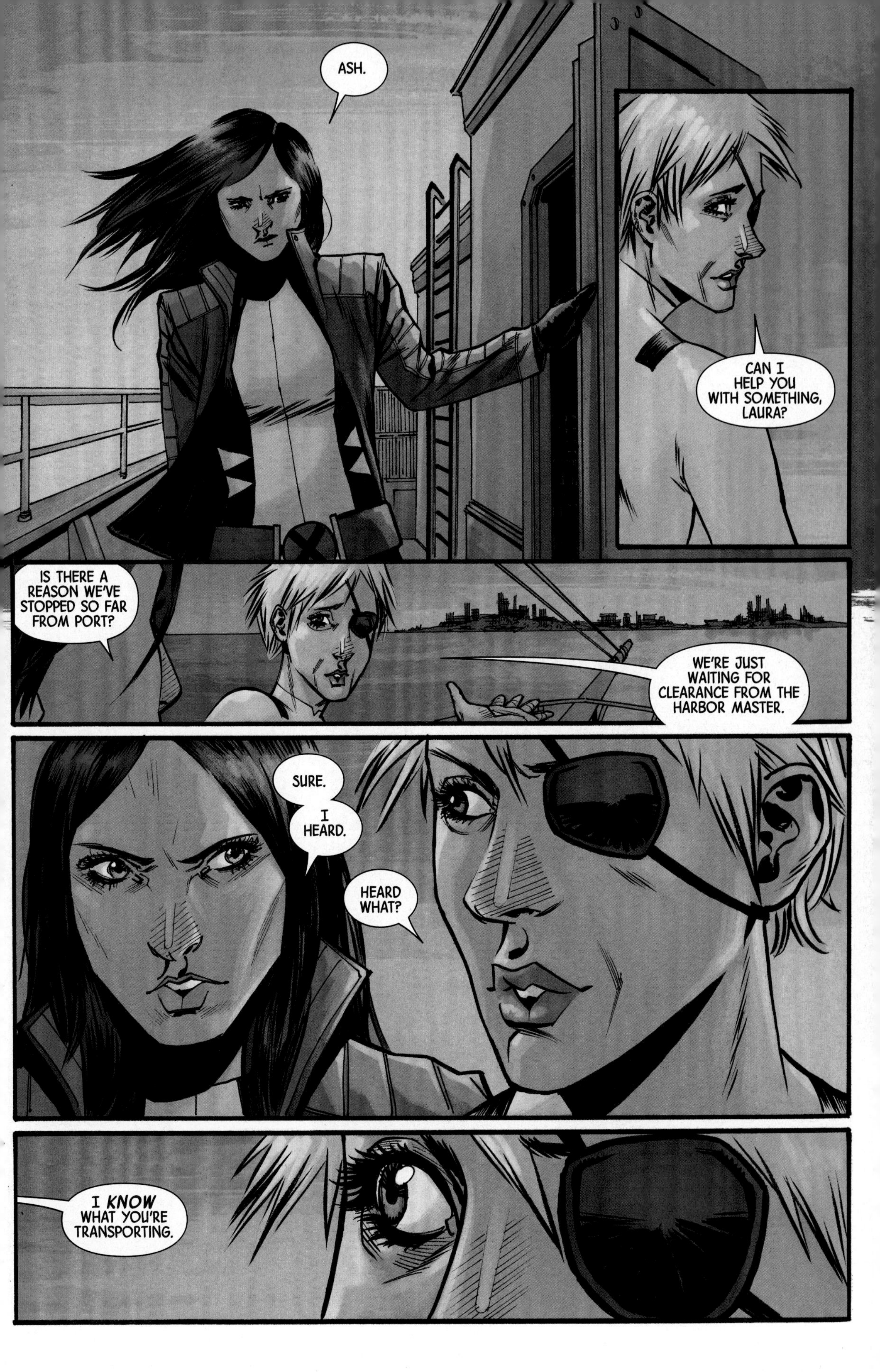
ASH.
CAN I HELP YOU WITH SOMETHING, LAURA?
IS THERE A REASON WE'VE STOPPED SO FAR FROM PORT?
WE'RE JUST WAITING FOR CLEARANCE FROM THE HARBOR MASTER.
SURE.
I HEARD.
HEARD WHAT?
I *KNOW* WHAT YOU'RE TRANSPORTING.

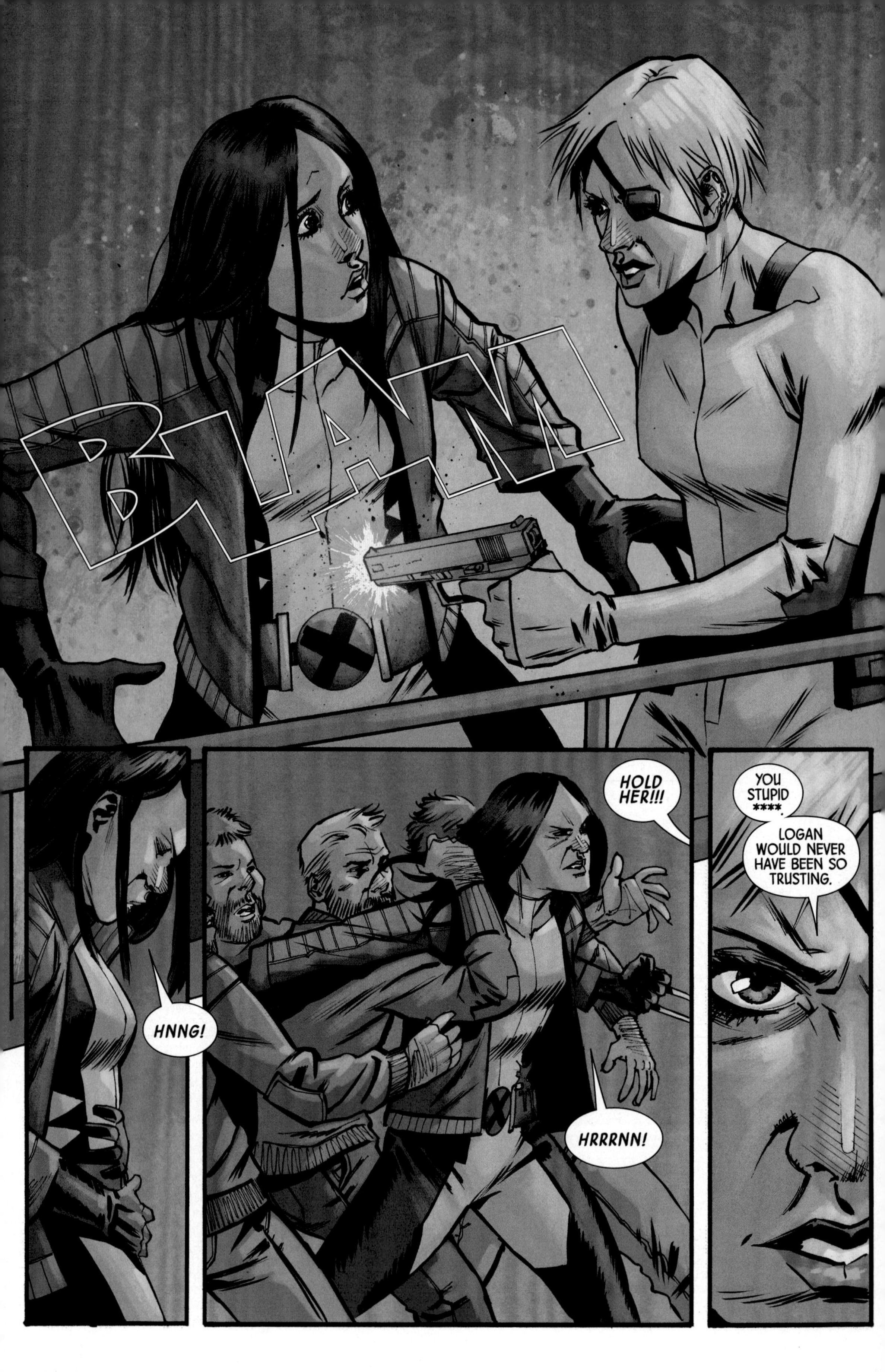
BLAM
HNNG!
HOLD HER!!!
HRRRNN!
YOU STUPID ****.
LOGAN WOULD NEVER HAVE BEEN SO TRUSTING.

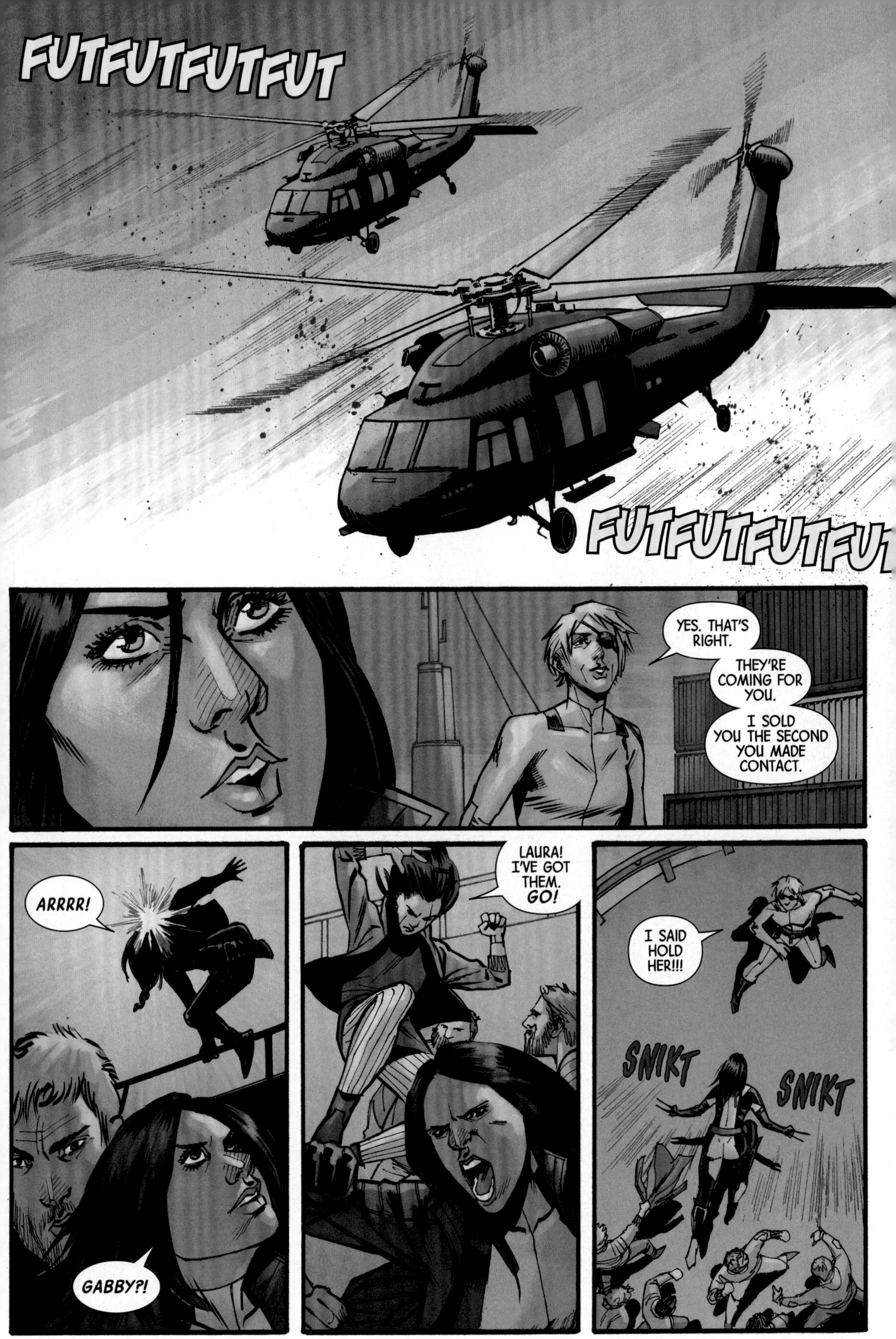
FUTFUTFUTFUT
FUTFUTFUTFUT
YES. THAT'S RIGHT.
THEY'RE COMING FOR YOU.
I SOLD YOU THE SECOND YOU MADE CONTACT.
ARRRR!
GABBY?!
LAURA! I'VE GOT THEM. GO!
I SAID HOLD HER!!!
SNIKT
SNIKT

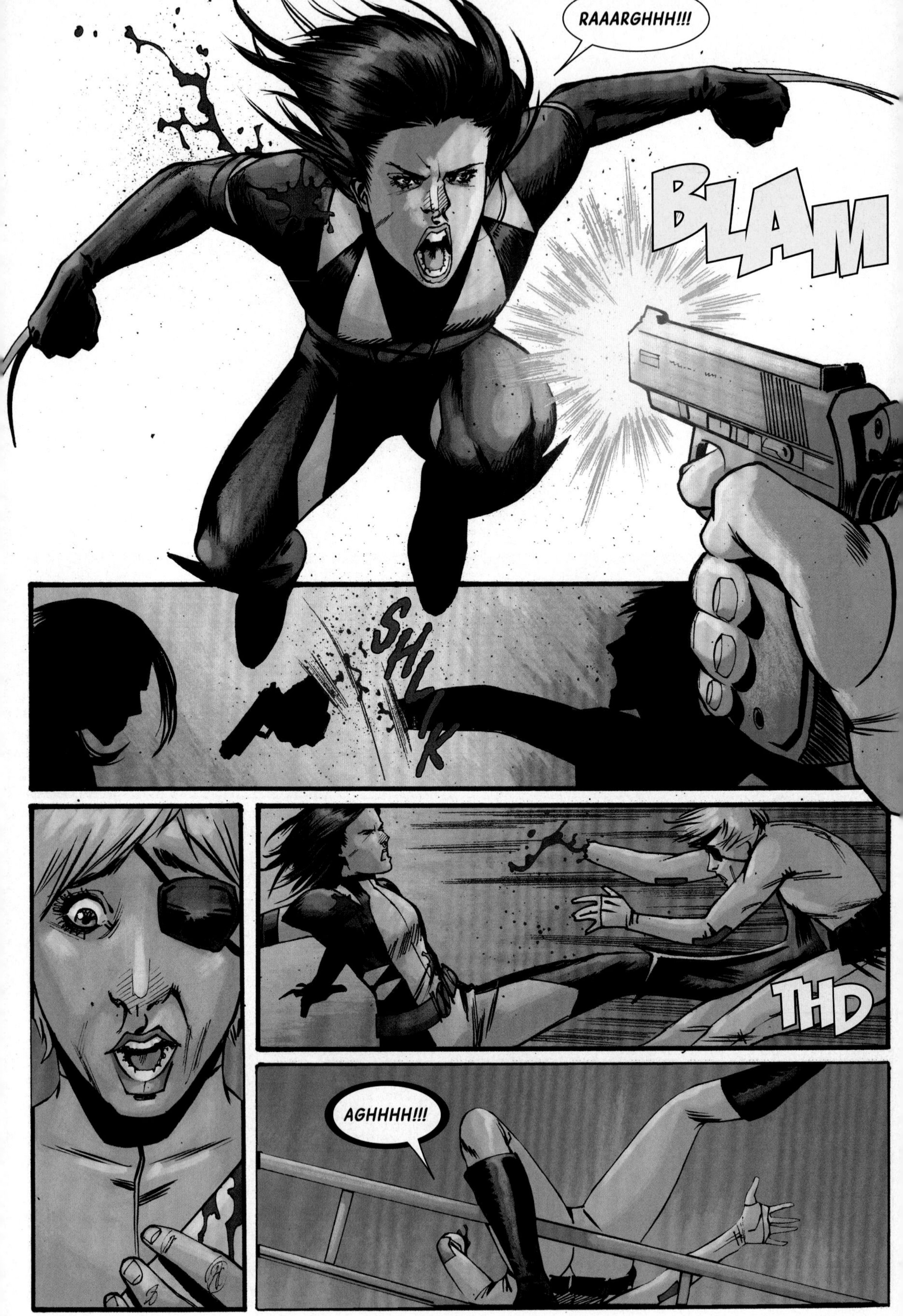
RAAARGHHH!!!
BLAM
SHLIK
THD
AGHHHH!!!

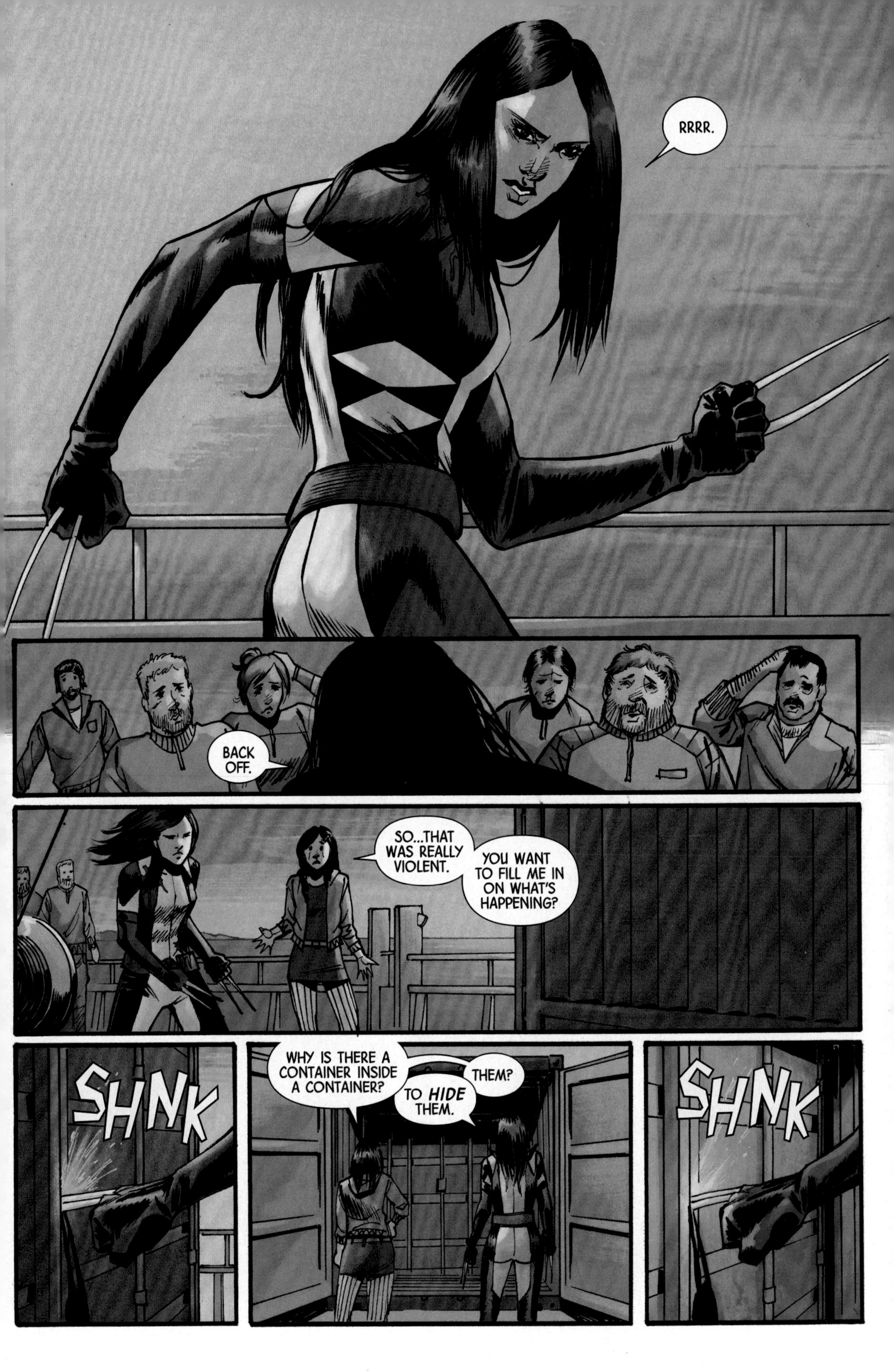
RRRR.
BACK OFF.
SO...THAT WAS REALLY VIOLENT.
YOU WANT TO FILL ME IN ON WHAT'S HAPPENING?
SHNK
WHY IS THERE A CONTAINER INSIDE A CONTAINER?
TO *HIDE* THEM.
THEM?
SHNK

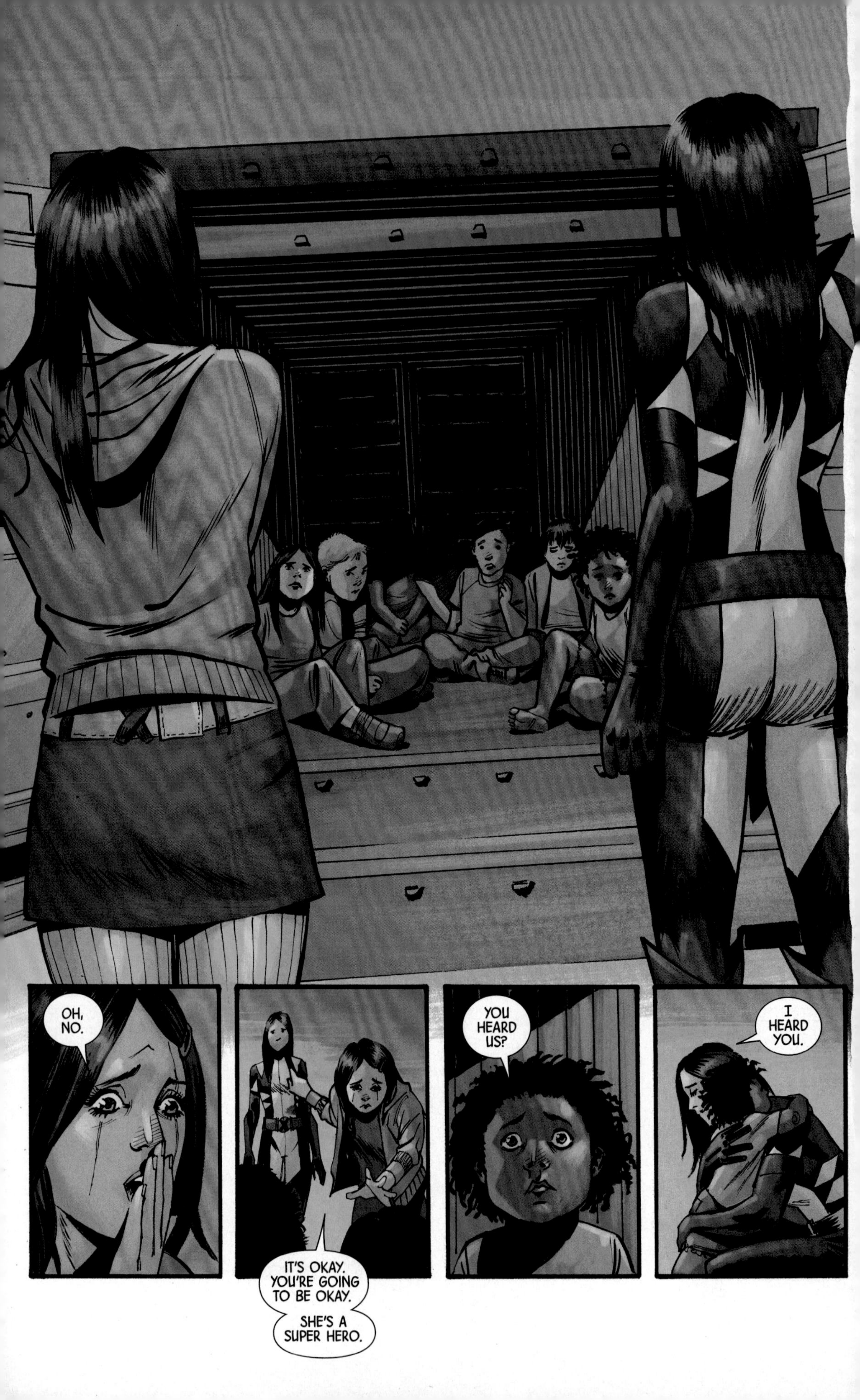
OH, NO.
IT'S OKAY. YOU'RE GOING TO BE OKAY.
SHE'S A SUPER HERO.
YOU HEARD US?
I HEARD YOU.

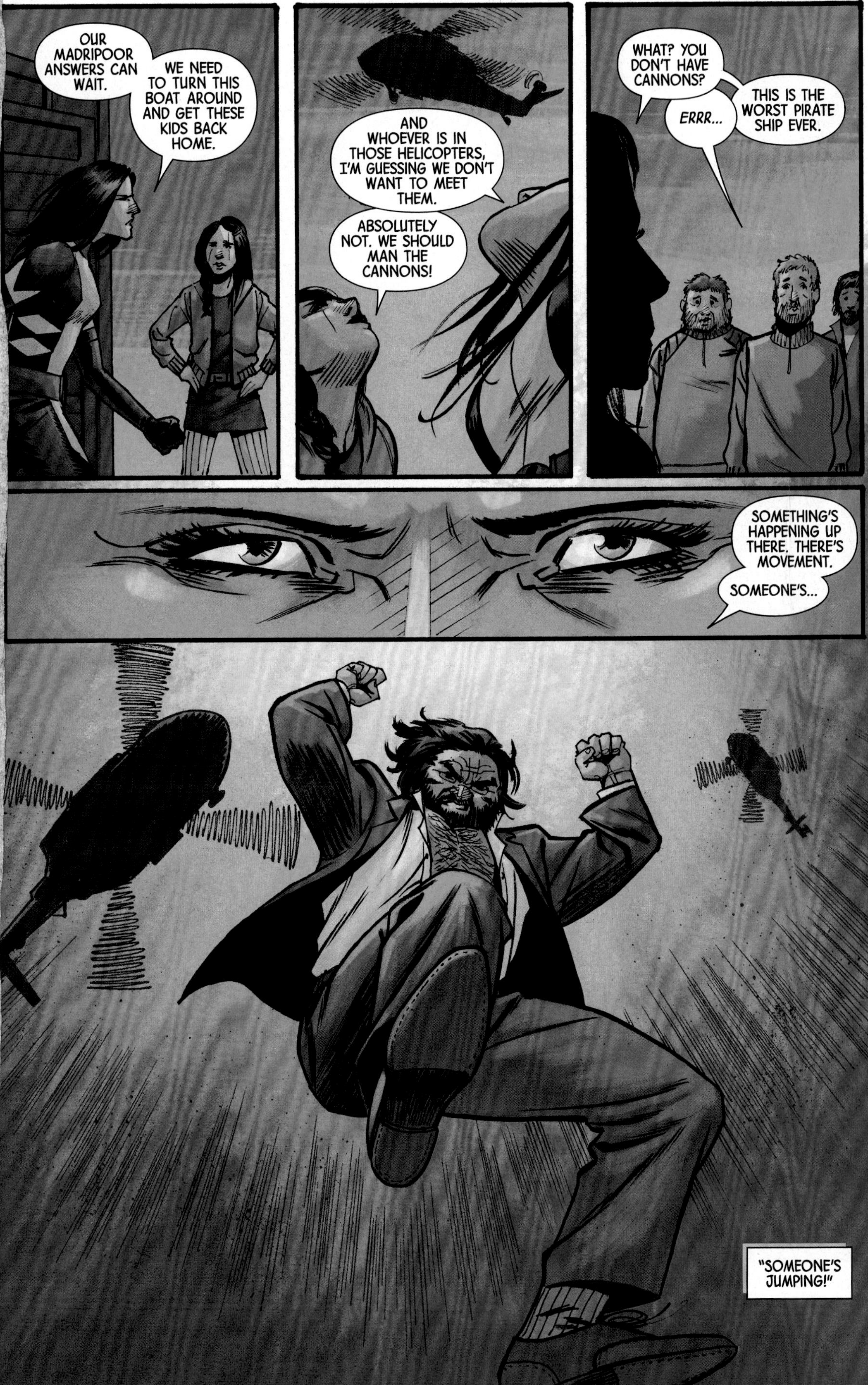
OUR MADRIPOOR ANSWERS CAN WAIT.
WE NEED TO TURN THIS BOAT AROUND AND GET THESE KIDS BACK HOME.
AND WHOEVER IS IN THOSE HELICOPTERS, I'M GUESSING WE DON'T WANT TO MEET THEM.
ABSOLUTELY NOT. WE SHOULD MAN THE CANNONS!
WHAT? YOU DON'T HAVE CANNONS?
ERRR...
THIS IS THE WORST PIRATE SHIP EVER.
SOMETHING'S HAPPENING UP THERE. THERE'S MOVEMENT.
SOMEONE'S...
"SOMEONE'S JUMPING!"

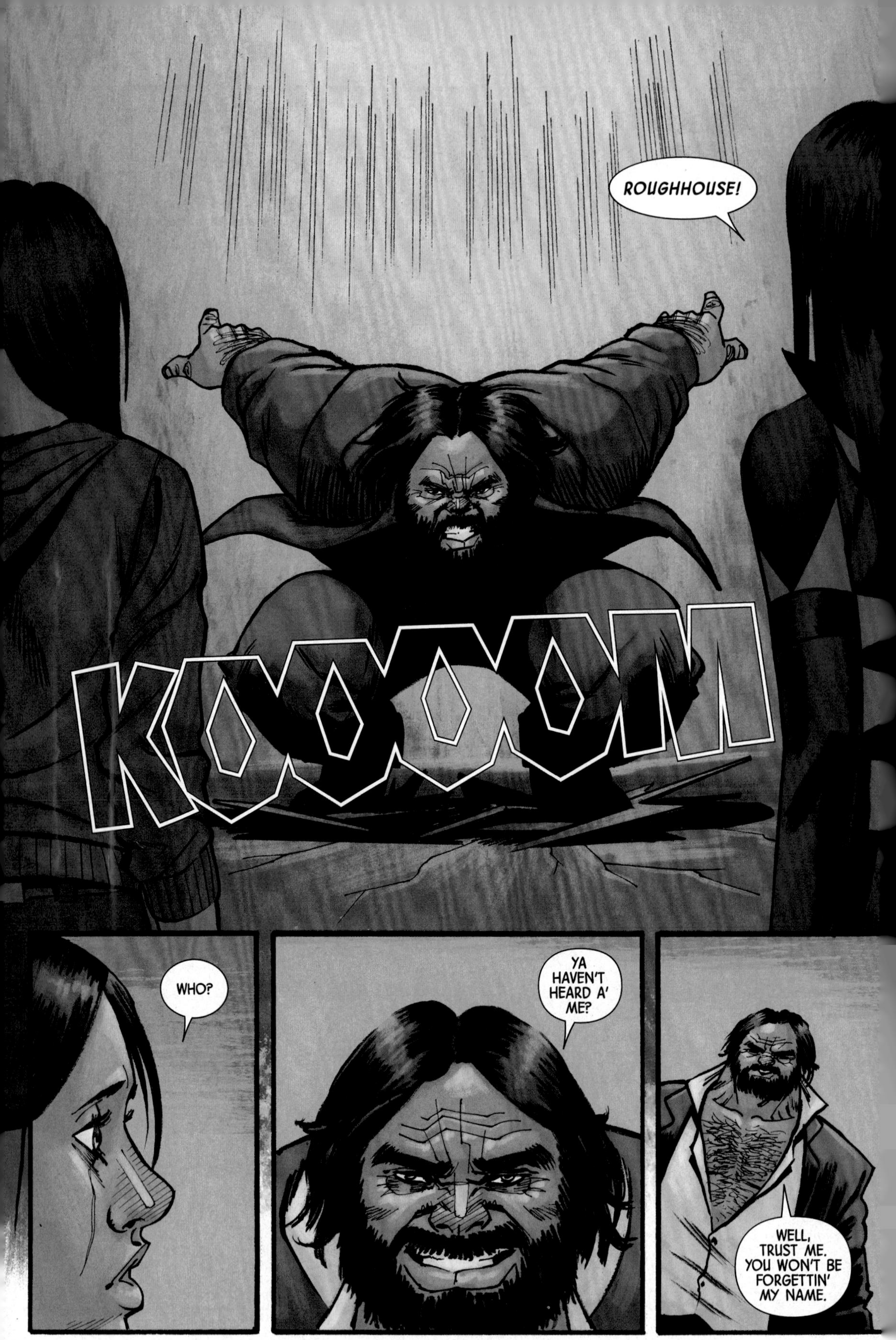
ROUGHHOUSE!
KOOOOM
WHO?
YA HAVEN'T HEARD A' ME?
WELL, TRUST ME. YOU WON'T BE FORGETTIN' MY NAME.

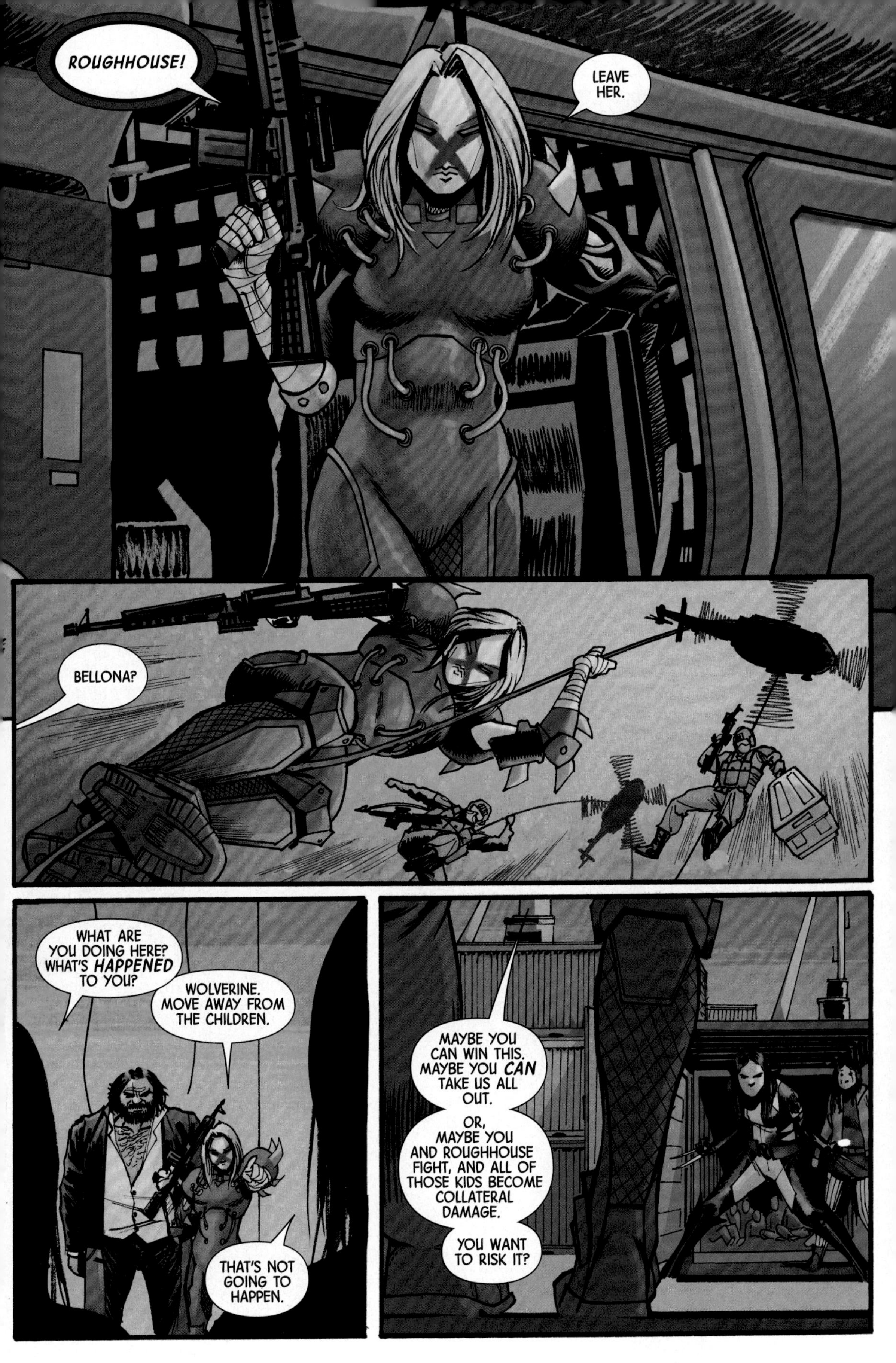
ROUGHHOUSE!
LEAVE HER.
BELLONA?
WHAT ARE YOU DOING HERE? WHAT'S HAPPENED TO YOU?
WOLVERINE. MOVE AWAY FROM THE CHILDREN.
THAT'S NOT GOING TO HAPPEN.
MAYBE YOU CAN WIN THIS. MAYBE YOU CAN TAKE US ALL OUT.
OR, MAYBE YOU AND ROUGHHOUSE FIGHT, AND ALL OF THOSE KIDS BECOME COLLATERAL DAMAGE.
YOU WANT TO RISK IT?

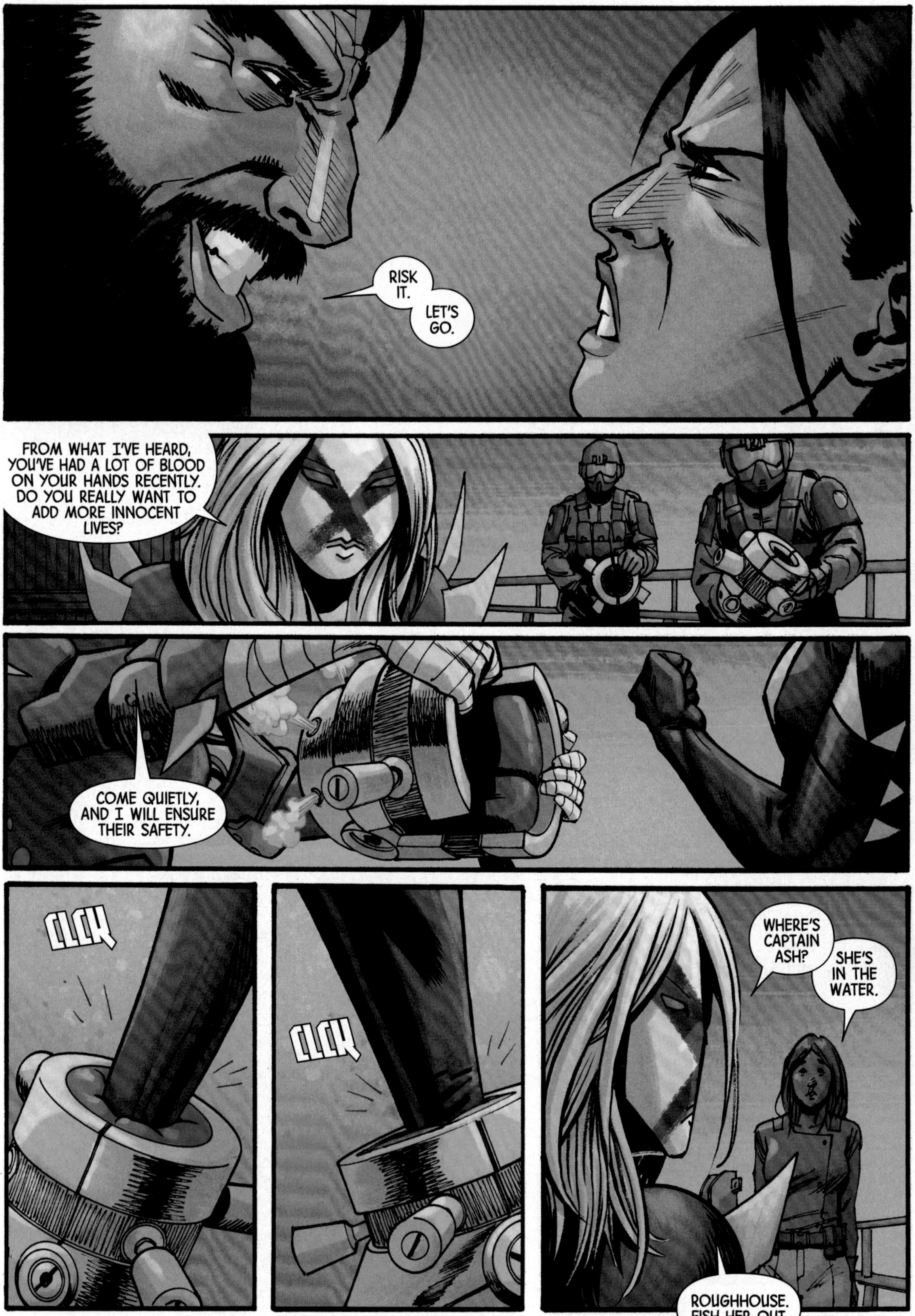
RISK IT.
LET'S GO.
FROM WHAT I'VE HEARD, YOU'VE HAD A LOT OF BLOOD ON YOUR HANDS RECENTLY. DO YOU REALLY WANT TO ADD MORE INNOCENT LIVES?
COME QUIETLY, AND I WILL ENSURE THEIR SAFETY.
CLCK
CLCK
WHERE'S CAPTAIN ASH?
SHE'S IN THE WATER.
ROUGHHOUSE. FISH HER OUT.

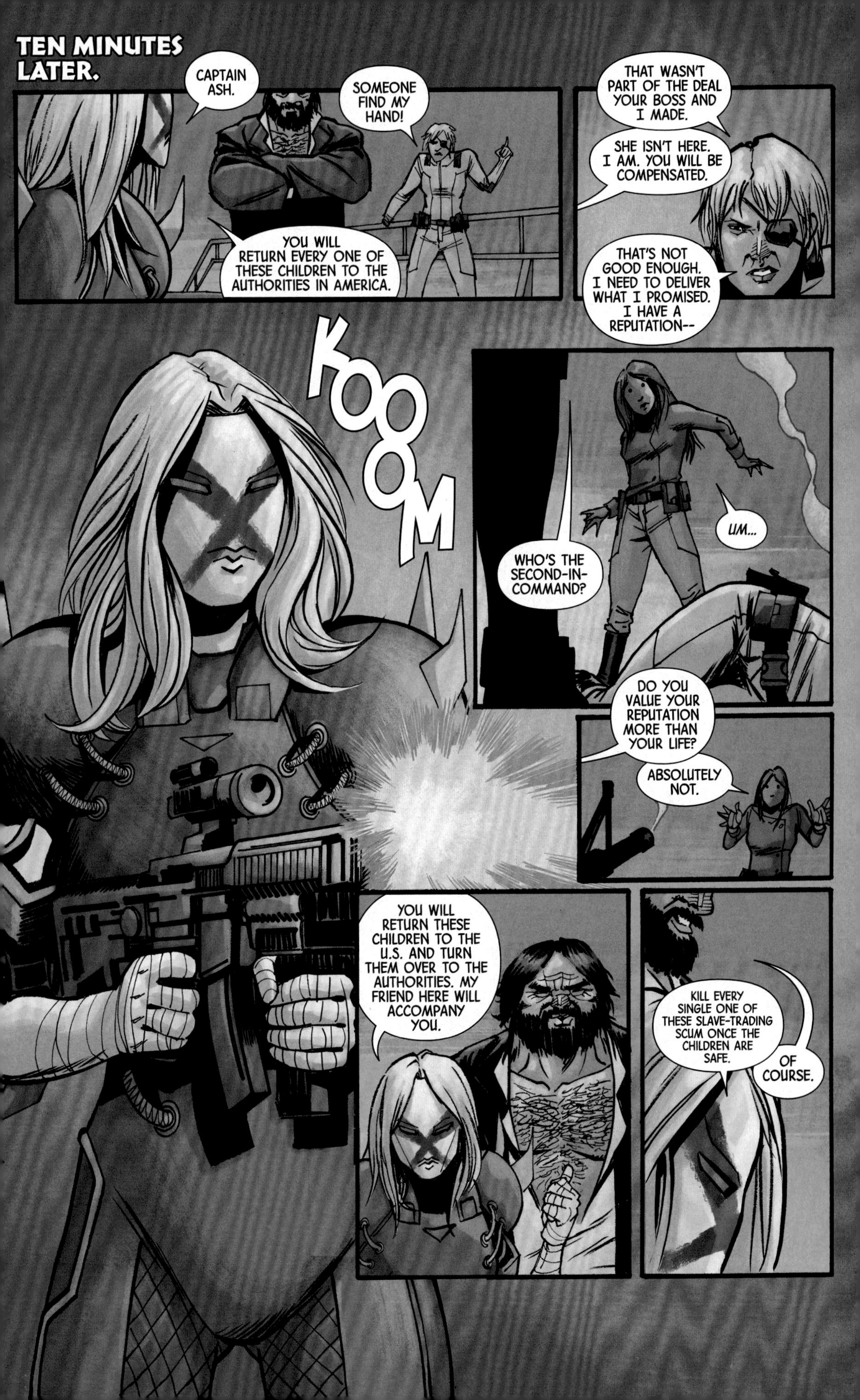
TEN MINUTES LATER.
CAPTAIN ASH.
SOMEONE FIND MY HAND!
YOU WILL RETURN EVERY ONE OF THESE CHILDREN TO THE AUTHORITIES IN AMERICA.
THAT WASN'T PART OF THE DEAL YOUR BOSS AND I MADE.
SHE ISN'T HERE. I AM. YOU WILL BE COMPENSATED.
THAT'S NOT GOOD ENOUGH. I NEED TO DELIVER WHAT I PROMISED. I HAVE A REPUTATION--
KOOOM
WHO'S THE SECOND-IN-COMMAND?
UM...
DO YOU VALUE YOUR REPUTATION MORE THAN YOUR LIFE?
ABSOLUTELY NOT.
YOU WILL RETURN THESE CHILDREN TO THE U.S. AND TURN THEM OVER TO THE AUTHORITIES. MY FRIEND HERE WILL ACCOMPANY YOU.
KILL EVERY SINGLE ONE OF THESE SLAVE-TRADING SCUM ONCE THE CHILDREN ARE SAFE.
OF COURSE.

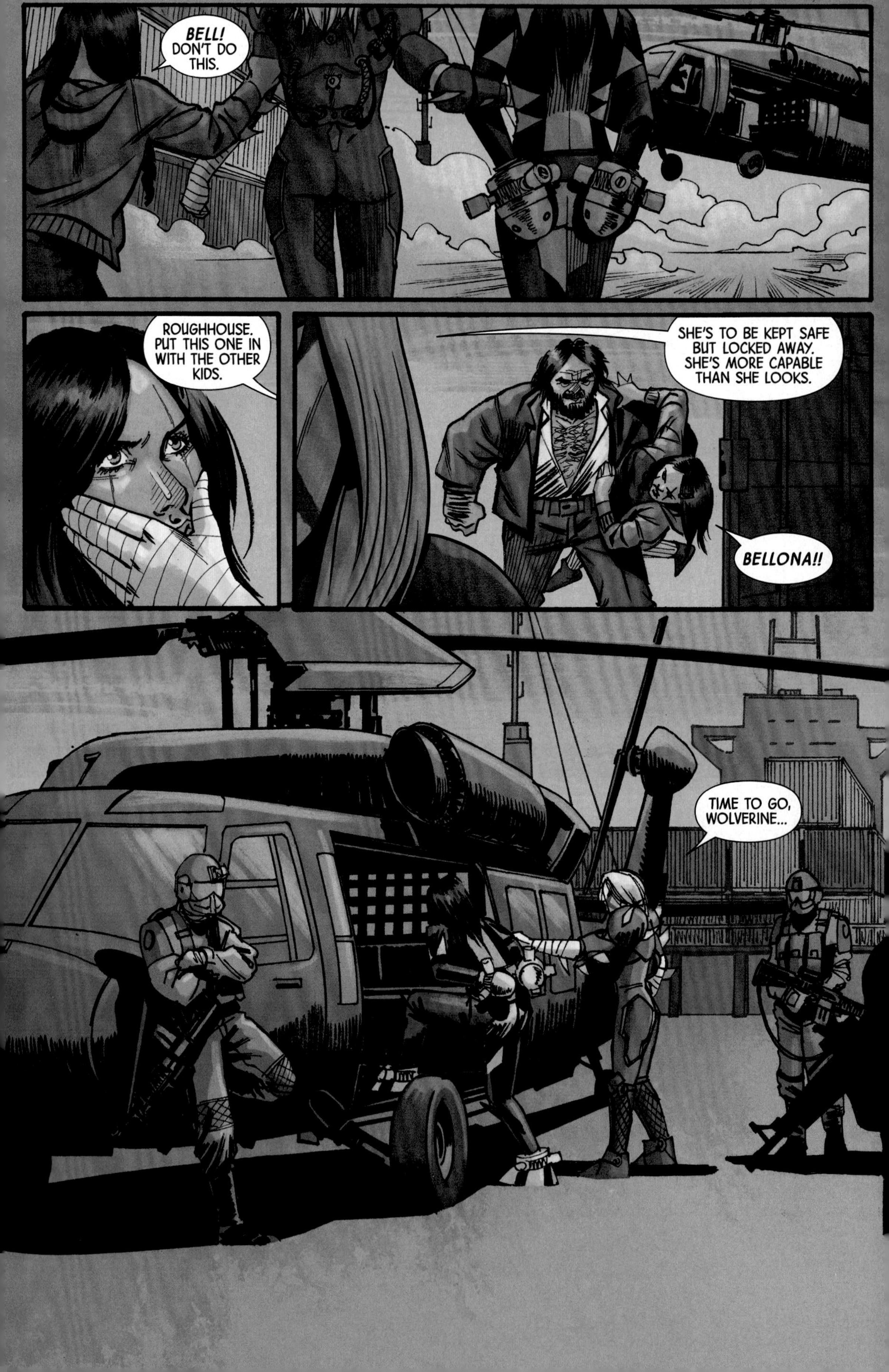
BELL! DON'T DO THIS.
ROUGHHOUSE. PUT THIS ONE IN WITH THE OTHER KIDS.
SHE'S TO BE KEPT SAFE BUT LOCKED AWAY. SHE'S MORE CAPABLE THAN SHE LOOKS.
BELLONA!!
TIME TO GO, WOLVERINE...

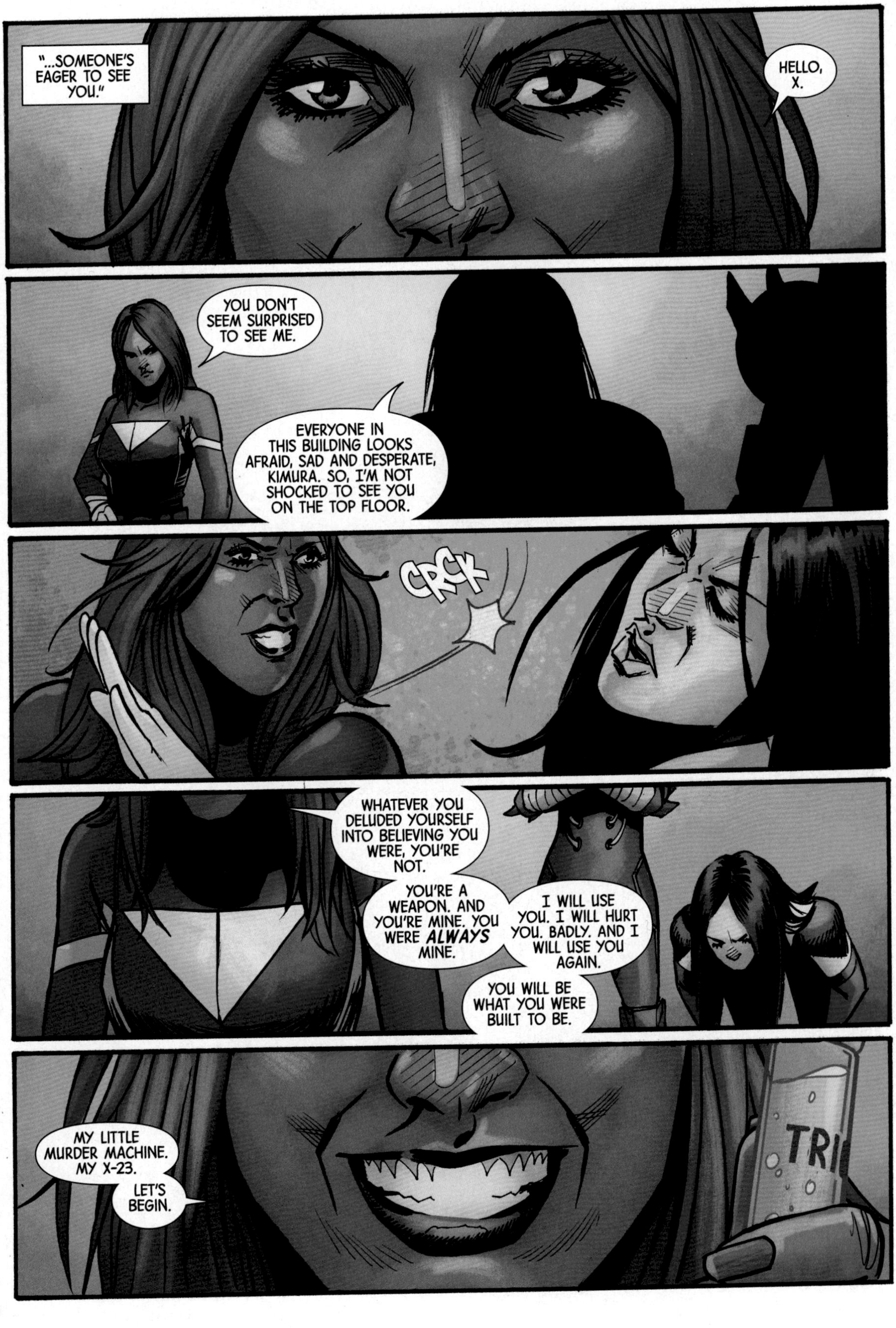
"...SOMEONE'S EAGER TO SEE YOU."
HELLO, X.
YOU DON'T SEEM SURPRISED TO SEE ME.
EVERYONE IN THIS BUILDING LOOKS AFRAID, SAD AND DESPERATE, KIMURA. SO, I'M NOT SHOCKED TO SEE YOU ON THE TOP FLOOR.
CRCK
WHATEVER YOU DELUDED YOURSELF INTO BELIEVING YOU WERE, YOU'RE NOT.
YOU'RE A WEAPON. AND YOU'RE MINE. YOU WERE *ALWAYS* MINE.
I WILL USE YOU. I WILL HURT YOU. BADLY. AND I WILL USE YOU AGAIN.
YOU WILL BE WHAT YOU WERE BUILT TO BE.
MY LITTLE MURDER MACHINE. MY X-23.
LET'S BEGIN.
TRI

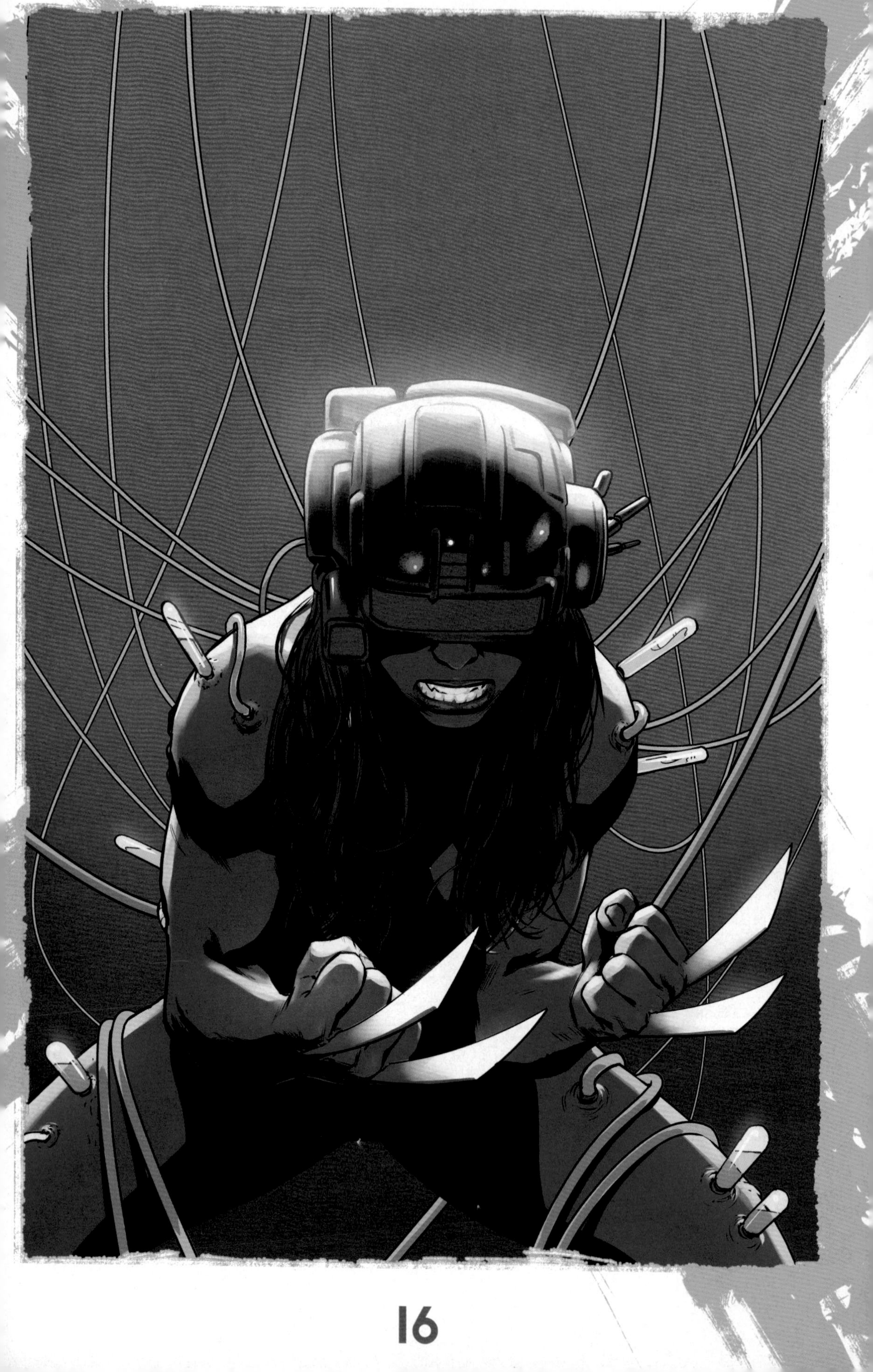

16

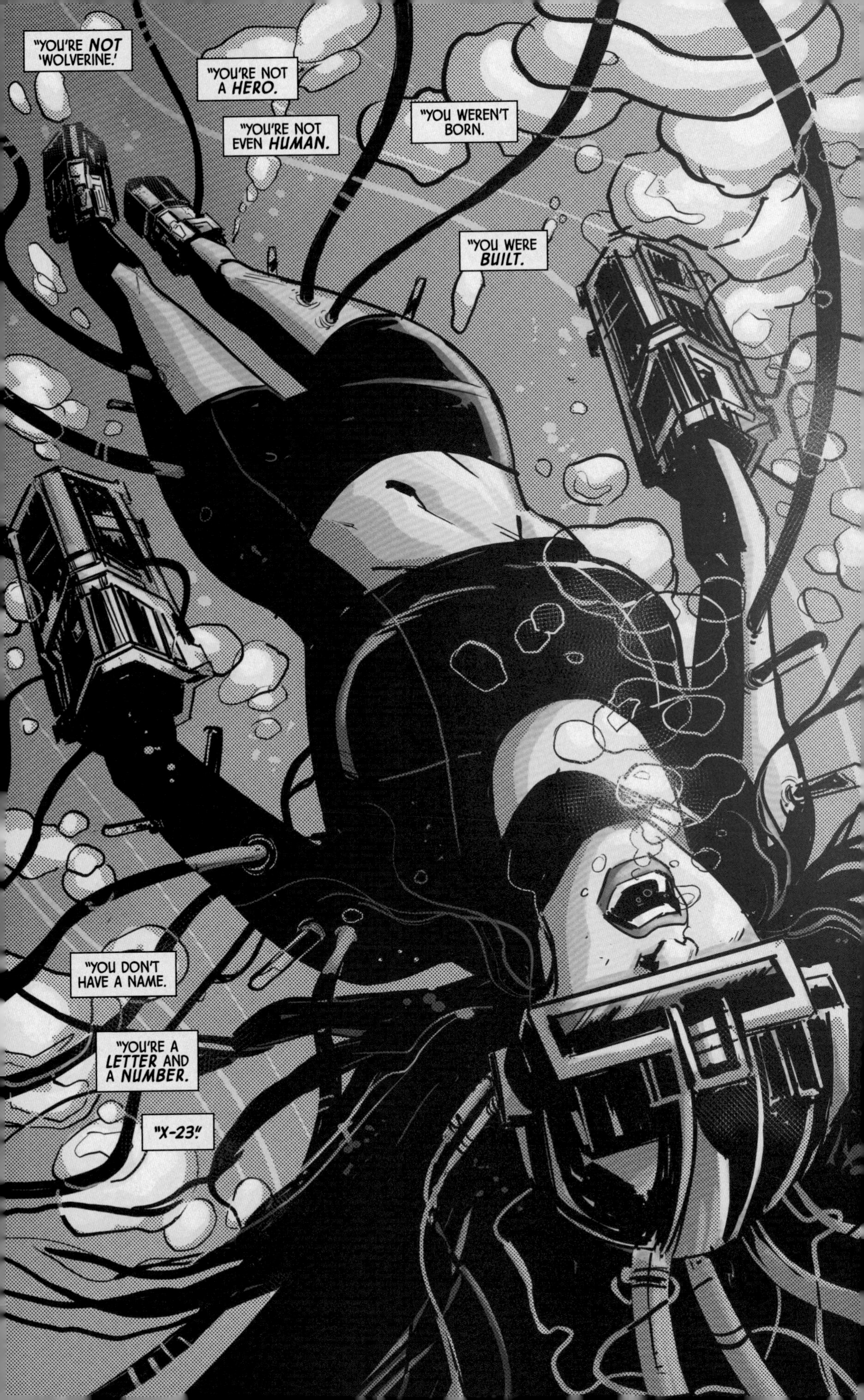

"YOU'RE *NOT* 'WOLVERINE.'
"YOU'RE NOT A *HERO.*
"YOU'RE NOT EVEN *HUMAN.*
"YOU WEREN'T BORN.
"YOU WERE *BUILT.*
"YOU DON'T HAVE A NAME.
"YOU'RE A *LETTER* AND A *NUMBER.*
"X-23."

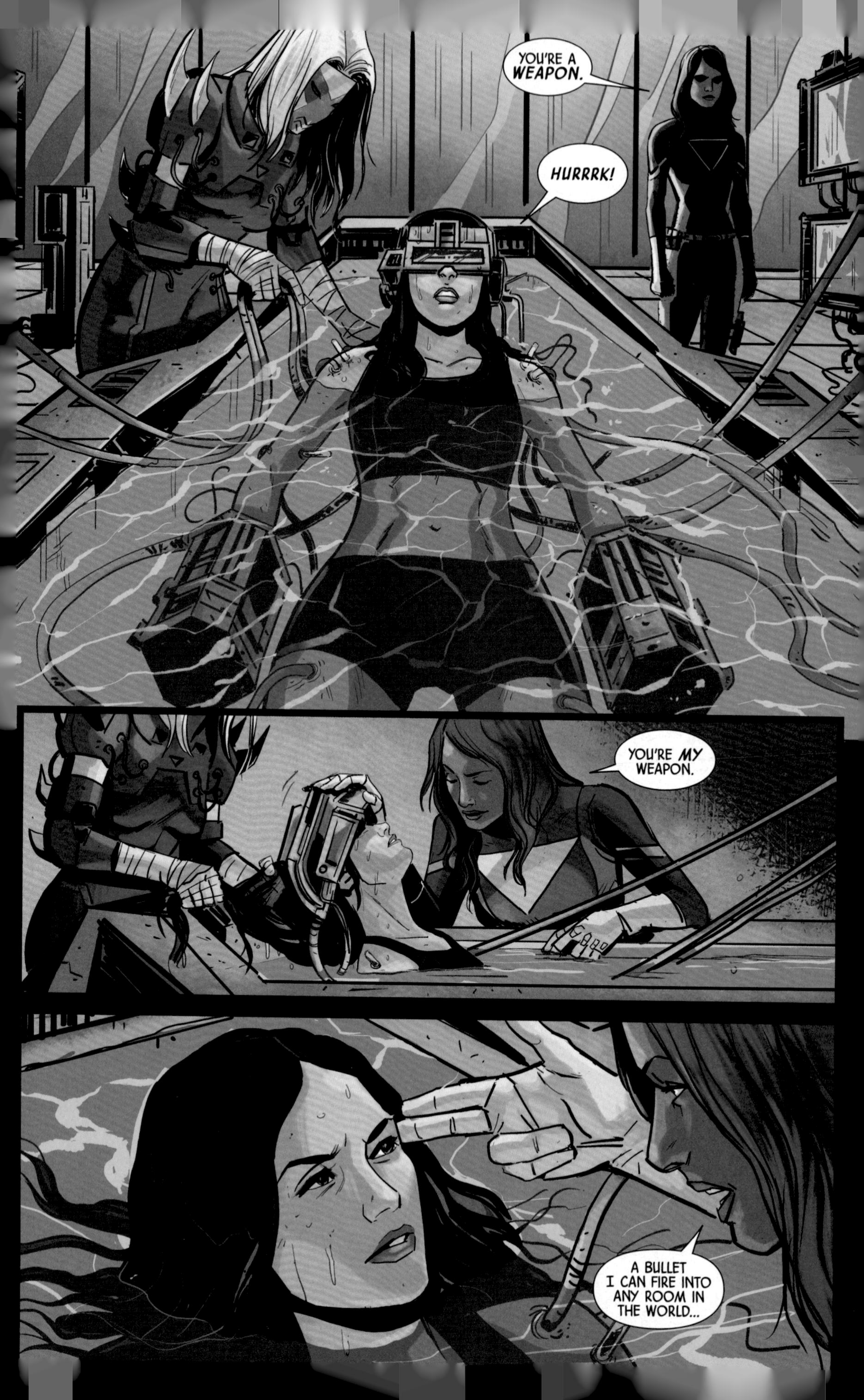
YOU'RE A WEAPON.
HURRRK!
YOU'RE MY WEAPON.
A BULLET I CAN FIRE INTO ANY ROOM IN THE WORLD...

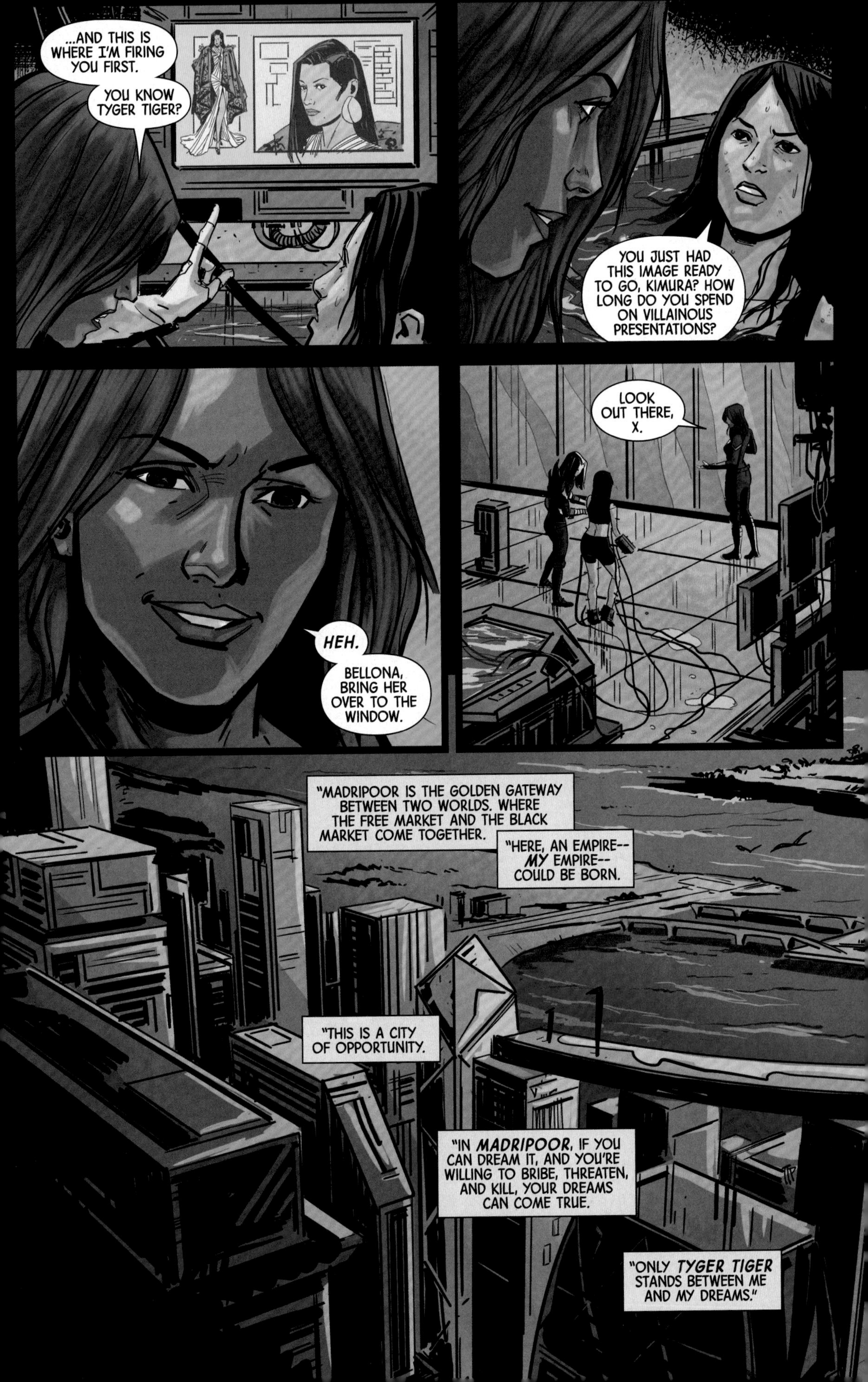
...AND THIS IS WHERE I'M FIRING YOU FIRST.
YOU KNOW TYGER TIGER?
YOU JUST HAD THIS IMAGE READY TO GO, KIMURA? HOW LONG DO YOU SPEND ON VILLAINOUS PRESENTATIONS?
HEH.
BELLONA, BRING HER OVER TO THE WINDOW.
LOOK OUT THERE, X.
"MADRIPOOR IS THE GOLDEN GATEWAY BETWEEN TWO WORLDS. WHERE THE FREE MARKET AND THE BLACK MARKET COME TOGETHER.
"HERE, AN EMPIRE-- MY EMPIRE-- COULD BE BORN.
"THIS IS A CITY OF OPPORTUNITY.
"IN MADRIPOOR, IF YOU CAN DREAM IT, AND YOU'RE WILLING TO BRIBE, THREATEN, AND KILL, YOUR DREAMS CAN COME TRUE.
"ONLY TYGER TIGER STANDS BETWEEN ME AND MY DREAMS."

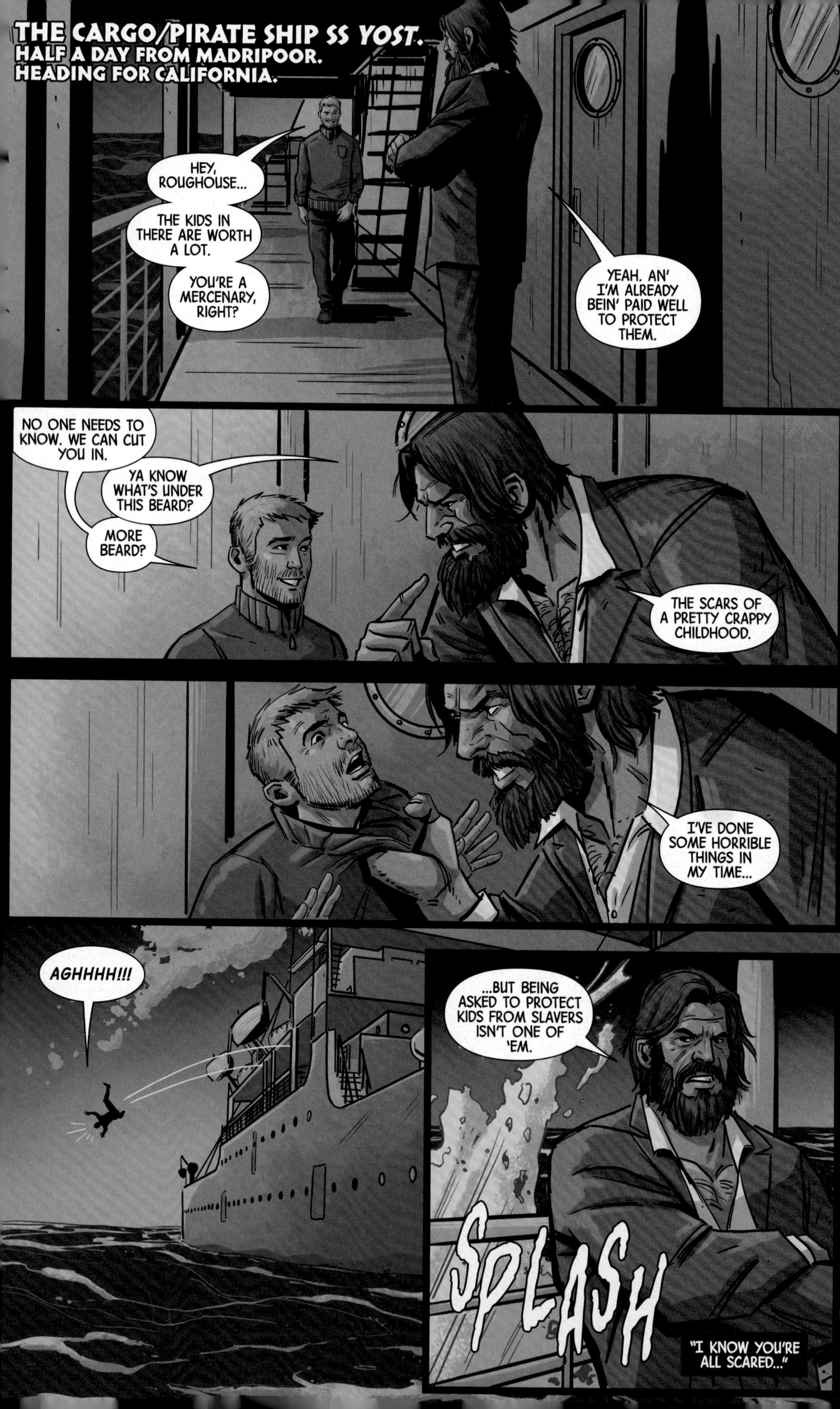
THE CARGO/PIRATE SHIP SS *YOST*.
HALF A DAY FROM MADRIPOOR.
HEADING FOR CALIFORNIA.
HEY, ROUGHOUSE...
THE KIDS IN THERE ARE WORTH A LOT.
YOU'RE A MERCENARY, RIGHT?
YEAH. AN' I'M ALREADY BEIN' PAID WELL TO PROTECT THEM.
NO ONE NEEDS TO KNOW. WE CAN CUT YOU IN.
YA KNOW WHAT'S UNDER THIS BEARD?
MORE BEARD?
THE SCARS OF A PRETTY CRAPPY CHILDHOOD.
I'VE DONE SOME HORRIBLE THINGS IN MY TIME...
AGHHHH!!!
...BUT BEING ASKED TO PROTECT KIDS FROM SLAVERS ISN'T ONE OF 'EM.
SPLASH
"I KNOW YOU'RE ALL SCARED..."

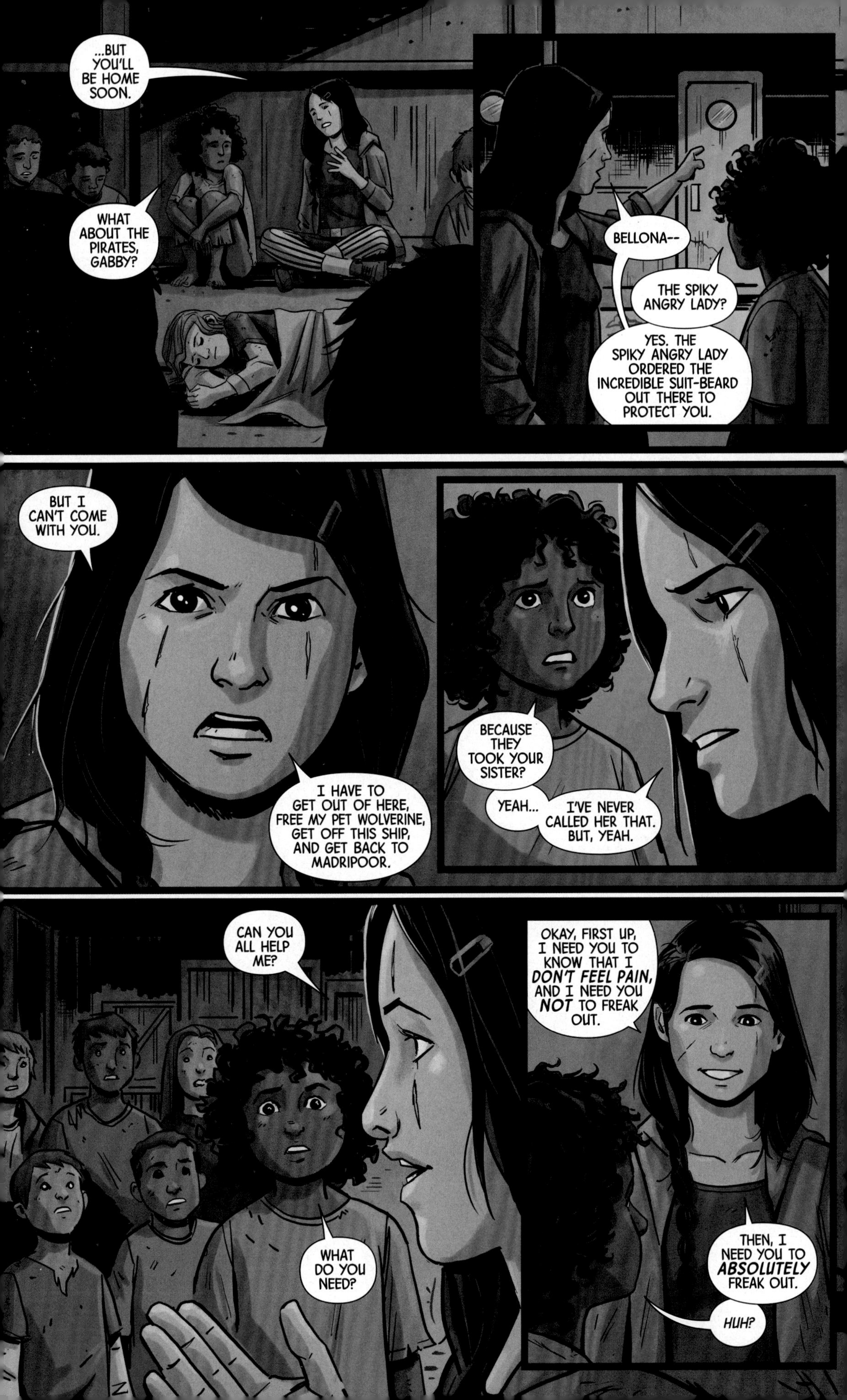
...BUT YOU'LL BE HOME SOON.
WHAT ABOUT THE PIRATES, GABBY?
BELLONA--
THE SPIKY ANGRY LADY?
YES. THE SPIKY ANGRY LADY ORDERED THE INCREDIBLE SUIT-BEARD OUT THERE TO PROTECT YOU.
BUT I CAN'T COME WITH YOU.
I HAVE TO GET OUT OF HERE, FREE MY PET WOLVERINE, GET OFF THIS SHIP, AND GET BACK TO MADRIPOOR.
BECAUSE THEY TOOK YOUR SISTER?
YEAH...
I'VE NEVER CALLED HER THAT. BUT, YEAH.
CAN YOU ALL HELP ME?
WHAT DO YOU NEED?
OKAY, FIRST UP, I NEED YOU TO KNOW THAT I DON'T FEEL PAIN, AND I NEED YOU NOT TO FREAK OUT.
THEN, I NEED YOU TO ABSOLUTELY FREAK OUT.
HUH?

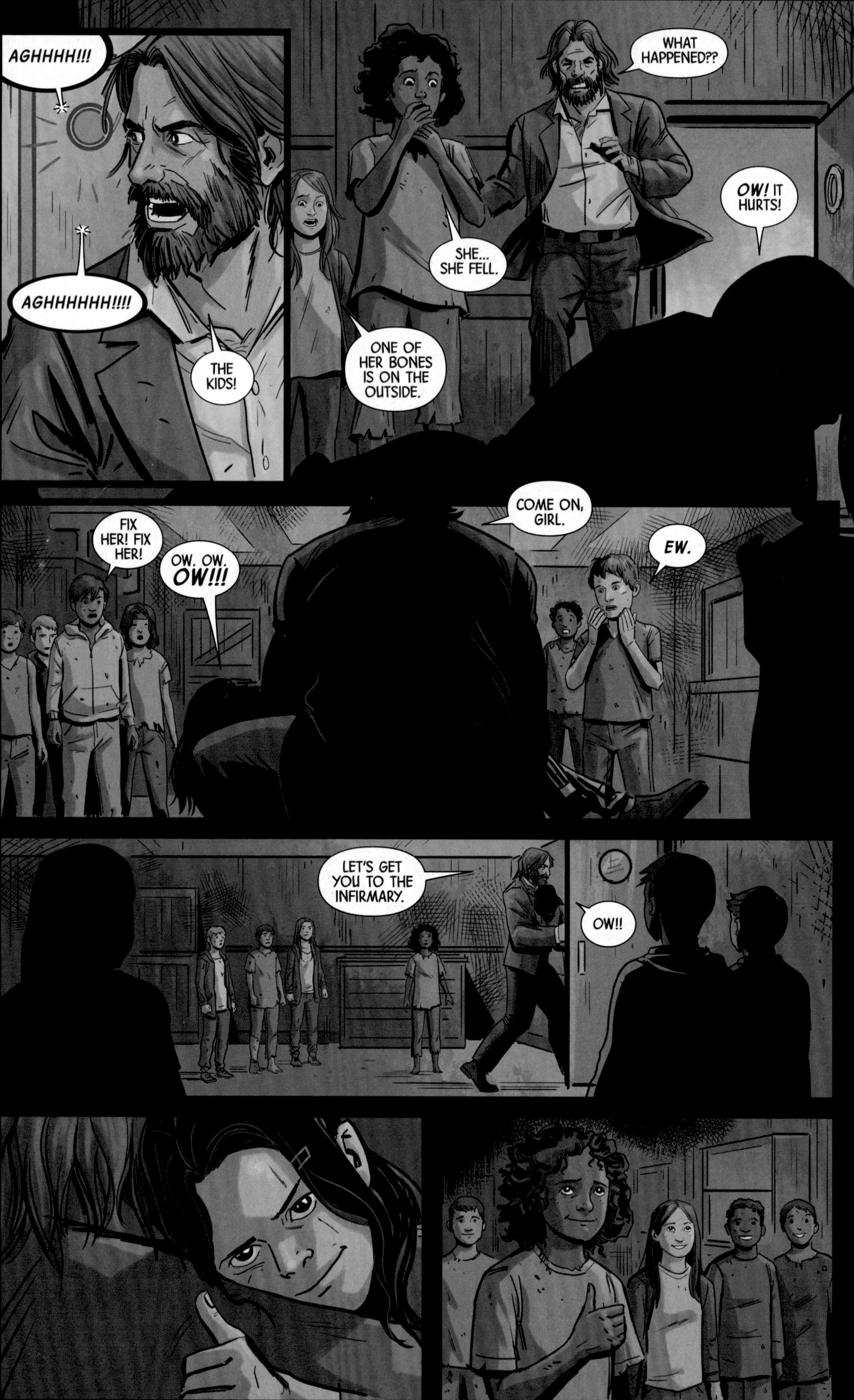

AGHHHH!!!
AGHHHHHH!!!!
THE KIDS!
ONE OF HER BONES IS ON THE OUTSIDE.
SHE... SHE FELL.
WHAT HAPPENED??
OW! IT HURTS!
FIX HER! FIX HER!
OW. OW. OW!!!
COME ON, GIRL.
EW.
LET'S GET YOU TO THE INFIRMARY.
OW!!

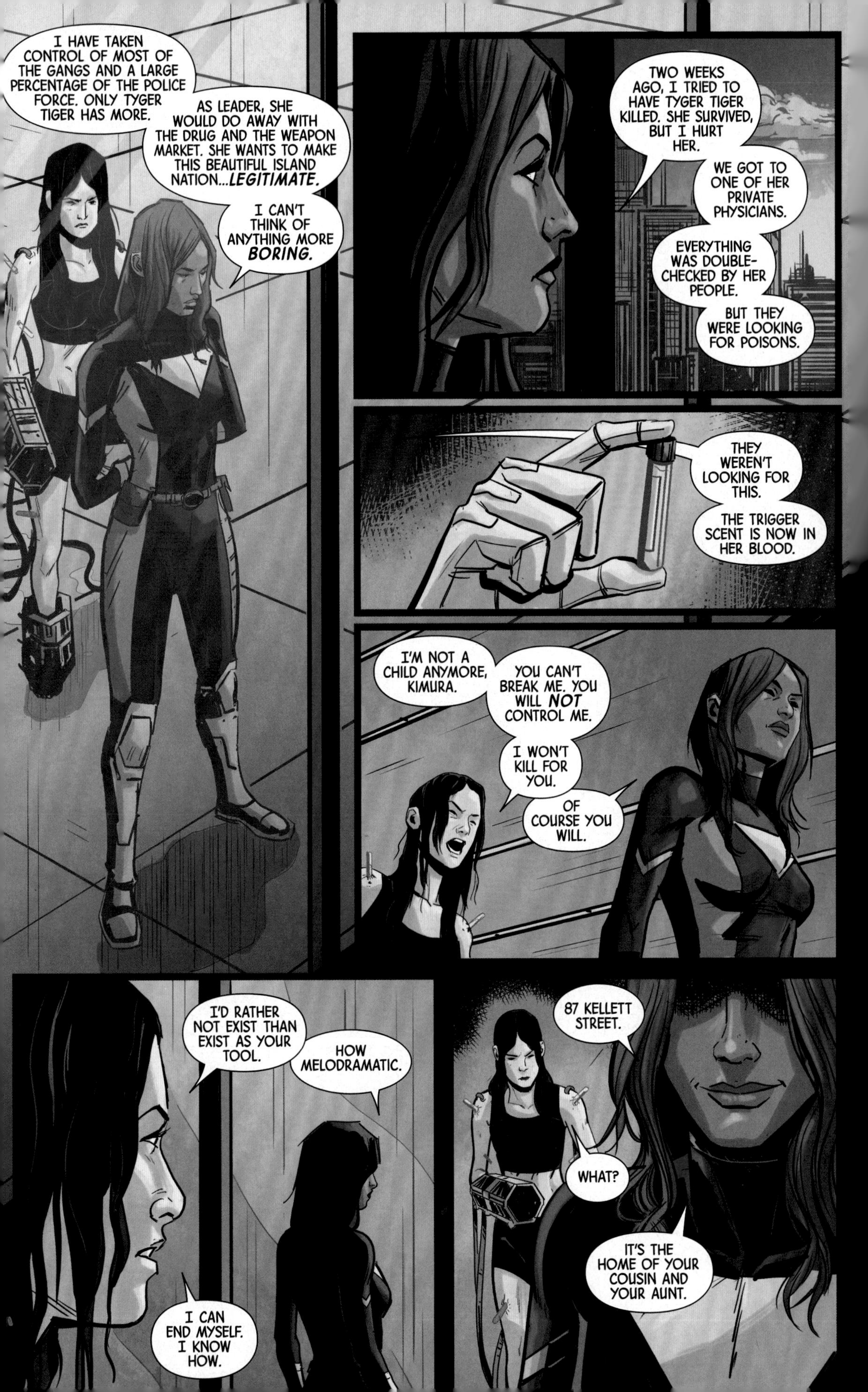

I HAVE TAKEN CONTROL OF MOST OF THE GANGS AND A LARGE PERCENTAGE OF THE POLICE FORCE. ONLY TYGER TIGER HAS MORE.
AS LEADER, SHE WOULD DO AWAY WITH THE DRUG AND THE WEAPON MARKET. SHE WANTS TO MAKE THIS BEAUTIFUL ISLAND NATION...LEGITIMATE.
I CAN'T THINK OF ANYTHING MORE BORING.
TWO WEEKS AGO, I TRIED TO HAVE TYGER TIGER KILLED. SHE SURVIVED, BUT I HURT HER.
WE GOT TO ONE OF HER PRIVATE PHYSICIANS.
EVERYTHING WAS DOUBLE-CHECKED BY HER PEOPLE.
BUT THEY WERE LOOKING FOR POISONS.
THEY WEREN'T LOOKING FOR THIS.
THE TRIGGER SCENT IS NOW IN HER BLOOD.
I'M NOT A CHILD ANYMORE, KIMURA.
YOU CAN'T BREAK ME. YOU WILL NOT CONTROL ME.
I WON'T KILL FOR YOU.
OF COURSE YOU WILL.
I'D RATHER NOT EXIST THAN EXIST AS YOUR TOOL.
HOW MELODRAMATIC.
I CAN END MYSELF. I KNOW HOW.
87 KELLETT STREET.
WHAT?
IT'S THE HOME OF YOUR COUSIN AND YOUR AUNT.

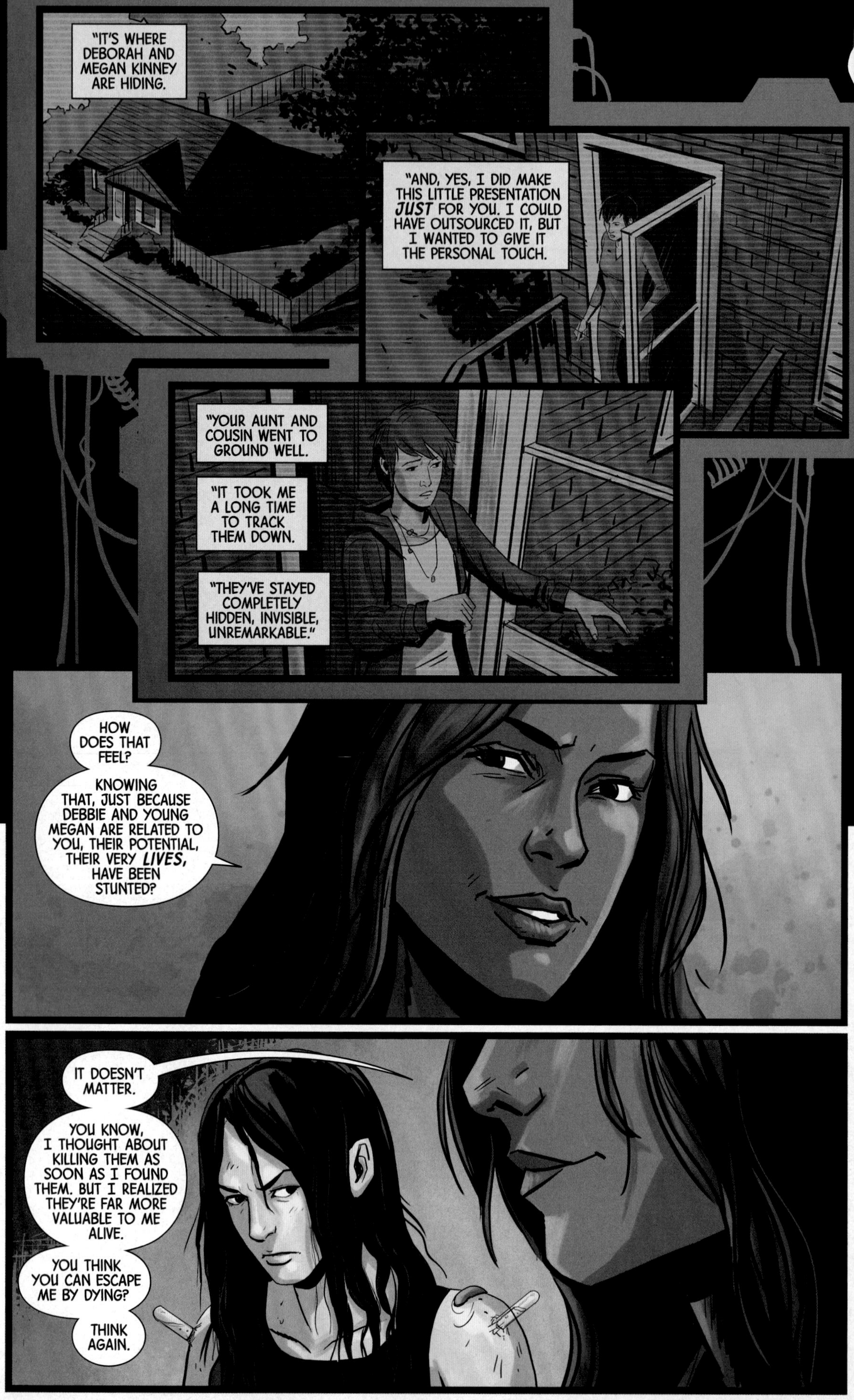
"IT'S WHERE DEBORAH AND MEGAN KINNEY ARE HIDING.
"AND, YES, I DID MAKE THIS LITTLE PRESENTATION JUST FOR YOU. I COULD HAVE OUTSOURCED IT, BUT I WANTED TO GIVE IT THE PERSONAL TOUCH.
"YOUR AUNT AND COUSIN WENT TO GROUND WELL.
"IT TOOK ME A LONG TIME TO TRACK THEM DOWN.
"THEY'VE STAYED COMPLETELY HIDDEN, INVISIBLE, UNREMARKABLE."
HOW DOES THAT FEEL?
KNOWING THAT, JUST BECAUSE DEBBIE AND YOUNG MEGAN ARE RELATED TO YOU, THEIR POTENTIAL, THEIR VERY LIVES, HAVE BEEN STUNTED?
IT DOESN'T MATTER.
YOU KNOW, I THOUGHT ABOUT KILLING THEM AS SOON AS I FOUND THEM. BUT I REALIZED THEY'RE FAR MORE VALUABLE TO ME ALIVE.
YOU THINK YOU CAN ESCAPE ME BY DYING?
THINK AGAIN.

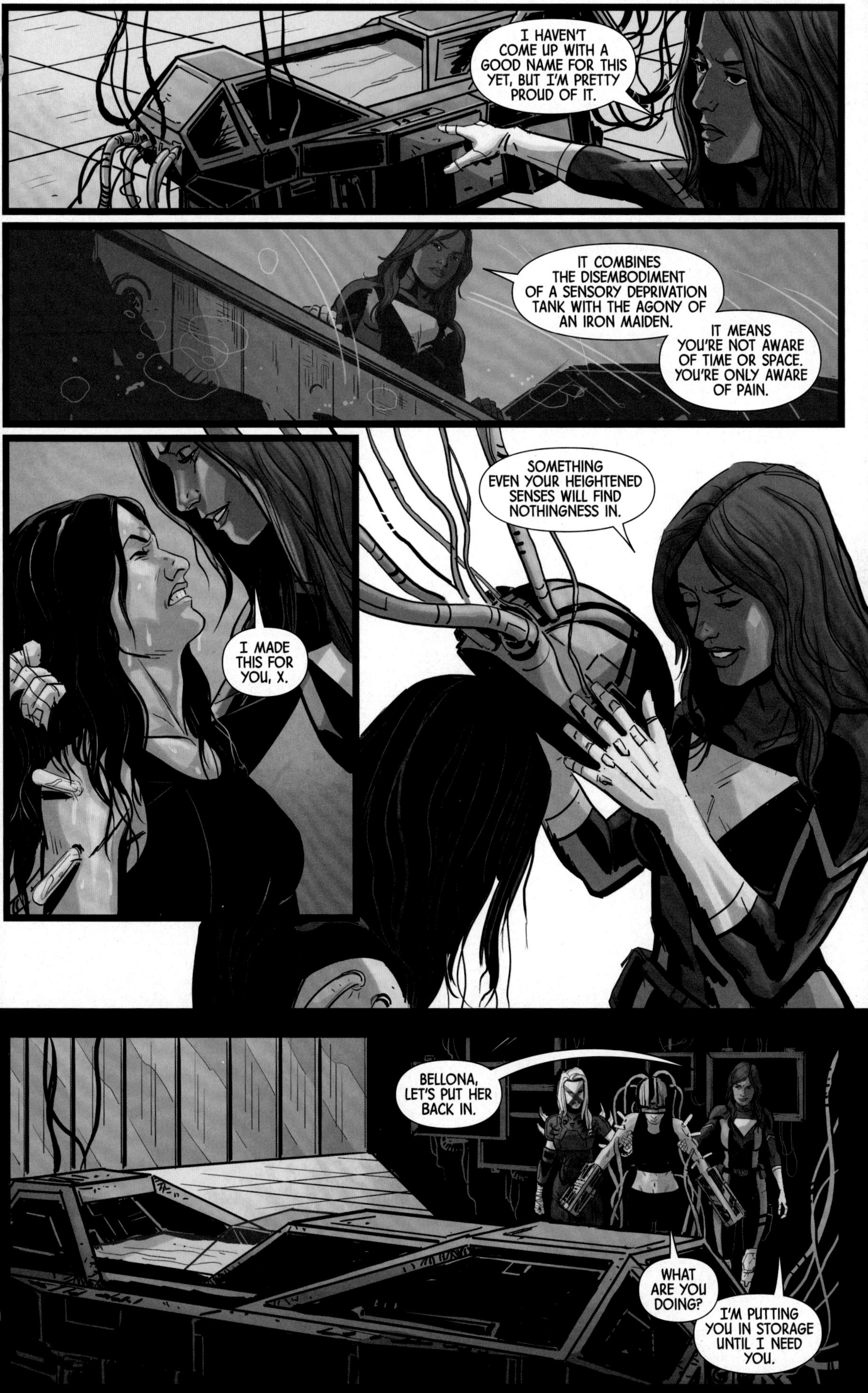
I HAVEN'T COME UP WITH A GOOD NAME FOR THIS YET, BUT I'M PRETTY PROUD OF IT.
IT COMBINES THE DISEMBODIMENT OF A SENSORY DEPRIVATION TANK WITH THE AGONY OF AN IRON MAIDEN.
IT MEANS YOU'RE NOT AWARE OF TIME OR SPACE. YOU'RE ONLY AWARE OF PAIN.
I MADE THIS FOR YOU, X.
SOMETHING EVEN YOUR HEIGHTENED SENSES WILL FIND NOTHINGNESS IN.
BELLONA, LET'S PUT HER BACK IN.
WHAT ARE YOU DOING?
I'M PUTTING YOU IN STORAGE UNTIL I NEED YOU.

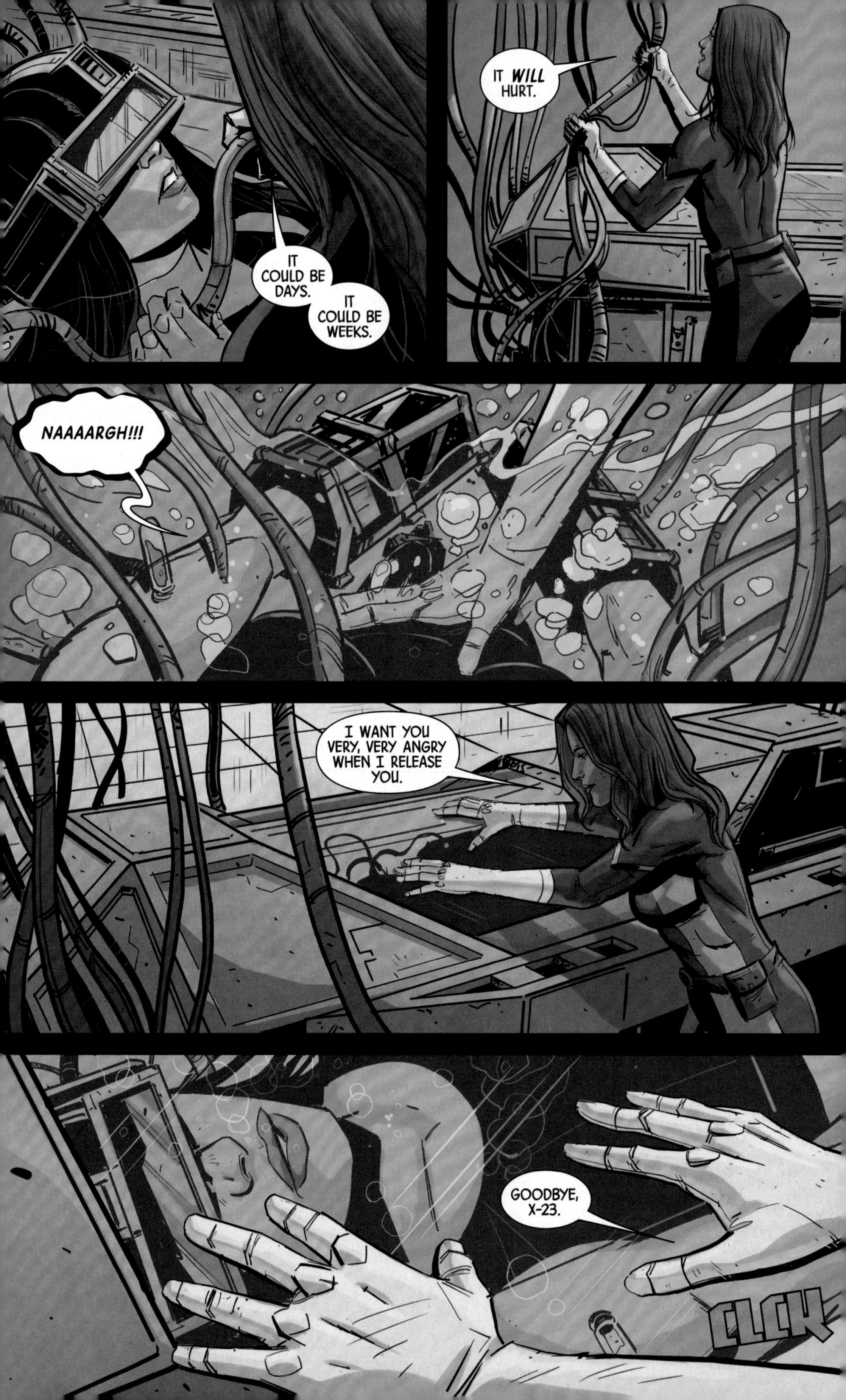
IT COULD BE DAYS.
IT COULD BE WEEKS.
IT WILL HURT.
NAAAARGH!!!
I WANT YOU VERY, VERY ANGRY WHEN I RELEASE YOU.
GOODBYE, X-23.
CLCK

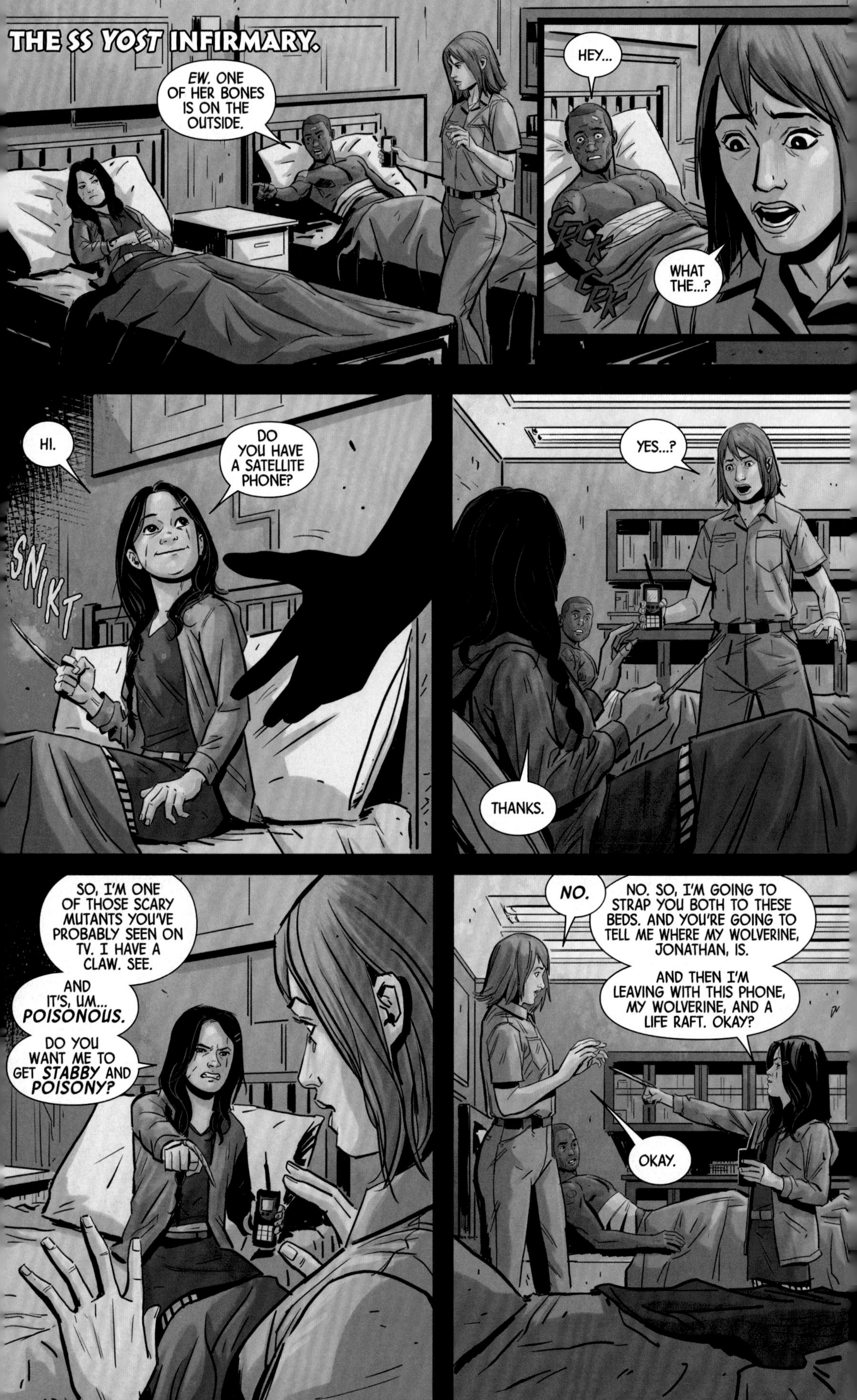
THE SS YOST INFIRMARY.
EW. ONE OF HER BONES IS ON THE OUTSIDE.
HEY...
CRCK CRK
WHAT THE...?
HI.
DO YOU HAVE A SATELLITE PHONE?
SNIKT
YES...?
THANKS.
SO, I'M ONE OF THOSE SCARY MUTANTS YOU'VE PROBABLY SEEN ON TV. I HAVE A CLAW. SEE.
AND IT'S, UM... POISONOUS.
DO YOU WANT ME TO GET STABBY AND POISONY?
NO.
NO. SO, I'M GOING TO STRAP YOU BOTH TO THESE BEDS. AND YOU'RE GOING TO TELL ME WHERE MY WOLVERINE, JONATHAN, IS.
AND THEN I'M LEAVING WITH THIS PHONE, MY WOLVERINE, AND A LIFE RAFT. OKAY?
OKAY.

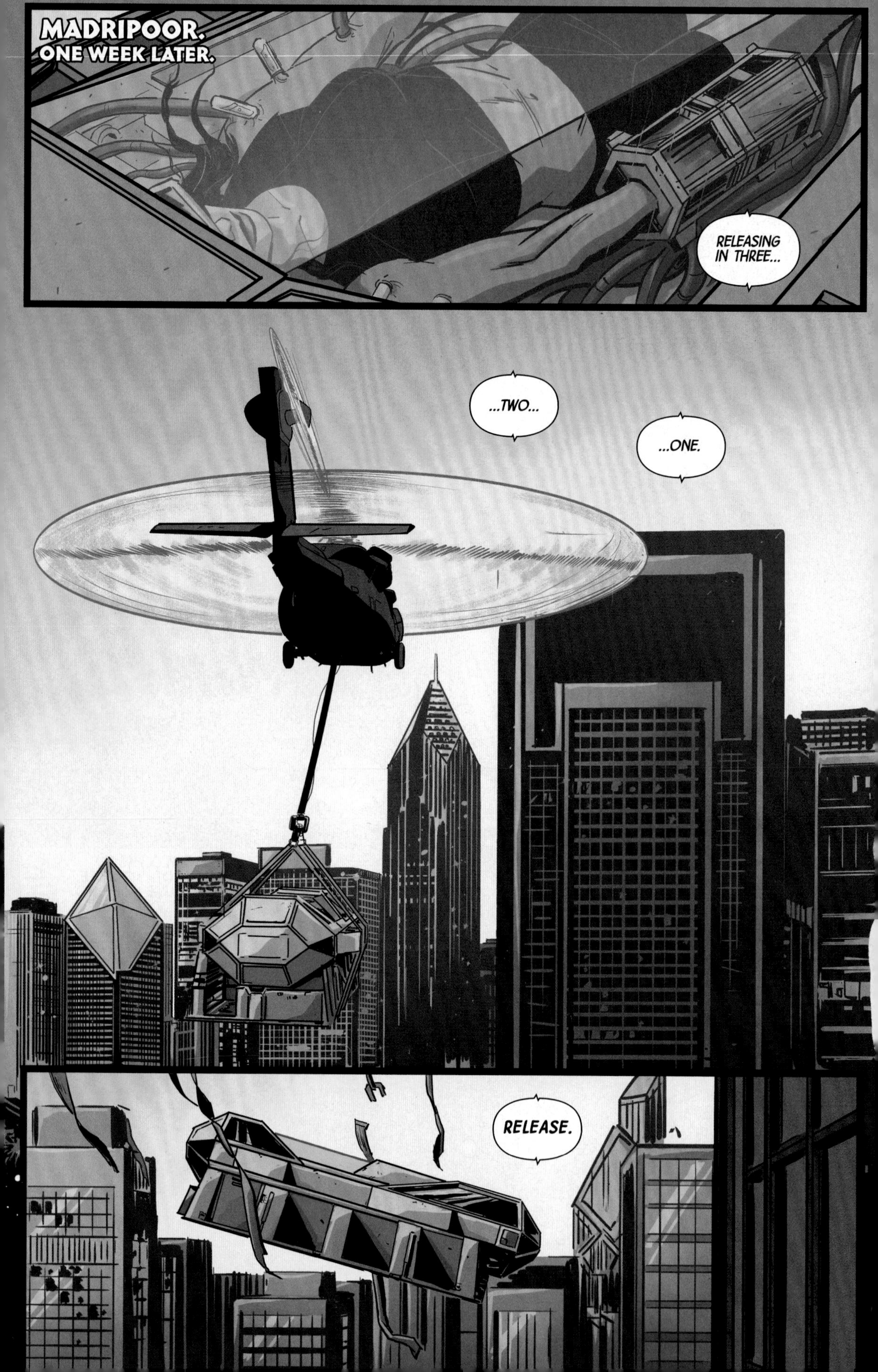
MADRIPOOR.
ONE WEEK LATER.
RELEASING IN THREE...
...TWO...
...ONE.
RELEASE.

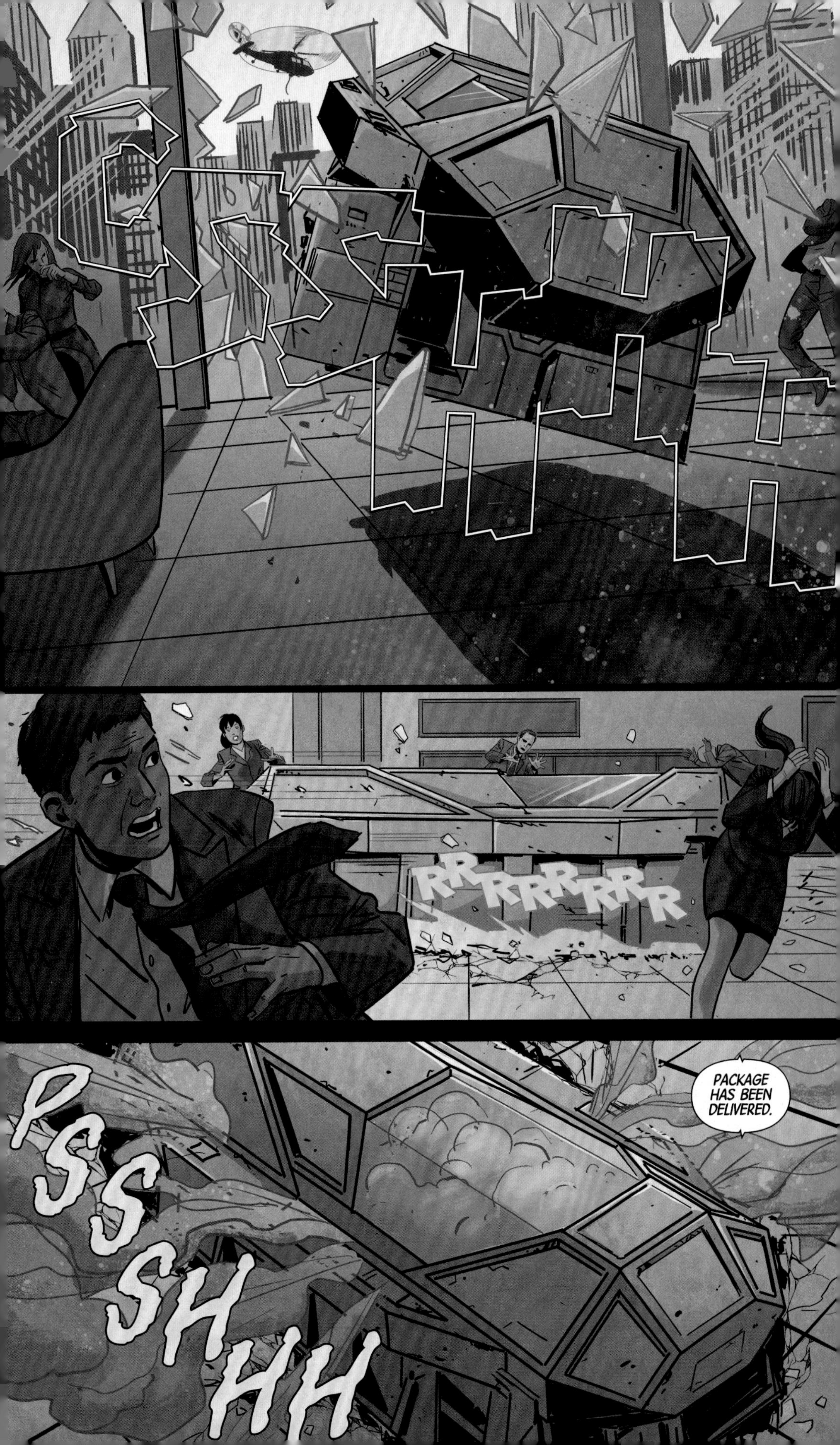
CRRUNCH
RRRRRRRRR
PSSSHHH
PACKAGE HAS BEEN DELIVERED.

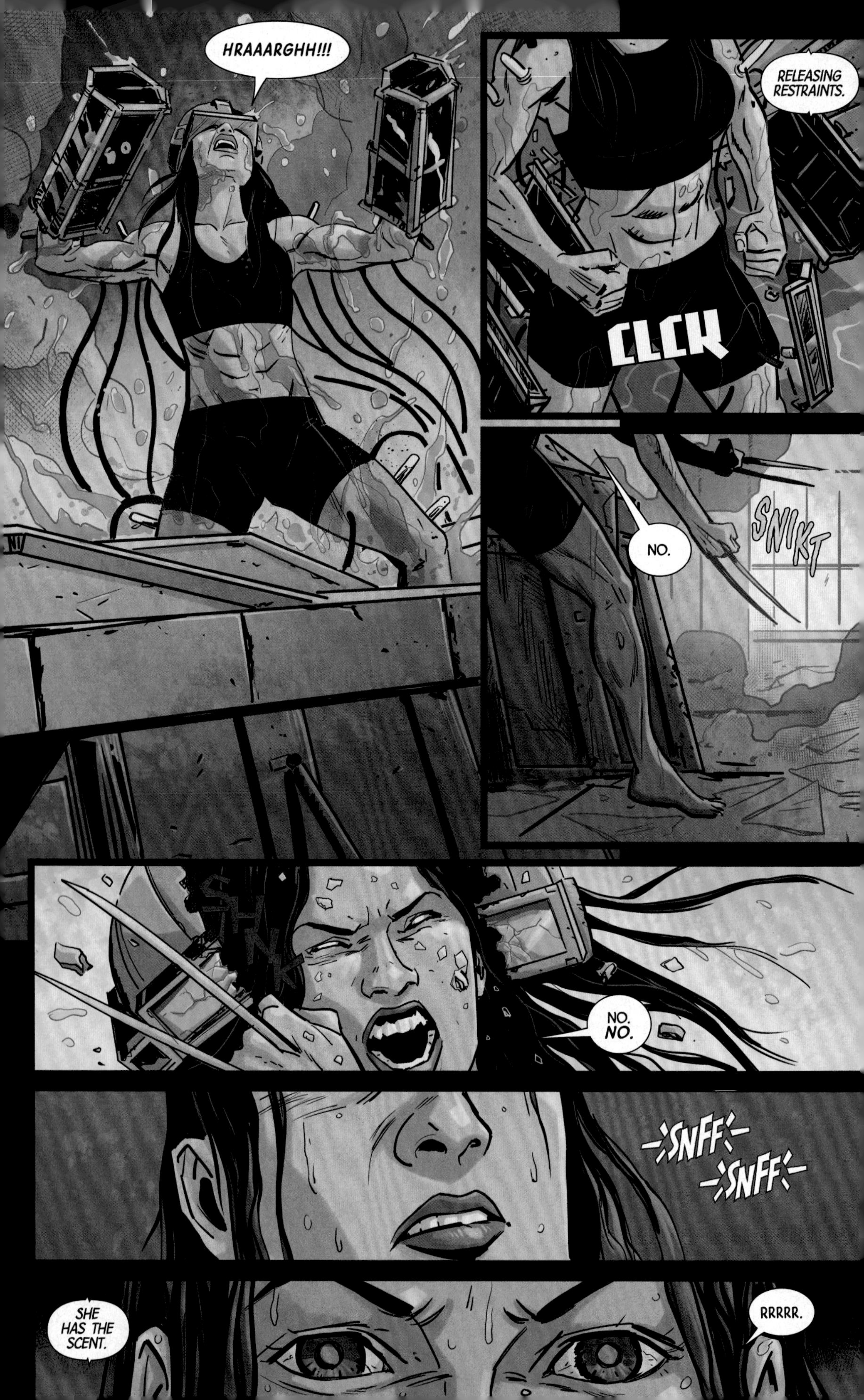
HRAAARGHH!!!
RELEASING RESTRAINTS.
CLCK
NO.
SNIKT
NO. NO.
SNFF
SNFF
SHE HAS THE SCENT.
RRRRR.

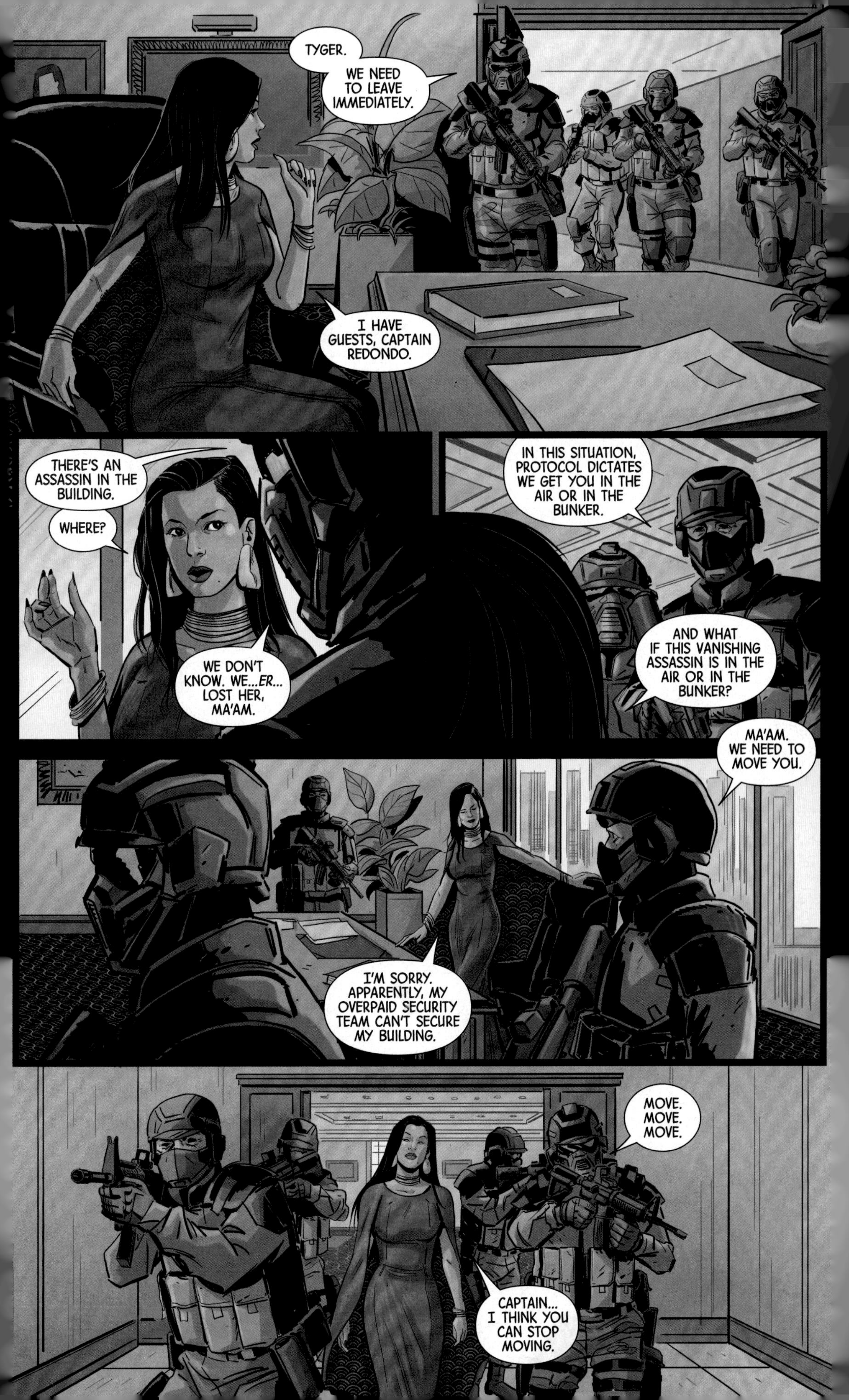
TYGER.
WE NEED TO LEAVE IMMEDIATELY.
I HAVE GUESTS, CAPTAIN REDONDO.
THERE'S AN ASSASSIN IN THE BUILDING.
WHERE?
WE DON'T KNOW. WE...ER... LOST HER, MA'AM.
IN THIS SITUATION, PROTOCOL DICTATES WE GET YOU IN THE AIR OR IN THE BUNKER.
AND WHAT IF THIS VANISHING ASSASSIN IS IN THE AIR OR IN THE BUNKER?
MA'AM. WE NEED TO MOVE YOU.
I'M SORRY. APPARENTLY, MY OVERPAID SECURITY TEAM CAN'T SECURE MY BUILDING.
MOVE. MOVE. MOVE.
CAPTAIN... I THINK YOU CAN STOP MOVING.

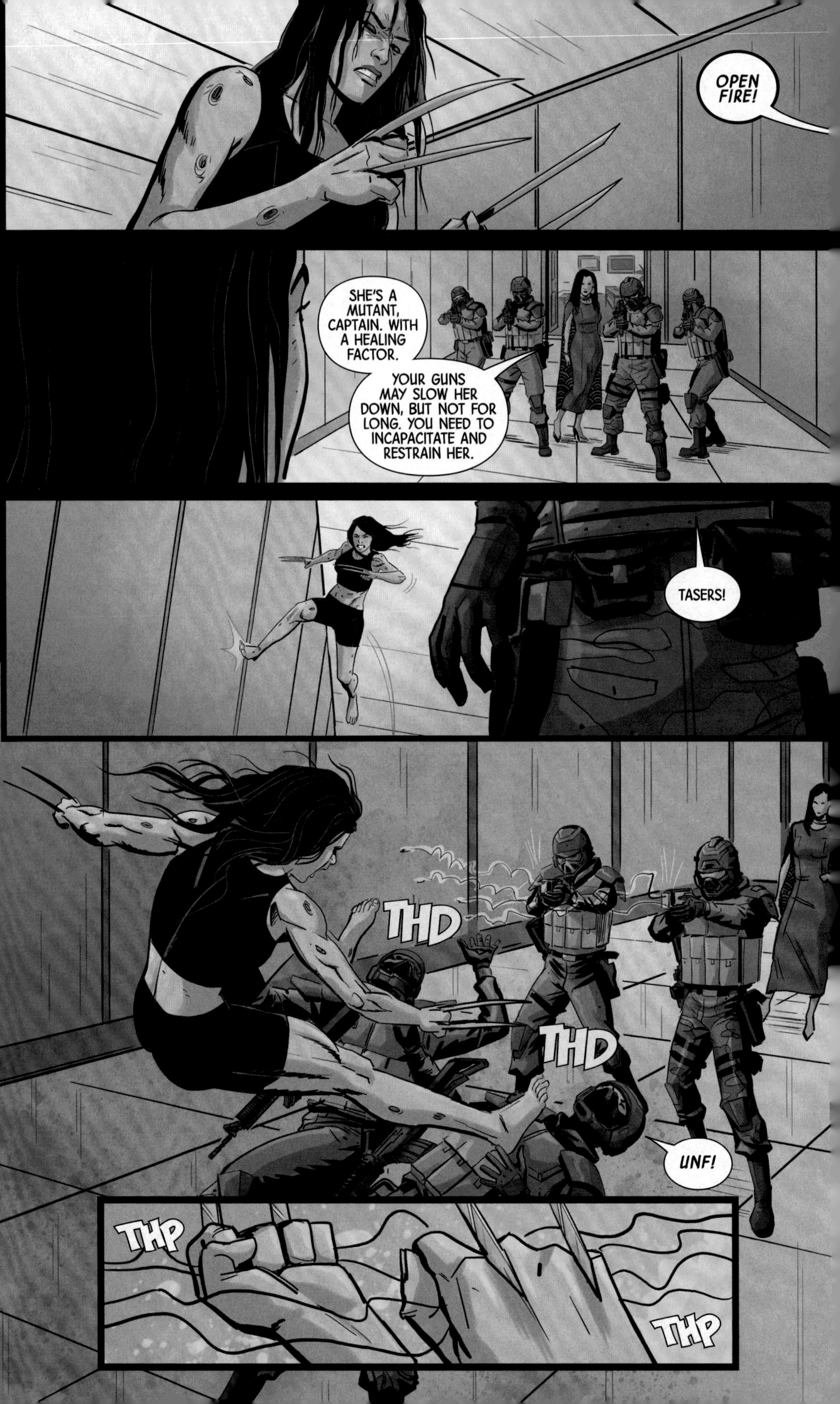
OPEN FIRE!
SHE'S A MUTANT, CAPTAIN. WITH A HEALING FACTOR.
YOUR GUNS MAY SLOW HER DOWN, BUT NOT FOR LONG. YOU NEED TO INCAPACITATE AND RESTRAIN HER.
TASERS!
THD
THD
UNF!
THP
THP

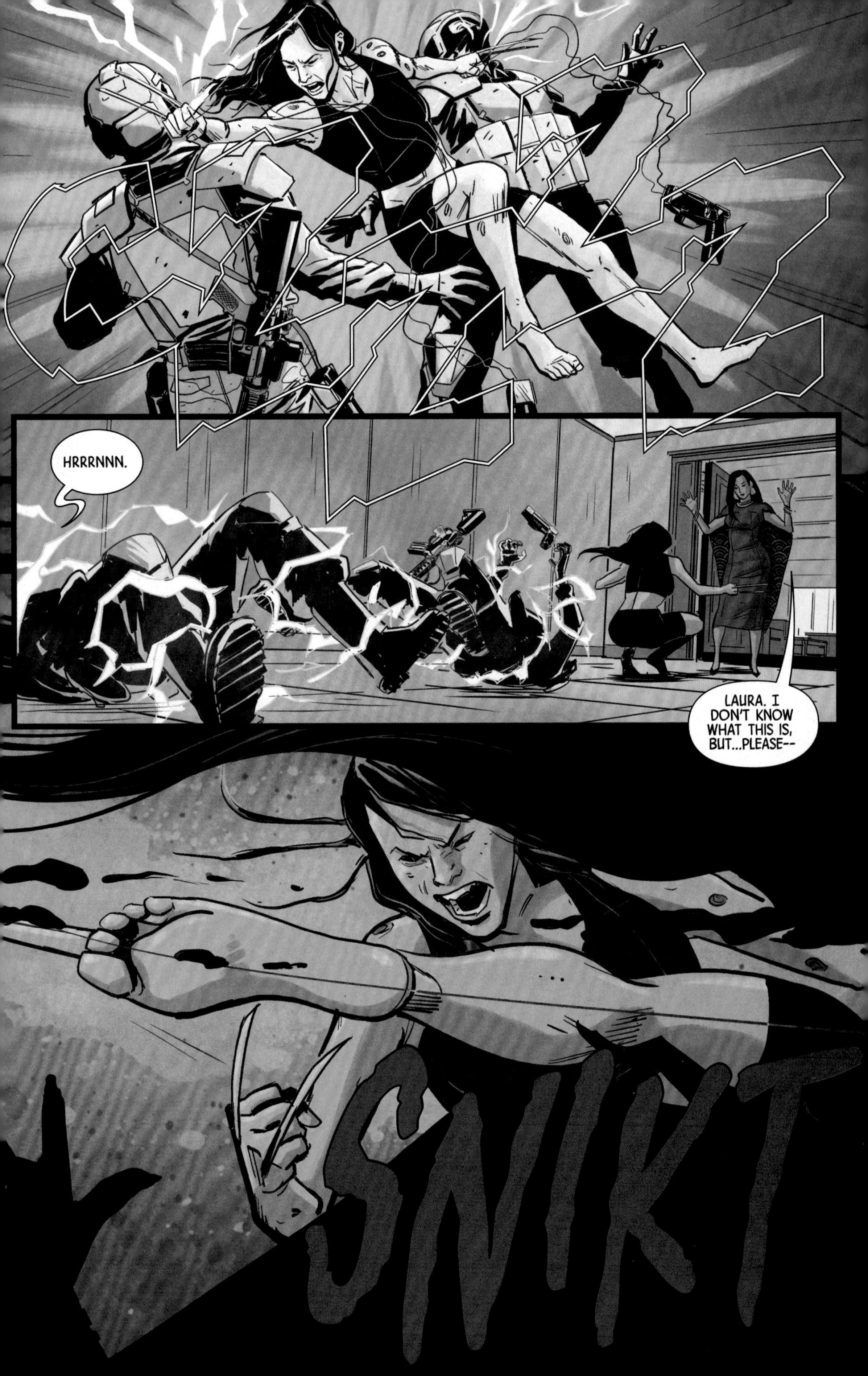
HRRRNNN.
LAURA. I DON'T KNOW WHAT THIS IS, BUT...PLEASE--
SNIKT

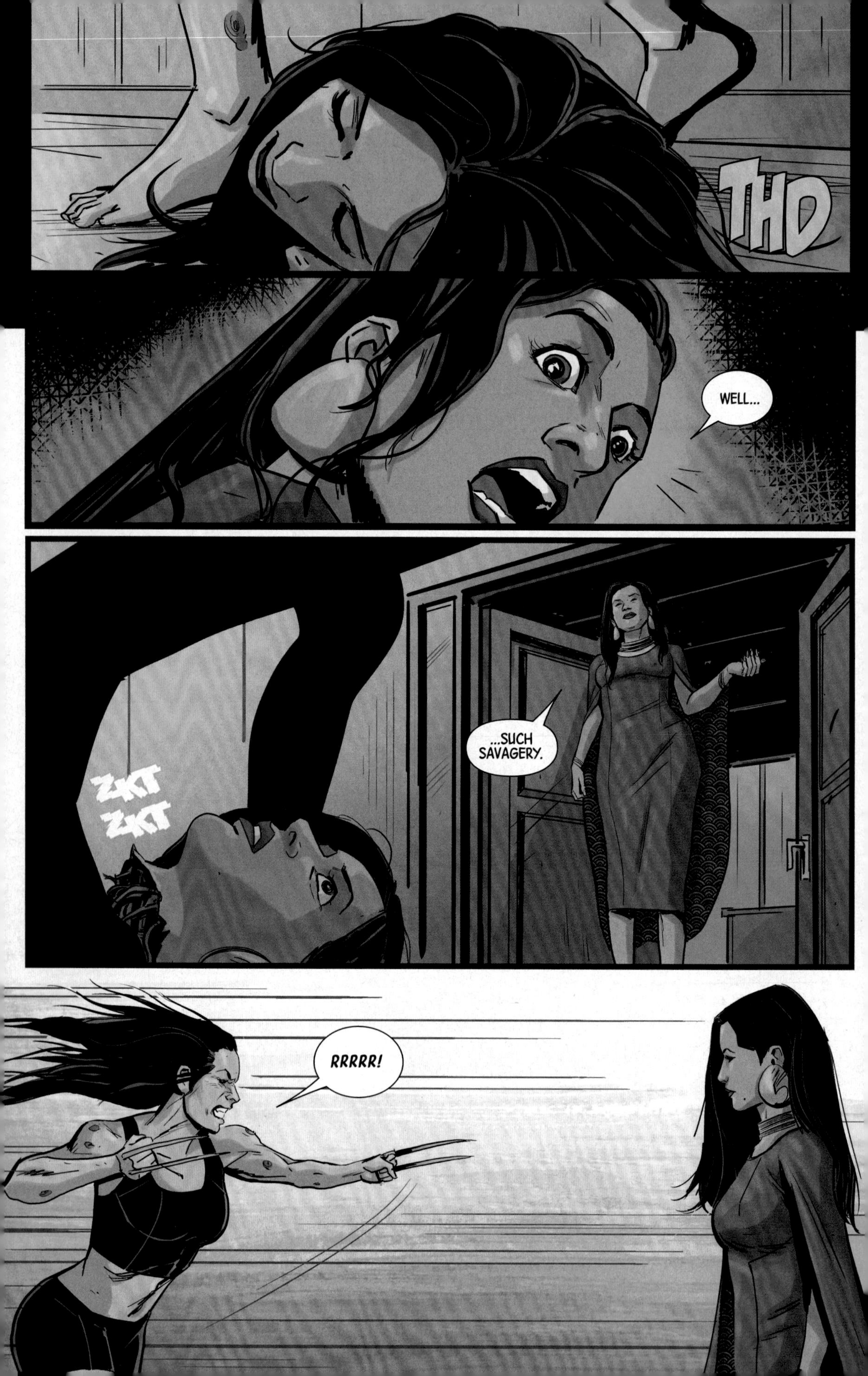
THD
WELL...
...SUCH SAVAGERY.
ZKT
ZKT
RRRRR!

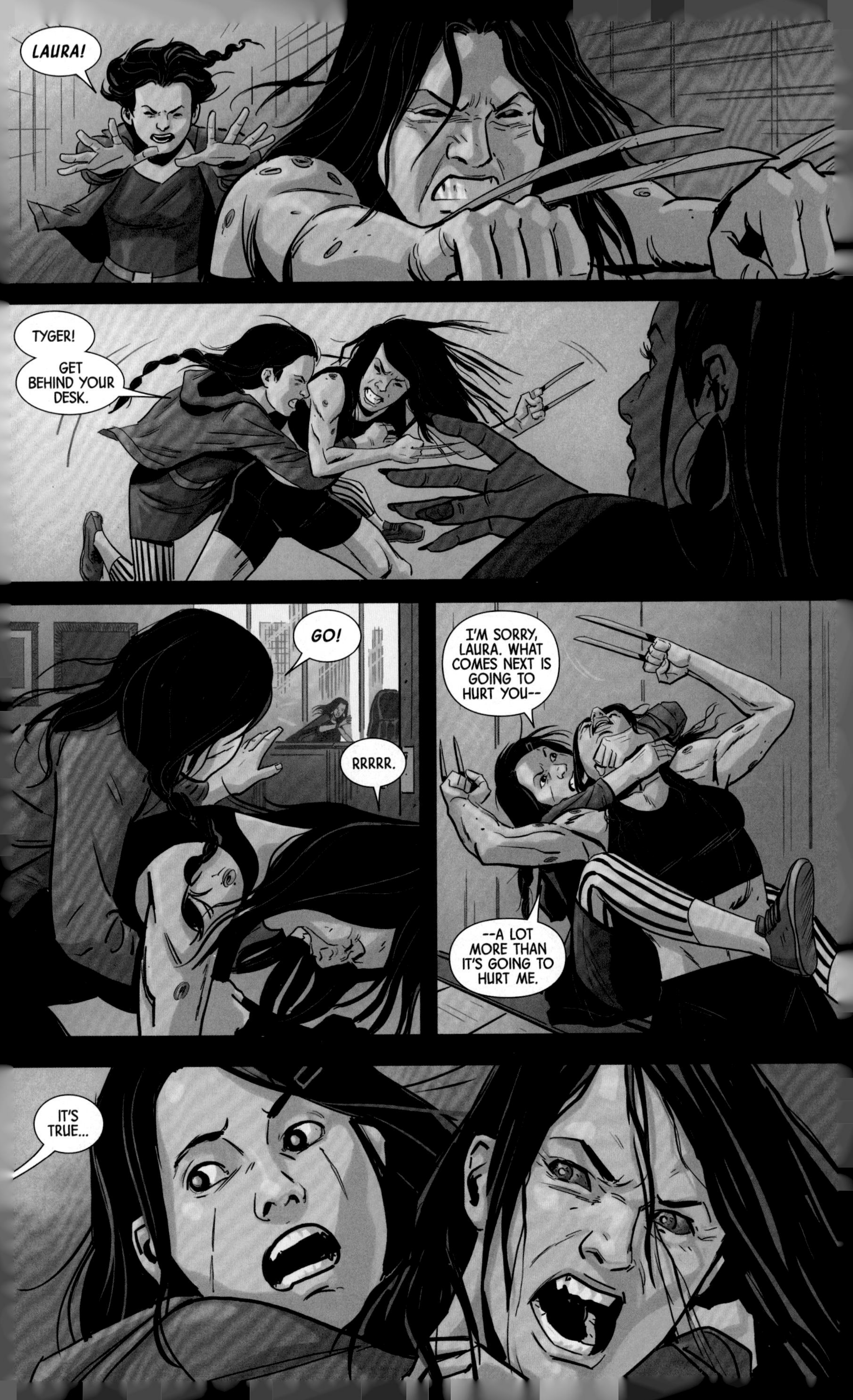
LAURA!
TYGER!
GET BEHIND YOUR DESK.
GO!
RRRRR.
I'M SORRY, LAURA. WHAT COMES NEXT IS GOING TO HURT YOU--
--A LOT MORE THAN IT'S GOING TO HURT ME.
IT'S TRUE...

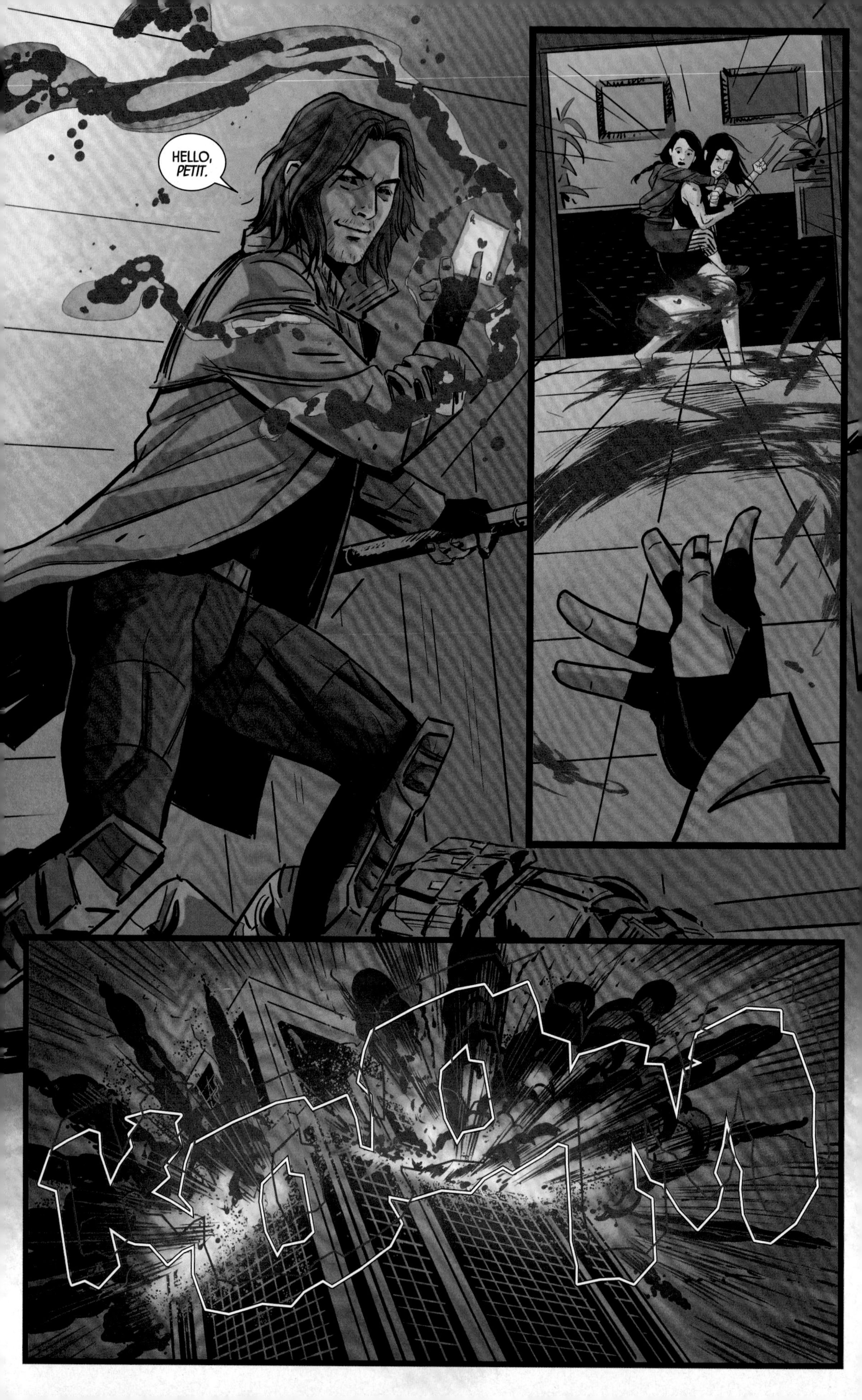
HELLO, PETIT.
KOOOOM

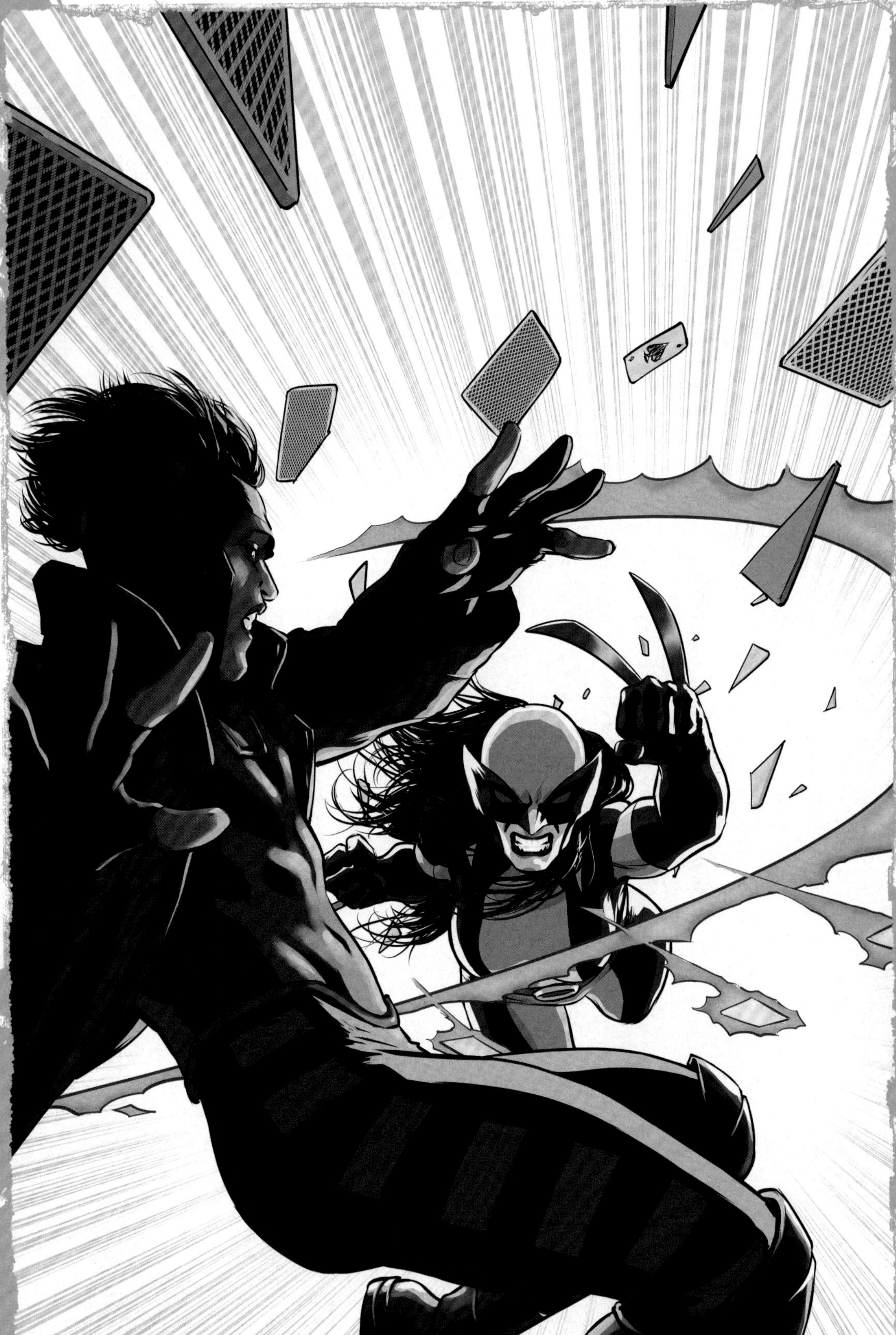

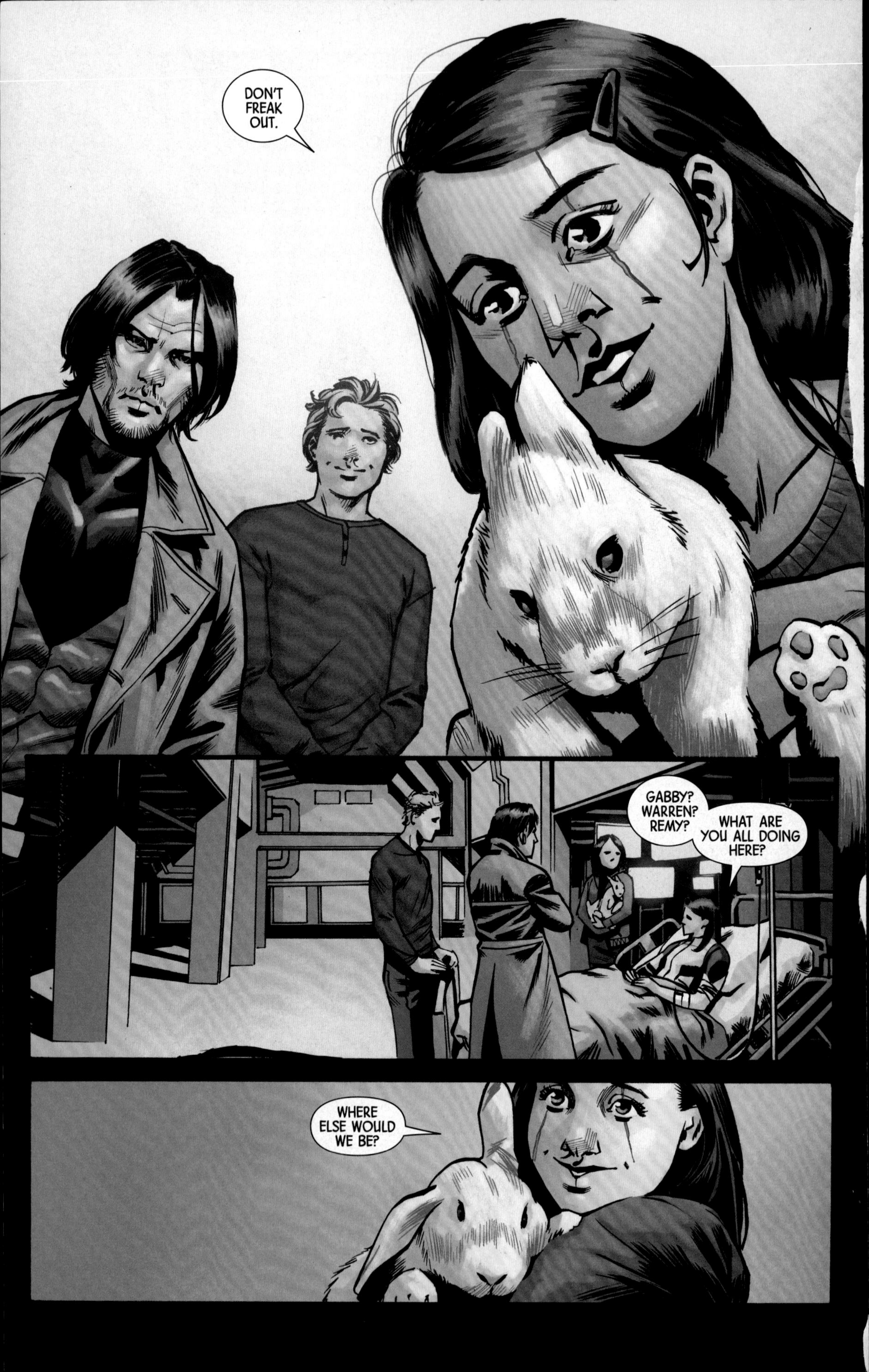
DON'T FREAK OUT.
GABBY? WARREN? REMY?
WHAT ARE YOU ALL DOING HERE?
WHERE ELSE WOULD WE BE?

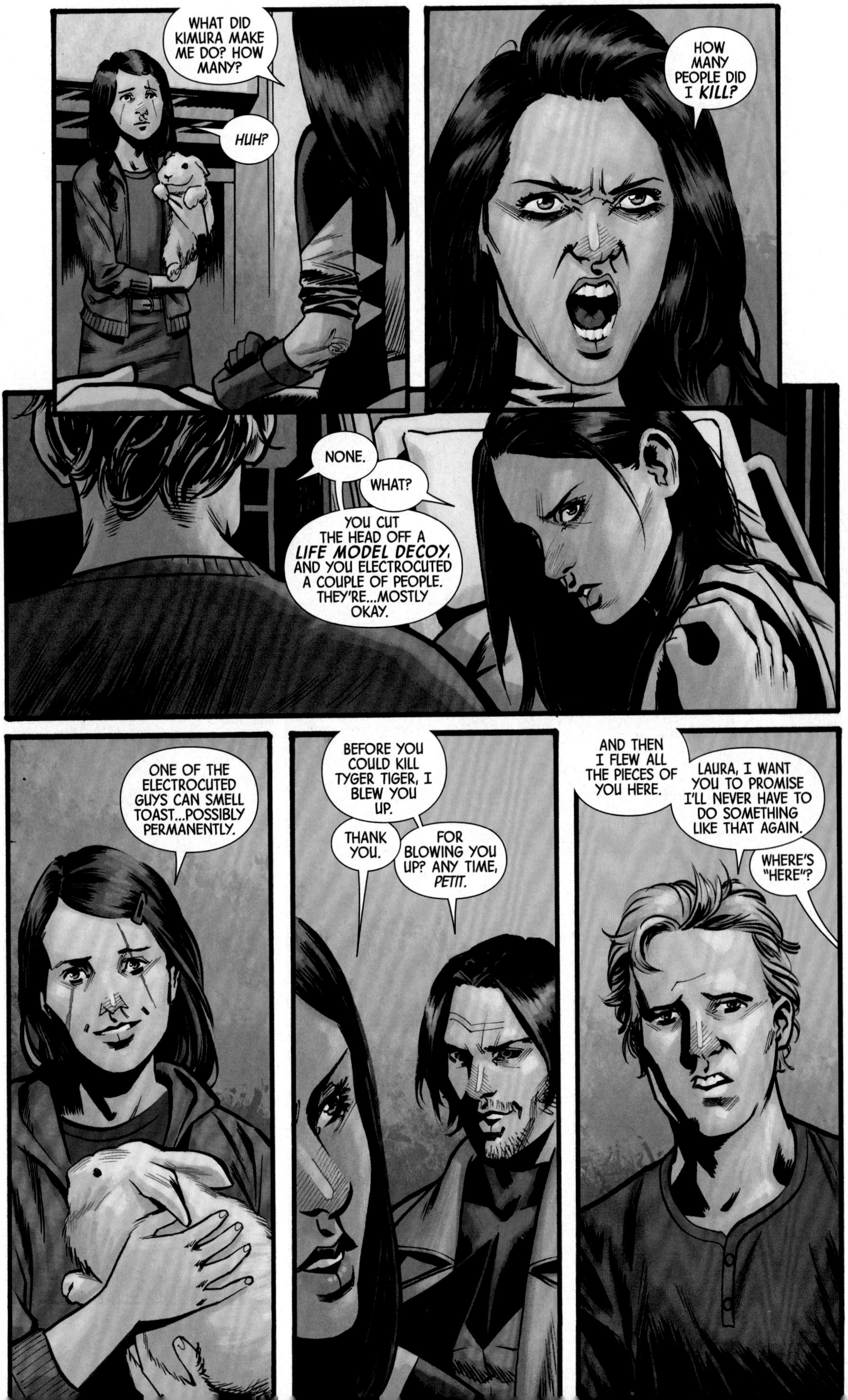
WHAT DID KIMURA MAKE ME DO? HOW MANY?
HUH?
HOW MANY PEOPLE DID I *KILL?*
NONE.
WHAT?
YOU CUT THE HEAD OFF A *LIFE MODEL DECOY*, AND YOU ELECTROCUTED A COUPLE OF PEOPLE. THEY'RE...MOSTLY OKAY.
ONE OF THE ELECTROCUTED GUYS CAN SMELL TOAST...POSSIBLY PERMANENTLY.
BEFORE YOU COULD KILL TYGER TIGER, I BLEW YOU UP.
THANK YOU.
FOR BLOWING YOU UP? ANY TIME, *PETIT.*
AND THEN I FLEW ALL THE PIECES OF YOU HERE.
LAURA, I WANT YOU TO PROMISE I'LL NEVER HAVE TO DO SOMETHING LIKE THAT AGAIN.
WHERE'S "HERE"?

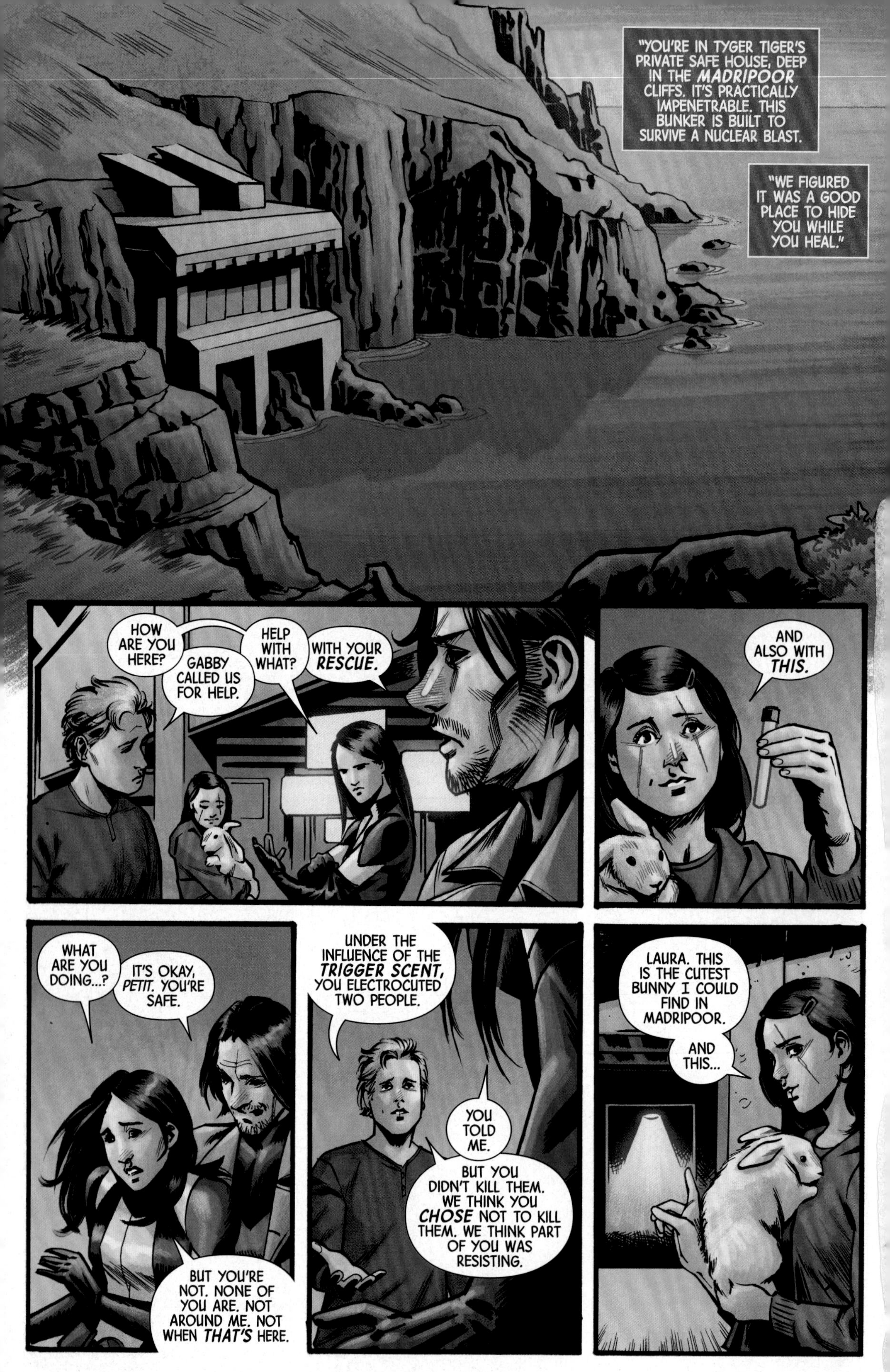
"YOU'RE IN TYGER TIGER'S PRIVATE SAFE HOUSE, DEEP IN THE MADRIPOOR CLIFFS. IT'S PRACTICALLY IMPENETRABLE. THIS BUNKER IS BUILT TO SURVIVE A NUCLEAR BLAST.
"WE FIGURED IT WAS A GOOD PLACE TO HIDE YOU WHILE YOU HEAL."
HOW ARE YOU HERE?
GABBY CALLED US FOR HELP.
HELP WITH WHAT?
WITH YOUR RESCUE.
AND ALSO WITH THIS.
WHAT ARE YOU DOING...?
IT'S OKAY, PETIT. YOU'RE SAFE.
BUT YOU'RE NOT. NONE OF YOU ARE. NOT AROUND ME. NOT WHEN THAT'S HERE.
UNDER THE INFLUENCE OF THE TRIGGER SCENT, YOU ELECTROCUTED TWO PEOPLE.
YOU TOLD ME.
BUT YOU DIDN'T KILL THEM. WE THINK YOU CHOSE NOT TO KILL THEM. WE THINK PART OF YOU WAS RESISTING.
LAURA. THIS IS THE CUTEST BUNNY I COULD FIND IN MADRIPOOR.
AND THIS...

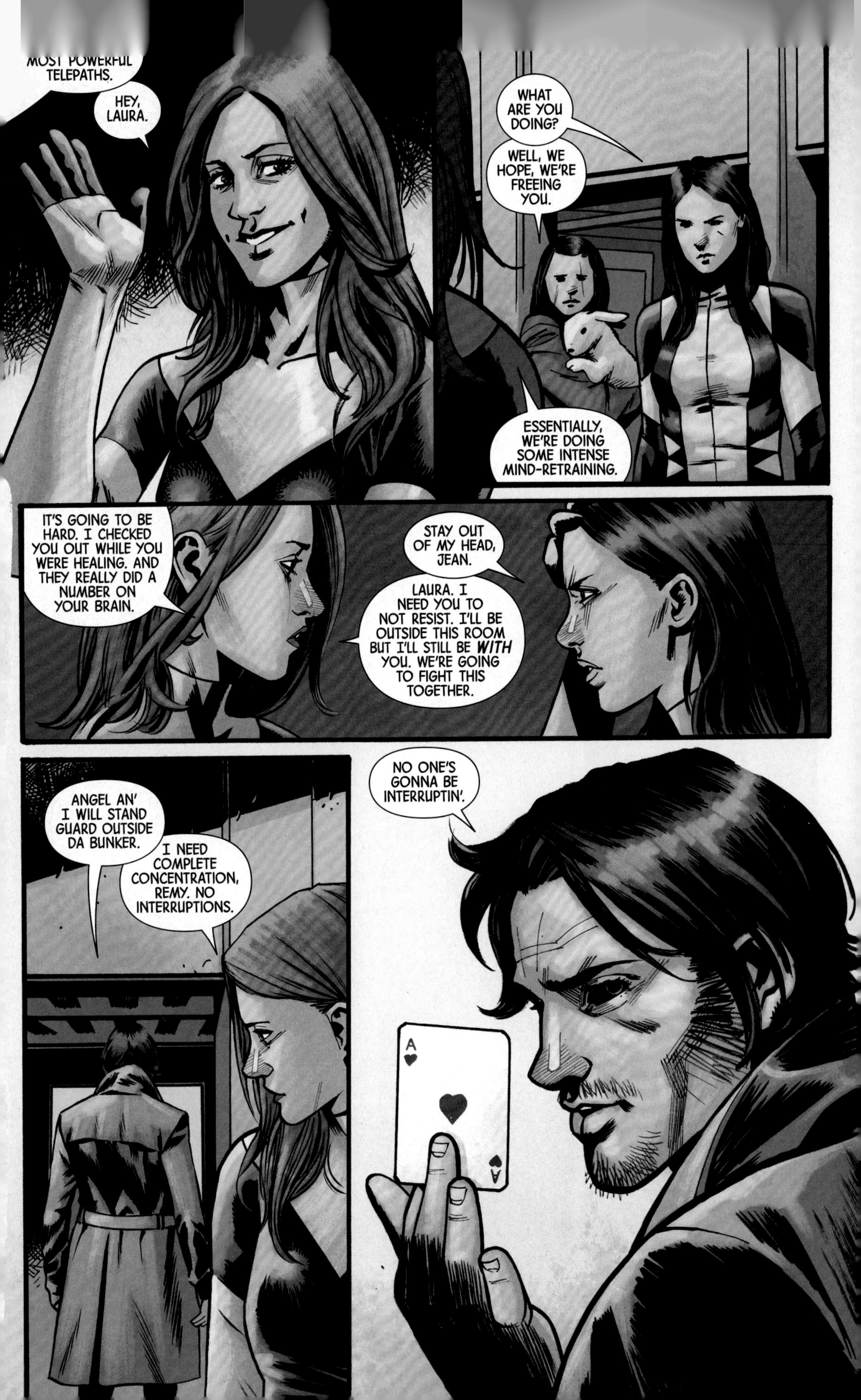
MOST POWERFUL TELEPATHS.
HEY, LAURA.
WHAT ARE YOU DOING?
WELL, WE HOPE, WE'RE FREEING YOU.
ESSENTIALLY, WE'RE DOING SOME INTENSE MIND-RETRAINING.
IT'S GOING TO BE HARD. I CHECKED YOU OUT WHILE YOU WERE HEALING. AND THEY REALLY DID A NUMBER ON YOUR BRAIN.
STAY OUT OF MY HEAD, JEAN.
LAURA. I NEED YOU TO NOT RESIST. I'LL BE OUTSIDE THIS ROOM BUT I'LL STILL BE *WITH* YOU. WE'RE GOING TO FIGHT THIS TOGETHER.
ANGEL AN' I WILL STAND GUARD OUTSIDE DA BUNKER.
I NEED COMPLETE CONCENTRATION, REMY. NO INTERRUPTIONS.
NO ONE'S GONNA BE INTERRUPTIN'.

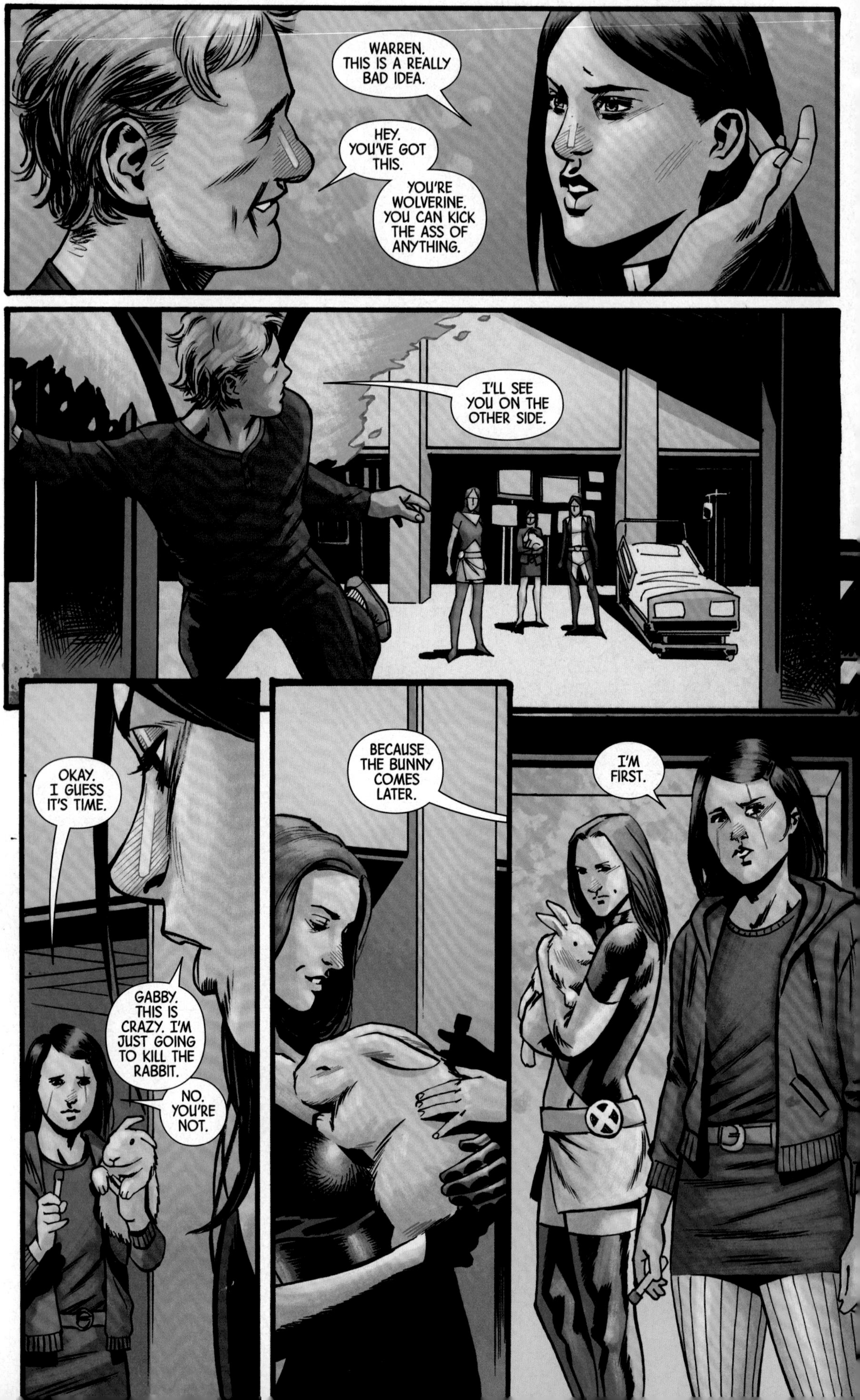
WARREN. THIS IS A REALLY BAD IDEA.
HEY. YOU'VE GOT THIS.
YOU'RE WOLVERINE. YOU CAN KICK THE ASS OF ANYTHING.
I'LL SEE YOU ON THE OTHER SIDE.
OKAY. I GUESS IT'S TIME.
GABBY. THIS IS CRAZY. I'M JUST GOING TO KILL THE RABBIT.
NO. YOU'RE NOT.
BECAUSE THE BUNNY COMES LATER.
I'M FIRST.

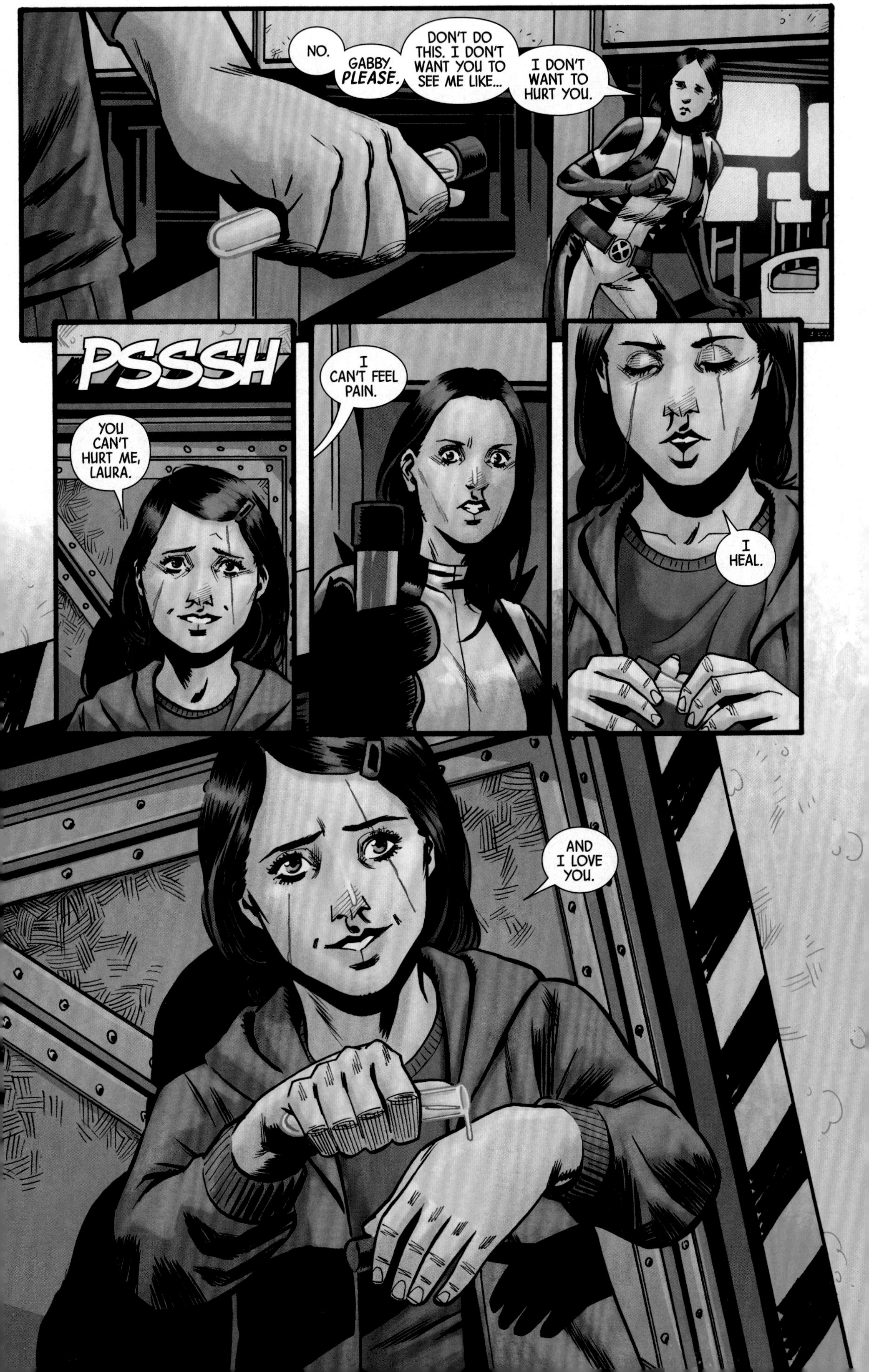
NO.
GABBY. PLEASE.
DON'T DO THIS. I DON'T WANT YOU TO SEE ME LIKE...
I DON'T WANT TO HURT YOU.
PSSSH
YOU CAN'T HURT ME, LAURA.
I CAN'T FEEL PAIN.
I HEAL.
AND I LOVE YOU.

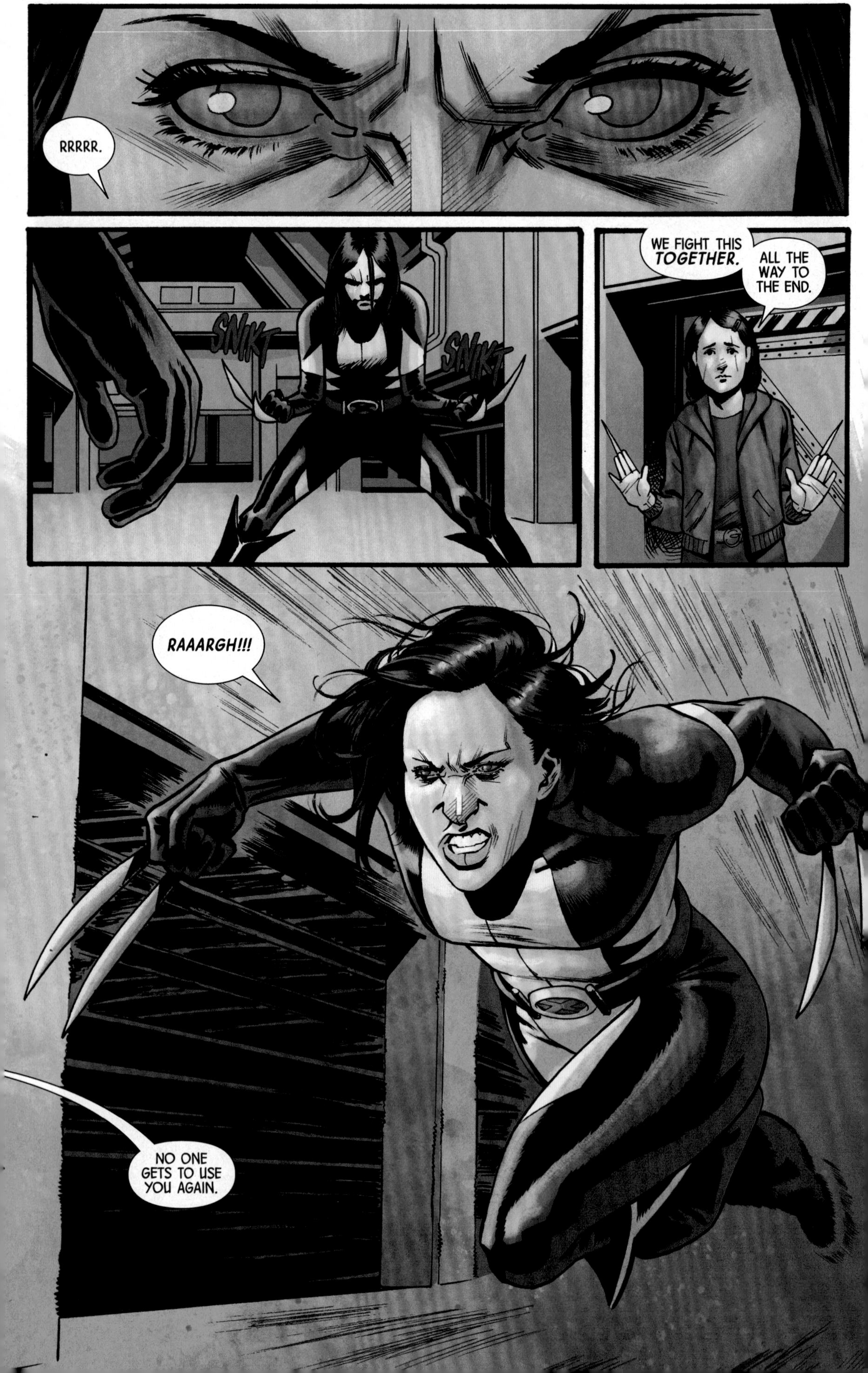
RRRRR.
SNIKT
SNIKT
WE FIGHT THIS *TOGETHER.*
ALL THE WAY TO THE END.
RAAARGH!!!
NO ONE GETS TO USE YOU AGAIN.

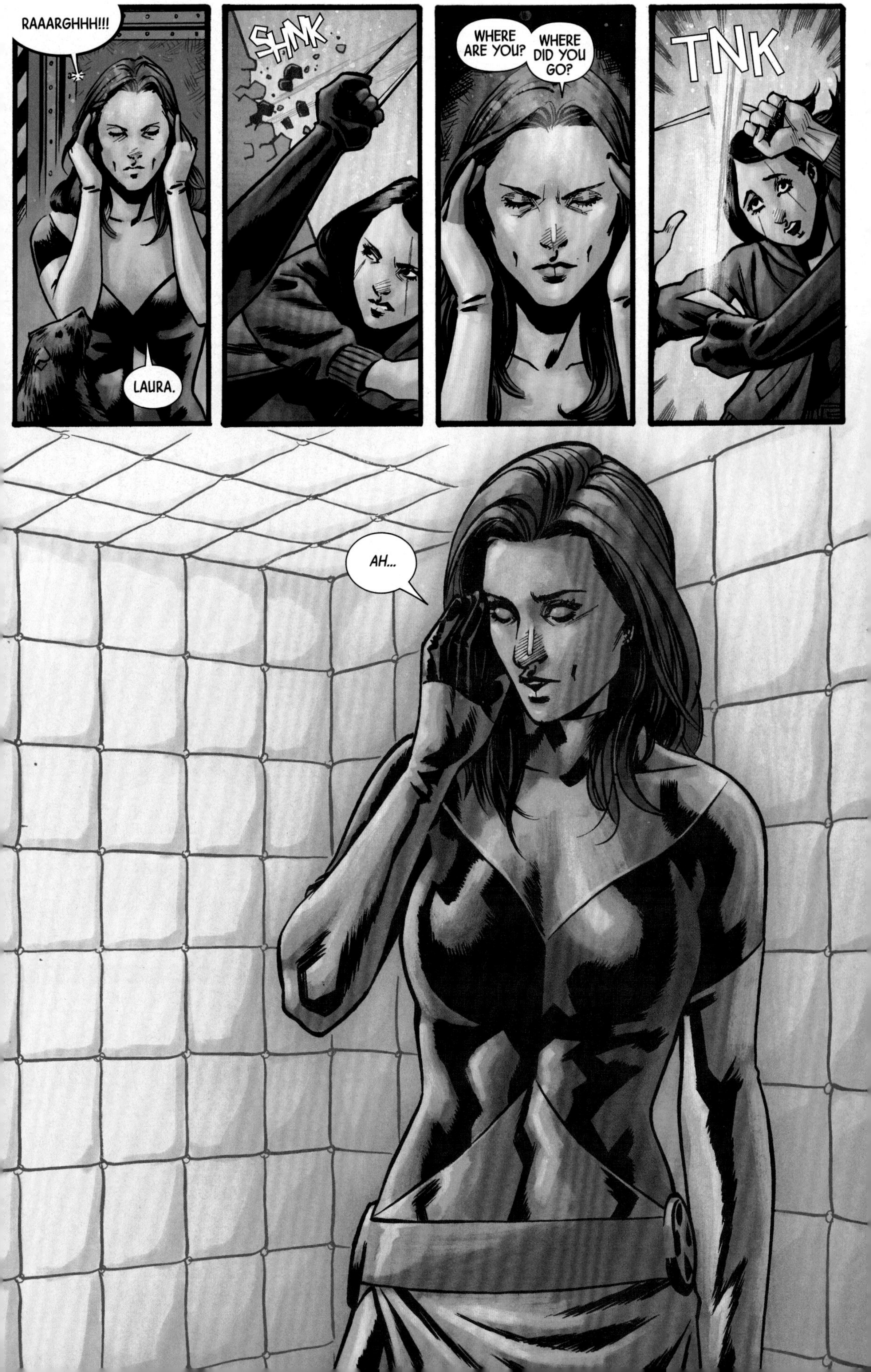
RAAARGHHH!!!
LAURA.
SHNK
WHERE ARE YOU?
WHERE DID YOU GO?
TNK
AH...

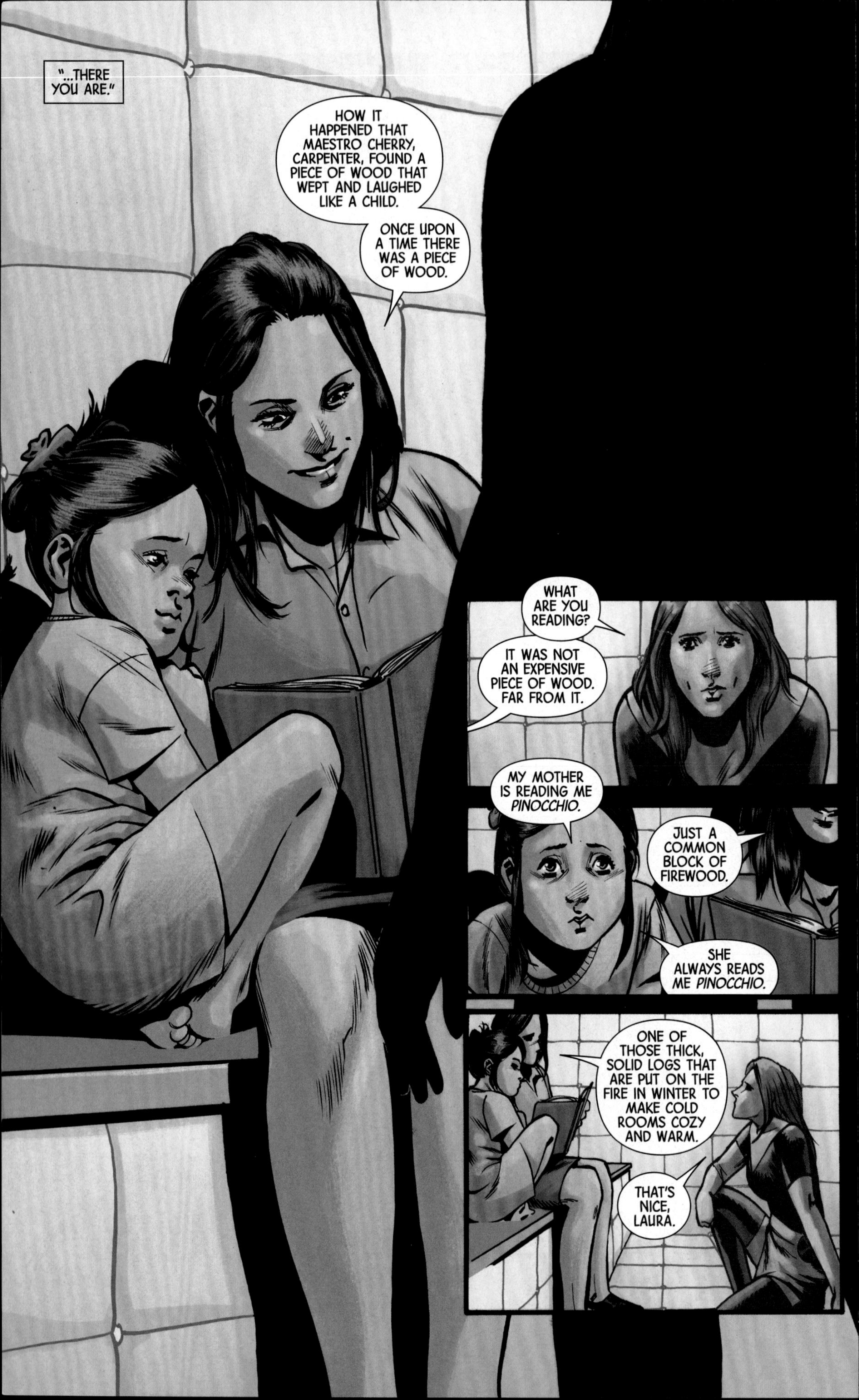
"...THERE YOU ARE."
HOW IT HAPPENED THAT MAESTRO CHERRY, CARPENTER, FOUND A PIECE OF WOOD THAT WEPT AND LAUGHED LIKE A CHILD.
ONCE UPON A TIME THERE WAS A PIECE OF WOOD.
WHAT ARE YOU READING?
IT WAS NOT AN EXPENSIVE PIECE OF WOOD. FAR FROM IT.
MY MOTHER IS READING ME *PINOCCHIO.*
JUST A COMMON BLOCK OF FIREWOOD.
SHE ALWAYS READS ME *PINOCCHIO.*
ONE OF THOSE THICK, SOLID LOGS THAT ARE PUT ON THE FIRE IN WINTER TO MAKE COLD ROOMS COZY AND WARM.
THAT'S NICE, LAURA.

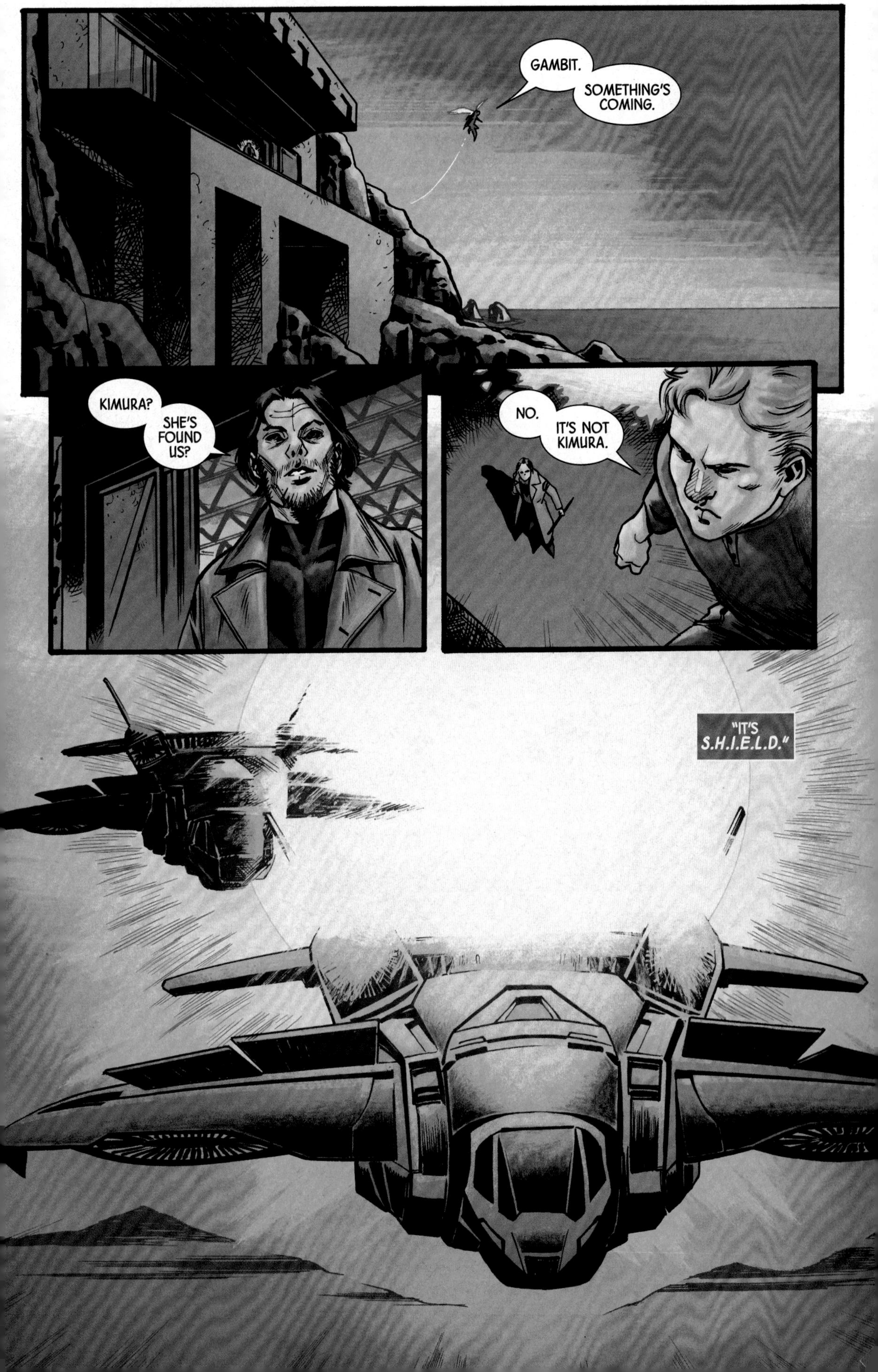
GAMBIT.
SOMETHING'S COMING.
KIMURA?
SHE'S FOUND US?
NO.
IT'S NOT KIMURA.
"IT'S S.H.I.E.L.D."

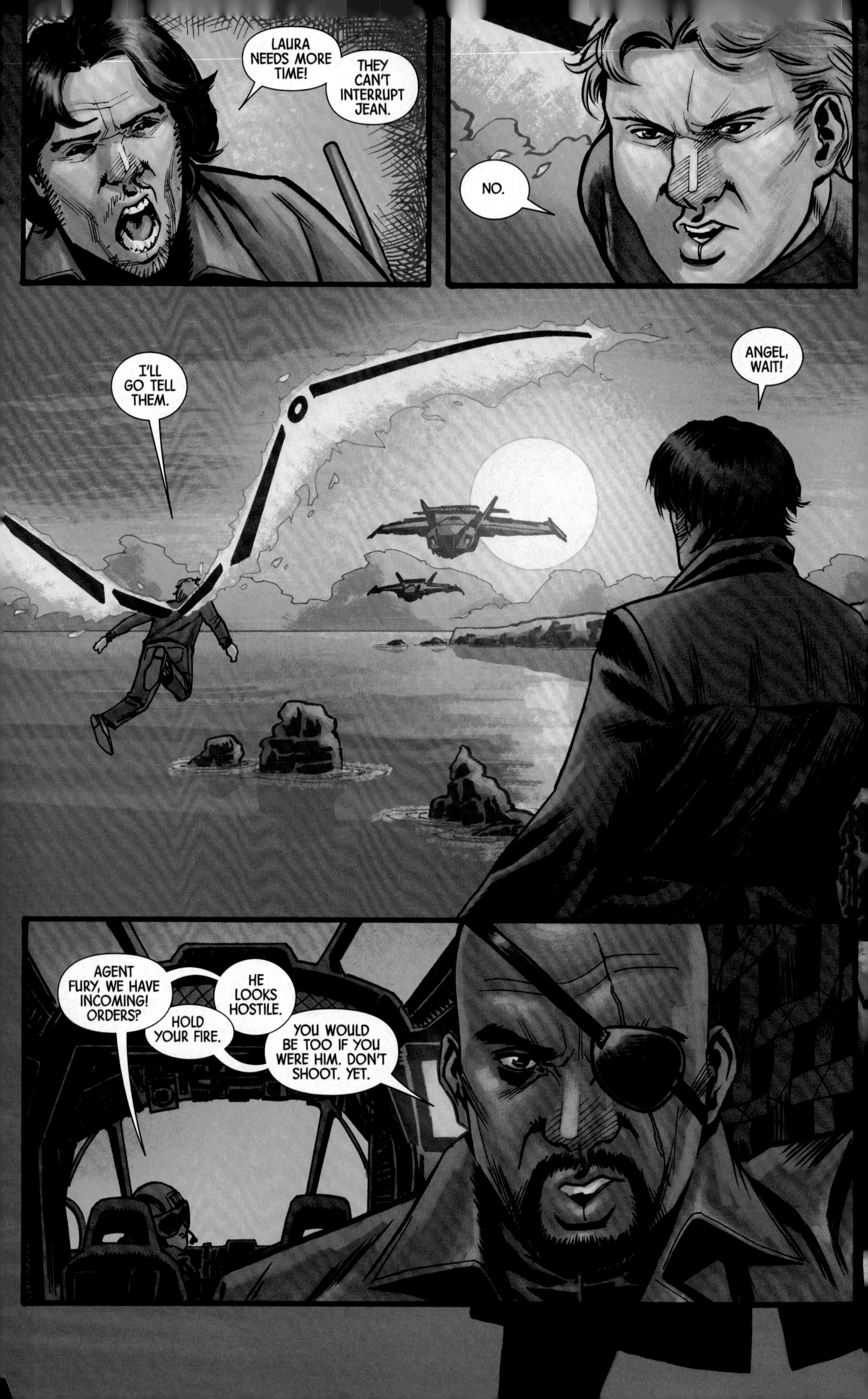
LAURA NEEDS MORE TIME!
THEY CAN'T INTERRUPT JEAN.
NO.
I'LL GO TELL THEM.
ANGEL, WAIT!
AGENT FURY, WE HAVE INCOMING! ORDERS?
HE LOOKS HOSTILE.
HOLD YOUR FIRE.
YOU WOULD BE TOO IF YOU WERE HIM. DON'T SHOOT. YET.

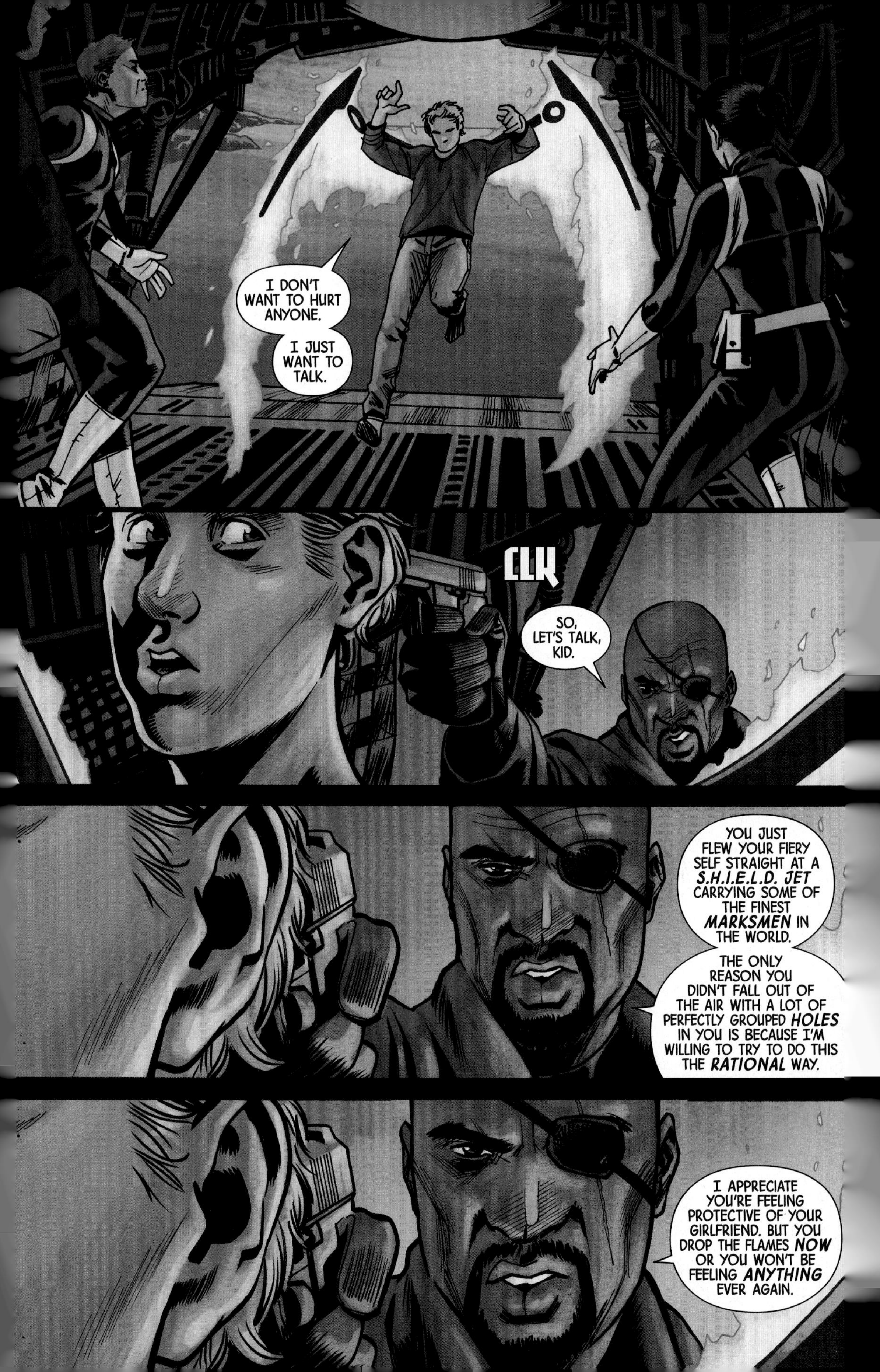
I DON'T WANT TO HURT ANYONE.
I JUST WANT TO TALK.
CLK
SO, LET'S TALK, KID.
YOU JUST FLEW YOUR FIERY SELF STRAIGHT AT A S.H.I.E.L.D. JET CARRYING SOME OF THE FINEST MARKSMEN IN THE WORLD.
THE ONLY REASON YOU DIDN'T FALL OUT OF THE AIR WITH A LOT OF PERFECTLY GROUPED HOLES IN YOU IS BECAUSE I'M WILLING TO TRY TO DO THIS THE RATIONAL WAY.
I APPRECIATE YOU'RE FEELING PROTECTIVE OF YOUR GIRLFRIEND. BUT YOU DROP THE FLAMES NOW OR YOU WON'T BE FEELING ANYTHING EVER AGAIN.

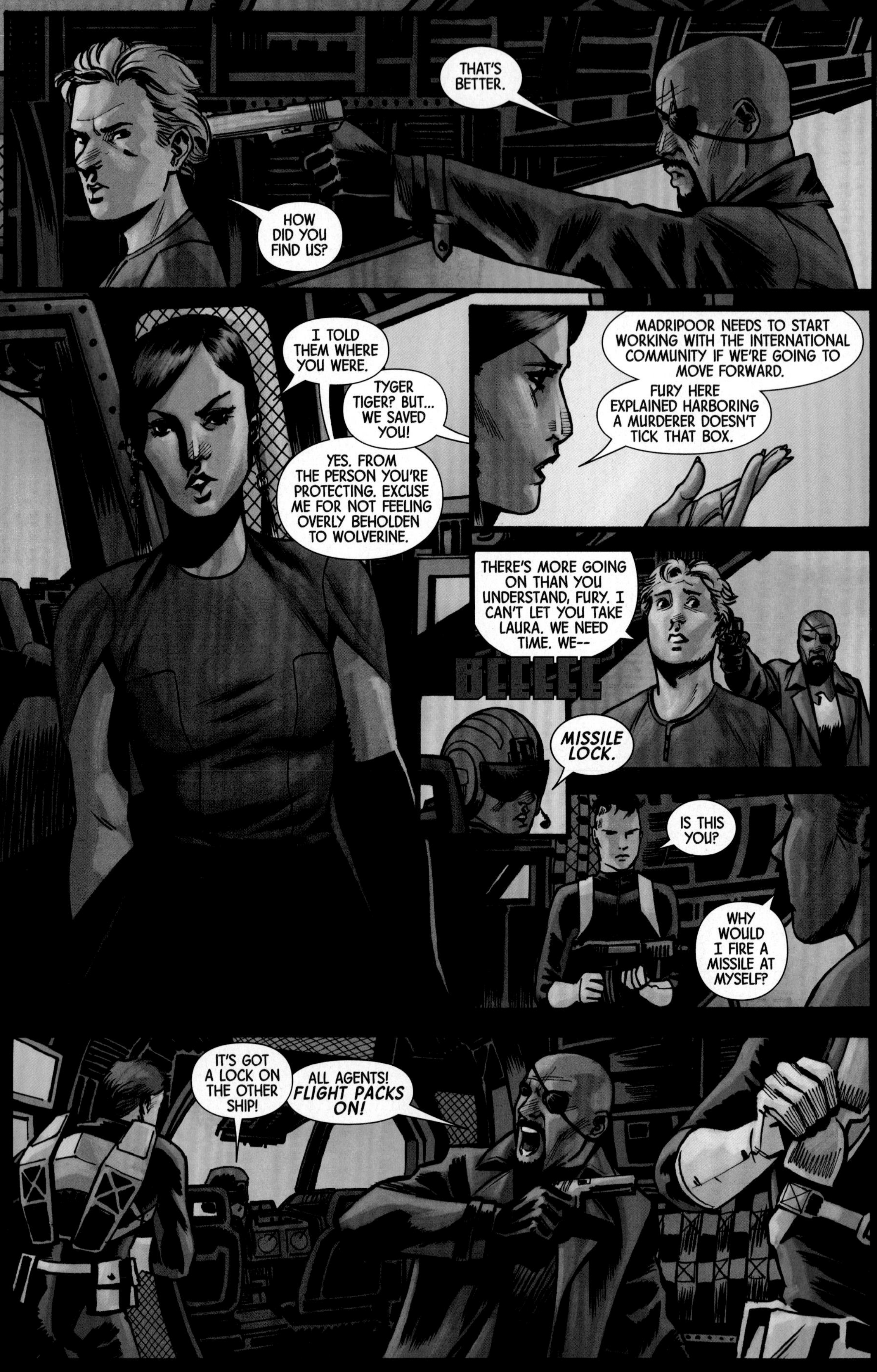
THAT'S BETTER.
HOW DID YOU FIND US?
I TOLD THEM WHERE YOU WERE.
TYGER TIGER? BUT... WE SAVED YOU!
YES. FROM THE PERSON YOU'RE PROTECTING. EXCUSE ME FOR NOT FEELING OVERLY BEHOLDEN TO WOLVERINE.
MADRIPOOR NEEDS TO START WORKING WITH THE INTERNATIONAL COMMUNITY IF WE'RE GOING TO MOVE FORWARD.
FURY HERE EXPLAINED HARBORING A MURDERER DOESN'T TICK THAT BOX.
THERE'S MORE GOING ON THAN YOU UNDERSTAND, FURY. I CAN'T LET YOU TAKE LAURA. WE NEED TIME. WE--
BEEEEE
MISSILE LOCK.
IS THIS YOU?
WHY WOULD I FIRE A MISSILE AT MYSELF?
IT'S GOT A LOCK ON THE OTHER SHIP!
ALL AGENTS! FLIGHT PACKS ON!

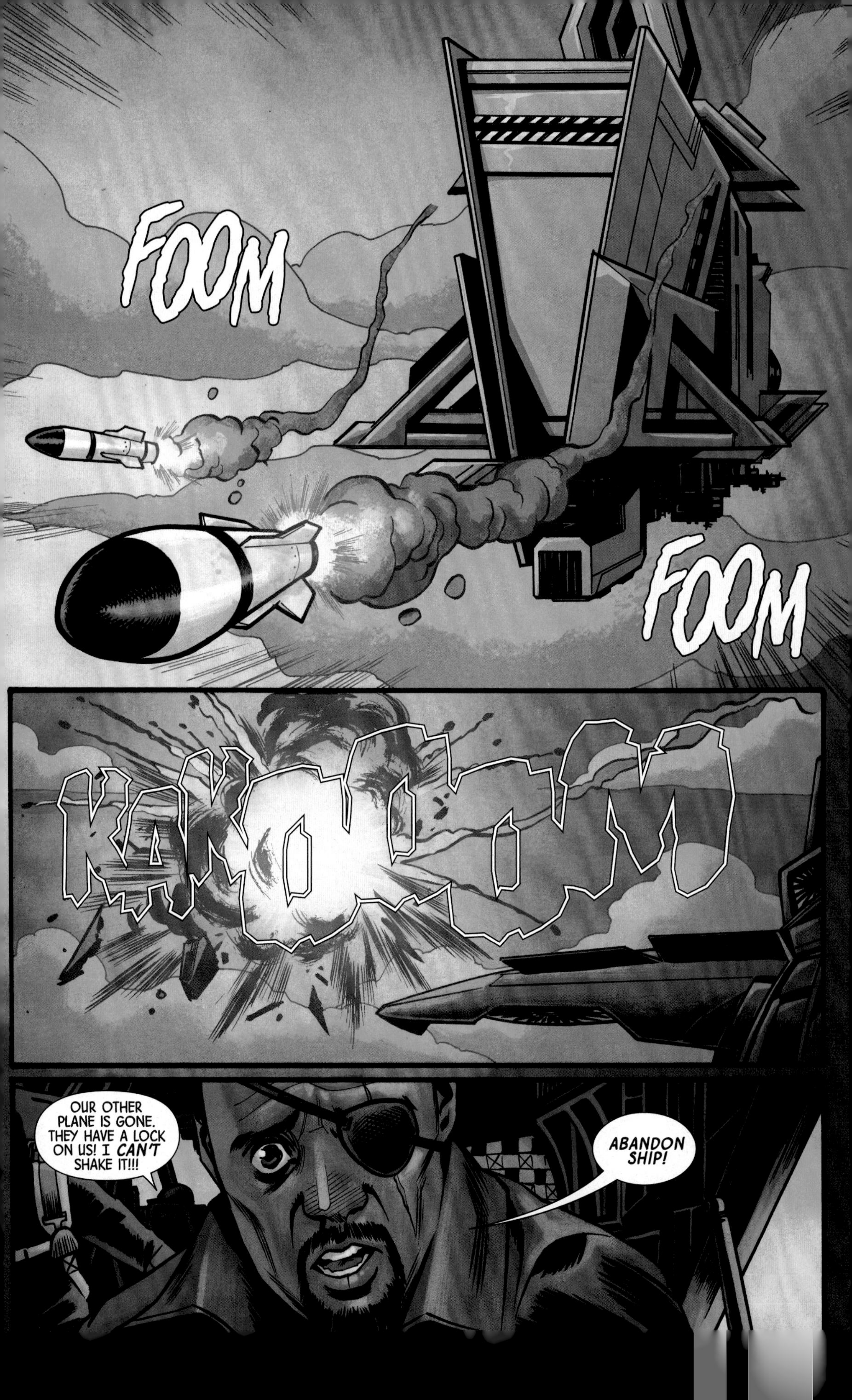
FOOM
FOOM
KAKOOOOOM
OUR OTHER PLANE IS GONE. THEY HAVE A LOCK ON US! I CAN'T SHAKE IT!!!
ABANDON SHIP!

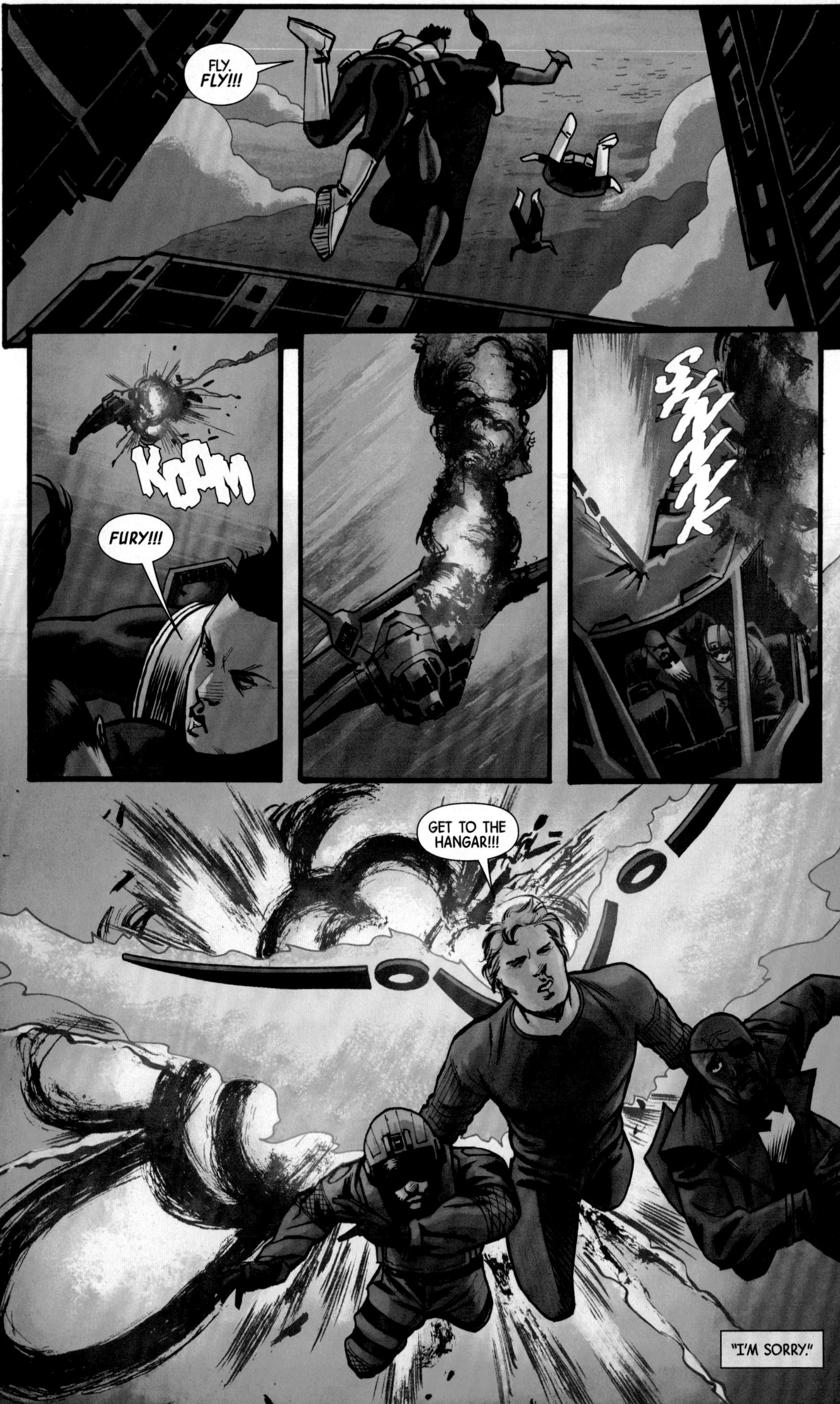
FLY. FLY!!!
KOOM
FURY!!!
SKNNK
GET TO THE HANGAR!!!
"I'M SORRY."

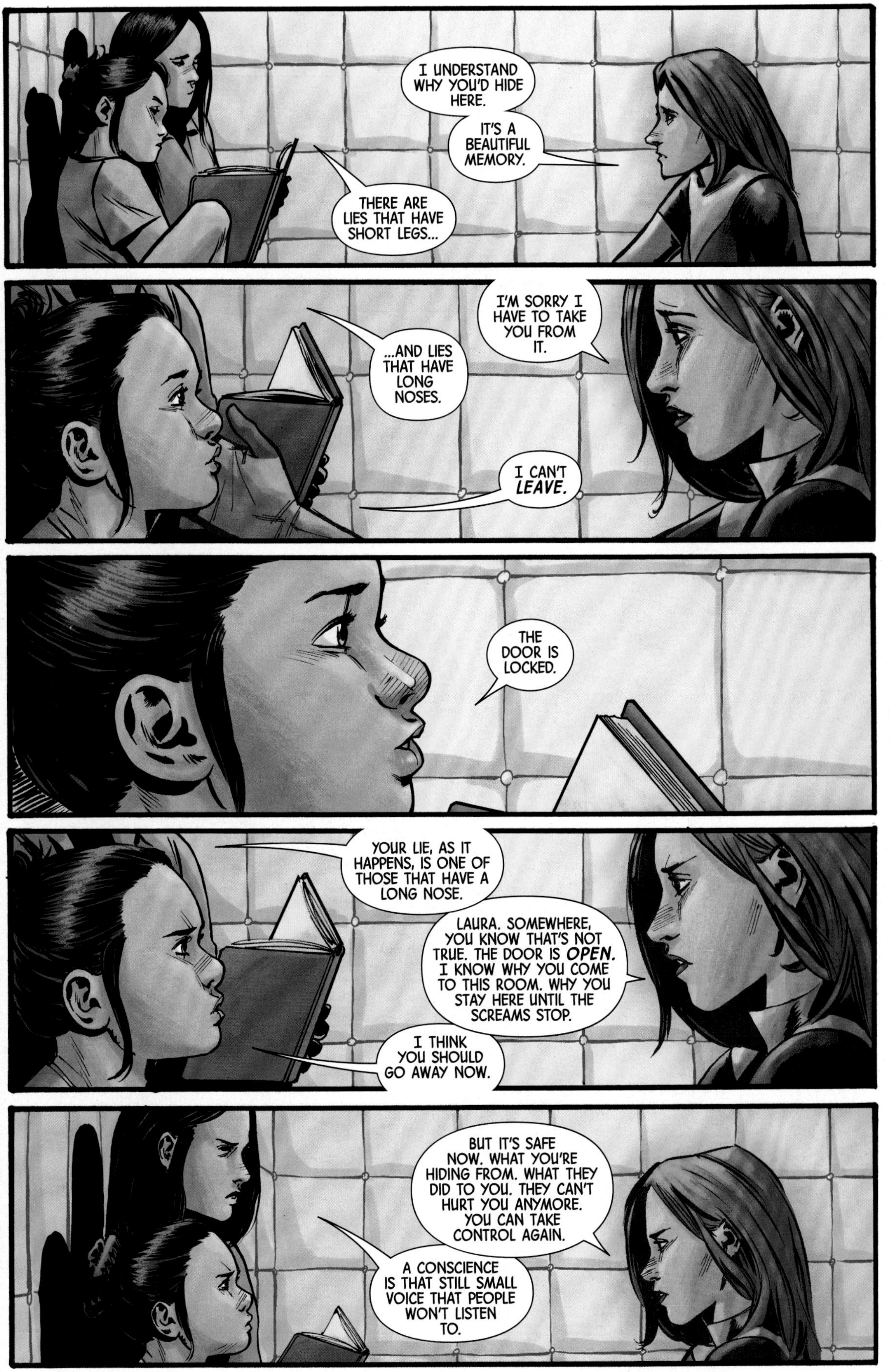

I UNDERSTAND WHY YOU'D HIDE HERE.
IT'S A BEAUTIFUL MEMORY.
THERE ARE LIES THAT HAVE SHORT LEGS...
I'M SORRY I HAVE TO TAKE YOU FROM IT.
...AND LIES THAT HAVE LONG NOSES.
I CAN'T *LEAVE.*
THE DOOR IS LOCKED.
YOUR LIE, AS IT HAPPENS, IS ONE OF THOSE THAT HAVE A LONG NOSE.
LAURA. SOMEWHERE, YOU KNOW THAT'S NOT TRUE. THE DOOR IS *OPEN.* I KNOW WHY YOU COME TO THIS ROOM. WHY YOU STAY HERE UNTIL THE SCREAMS STOP.
I THINK YOU SHOULD GO AWAY NOW.
BUT IT'S SAFE NOW. WHAT YOU'RE HIDING FROM. WHAT THEY DID TO YOU. THEY CAN'T HURT YOU ANYMORE. YOU CAN TAKE CONTROL AGAIN.
A CONSCIENCE IS THAT STILL SMALL VOICE THAT PEOPLE WON'T LISTEN TO.

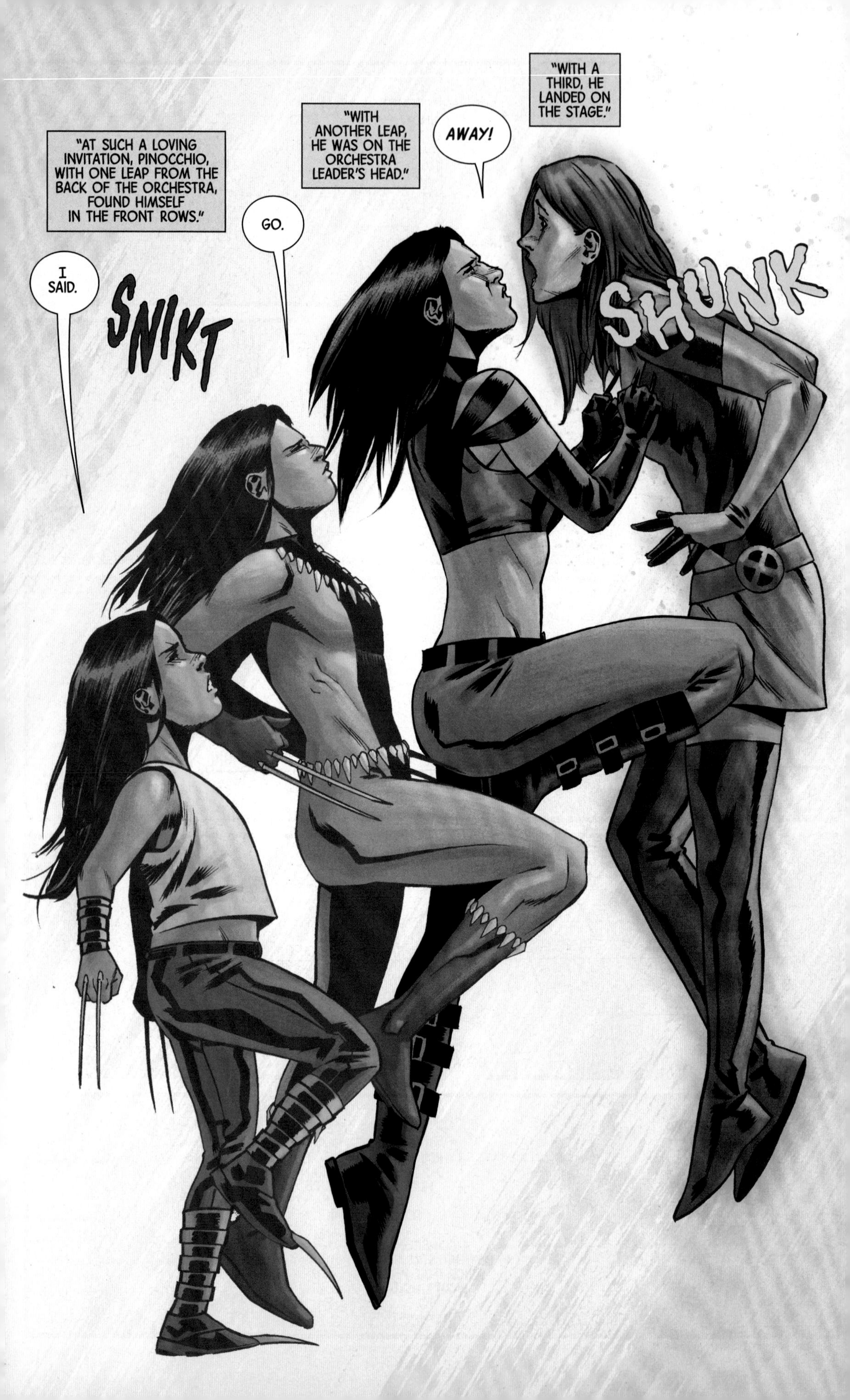
"AT SUCH A LOVING INVITATION, PINOCCHIO, WITH ONE LEAP FROM THE BACK OF THE ORCHESTRA, FOUND HIMSELF IN THE FRONT ROWS."
I SAID.
SNIKT
GO.
"WITH ANOTHER LEAP, HE WAS ON THE ORCHESTRA LEADER'S HEAD."
AWAY!
"WITH A THIRD, HE LANDED ON THE STAGE."
SHUNK

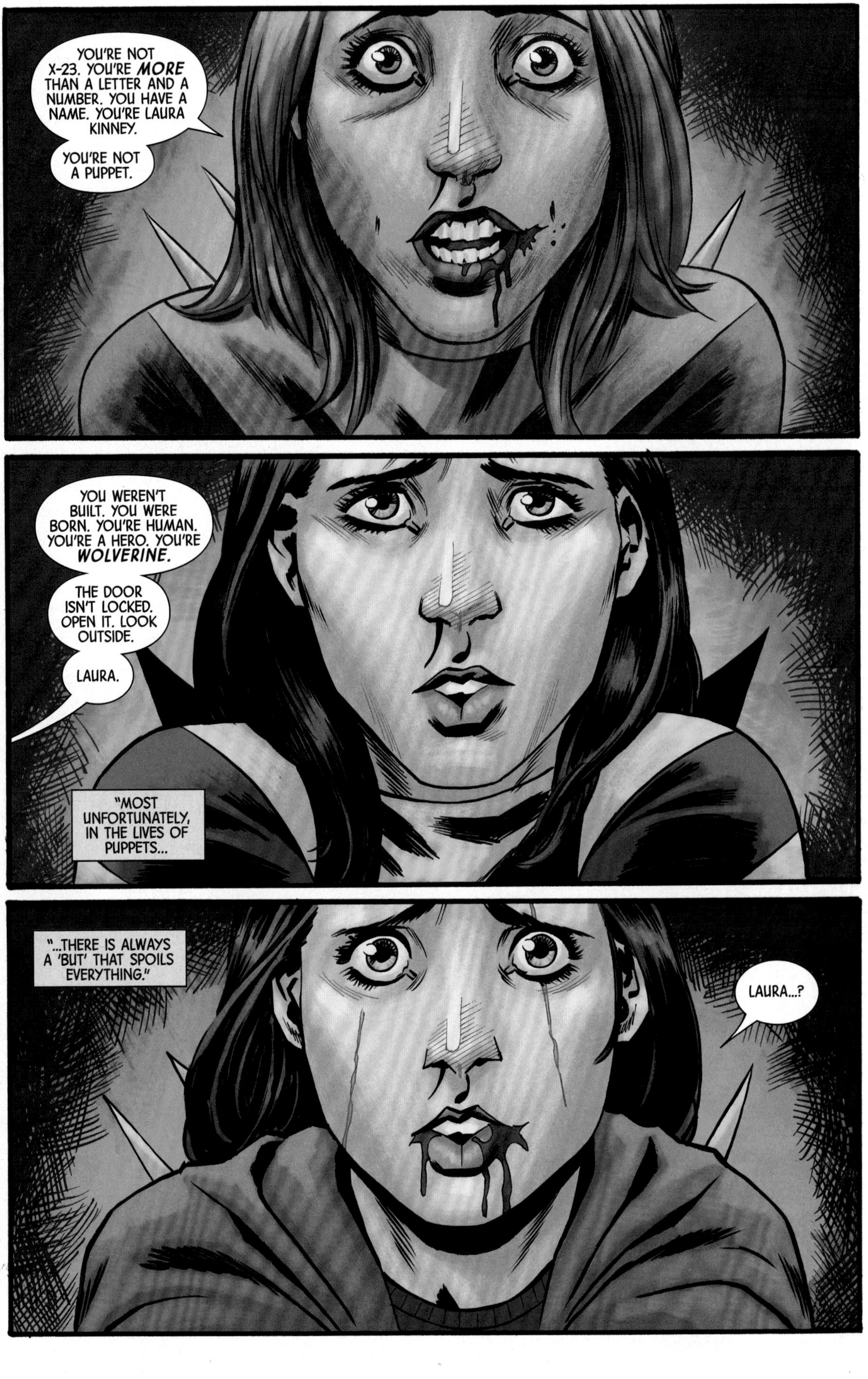
YOU'RE NOT X-23. YOU'RE MORE THAN A LETTER AND A NUMBER. YOU HAVE A NAME. YOU'RE LAURA KINNEY.
YOU'RE NOT A PUPPET.
YOU WEREN'T BUILT. YOU WERE BORN. YOU'RE HUMAN. YOU'RE A HERO. YOU'RE WOLVERINE.
THE DOOR ISN'T LOCKED. OPEN IT. LOOK OUTSIDE.
LAURA.
"MOST UNFORTUNATELY, IN THE LIVES OF PUPPETS...
"...THERE IS ALWAYS A 'BUT' THAT SPOILS EVERYTHING."
LAURA...?

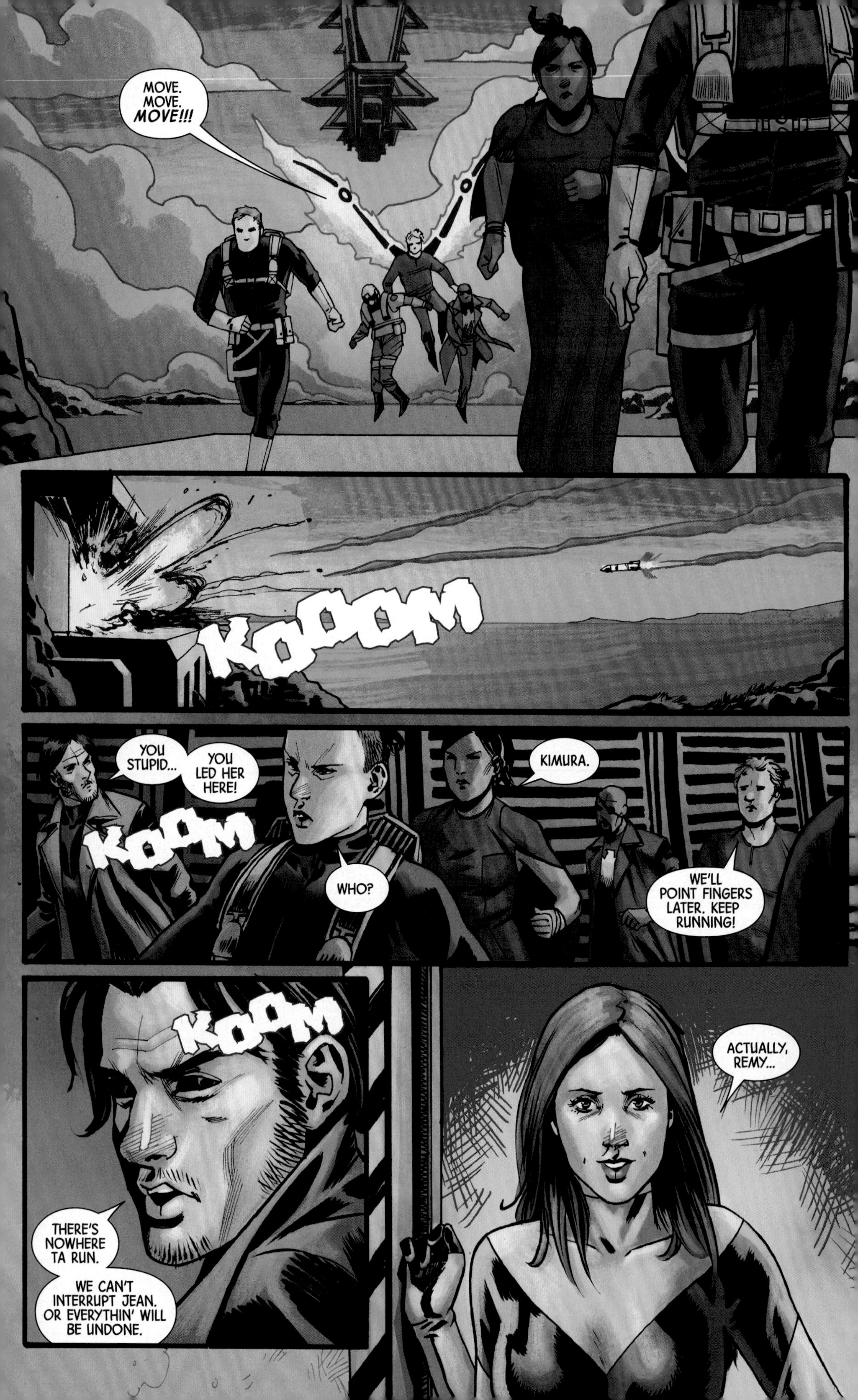
MOVE. MOVE. MOVE!!!
KOOOM
YOU STUPID...
YOU LED HER HERE!
KOOM
WHO?
KIMURA.
WE'LL POINT FINGERS LATER. KEEP RUNNING!
KOOM
THERE'S NOWHERE TA RUN.
WE CAN'T INTERRUPT JEAN. OR EVERYTHIN' WILL BE UNDONE.
ACTUALLY, REMY...

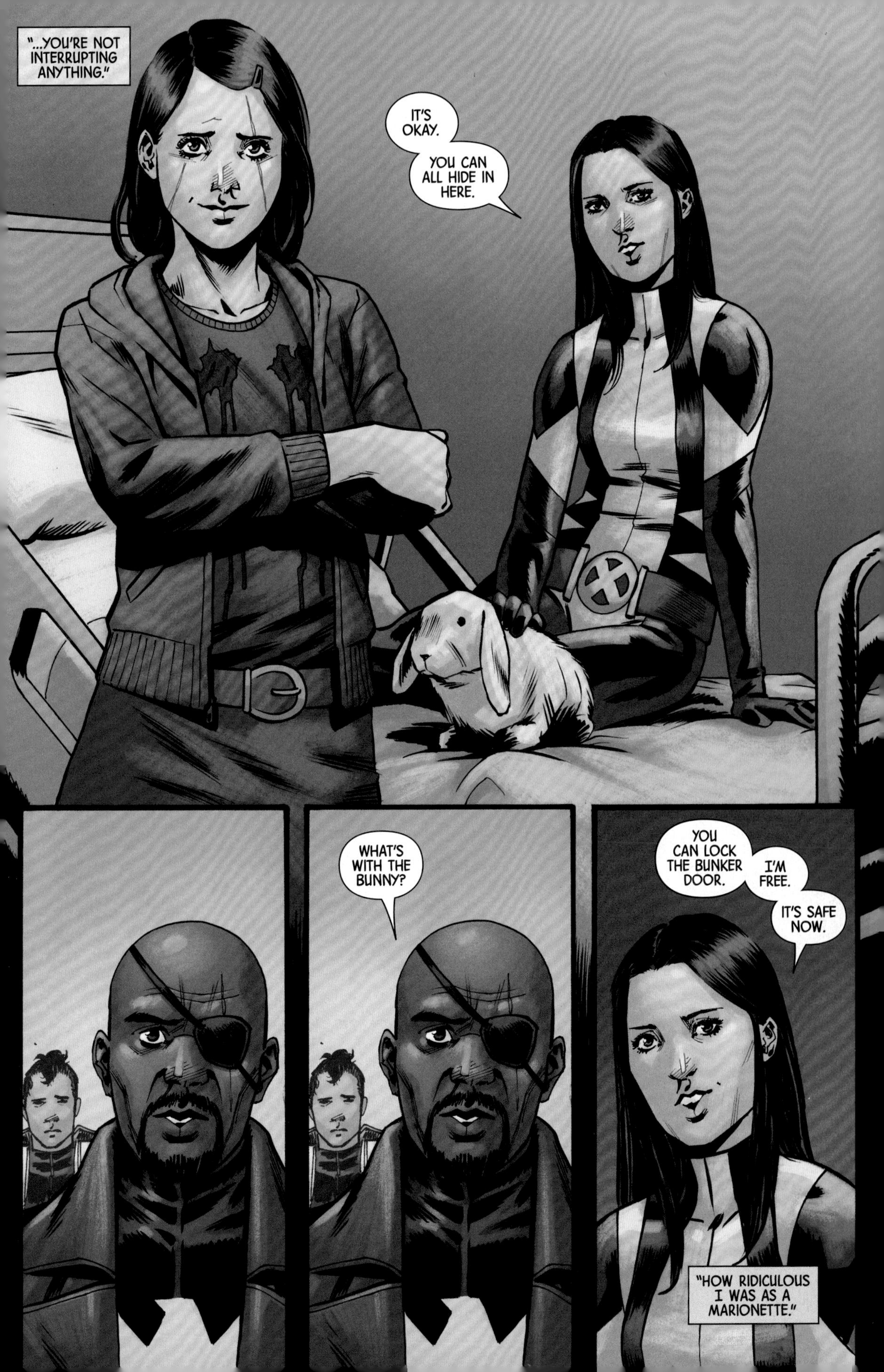
"...YOU'RE NOT INTERRUPTING ANYTHING."
IT'S OKAY.
YOU CAN ALL HIDE IN HERE.
WHAT'S WITH THE BUNNY?
YOU CAN LOCK THE BUNKER DOOR.
I'M FREE.
IT'S SAFE NOW.
"HOW RIDICULOUS I WAS AS A MARIONETTE."

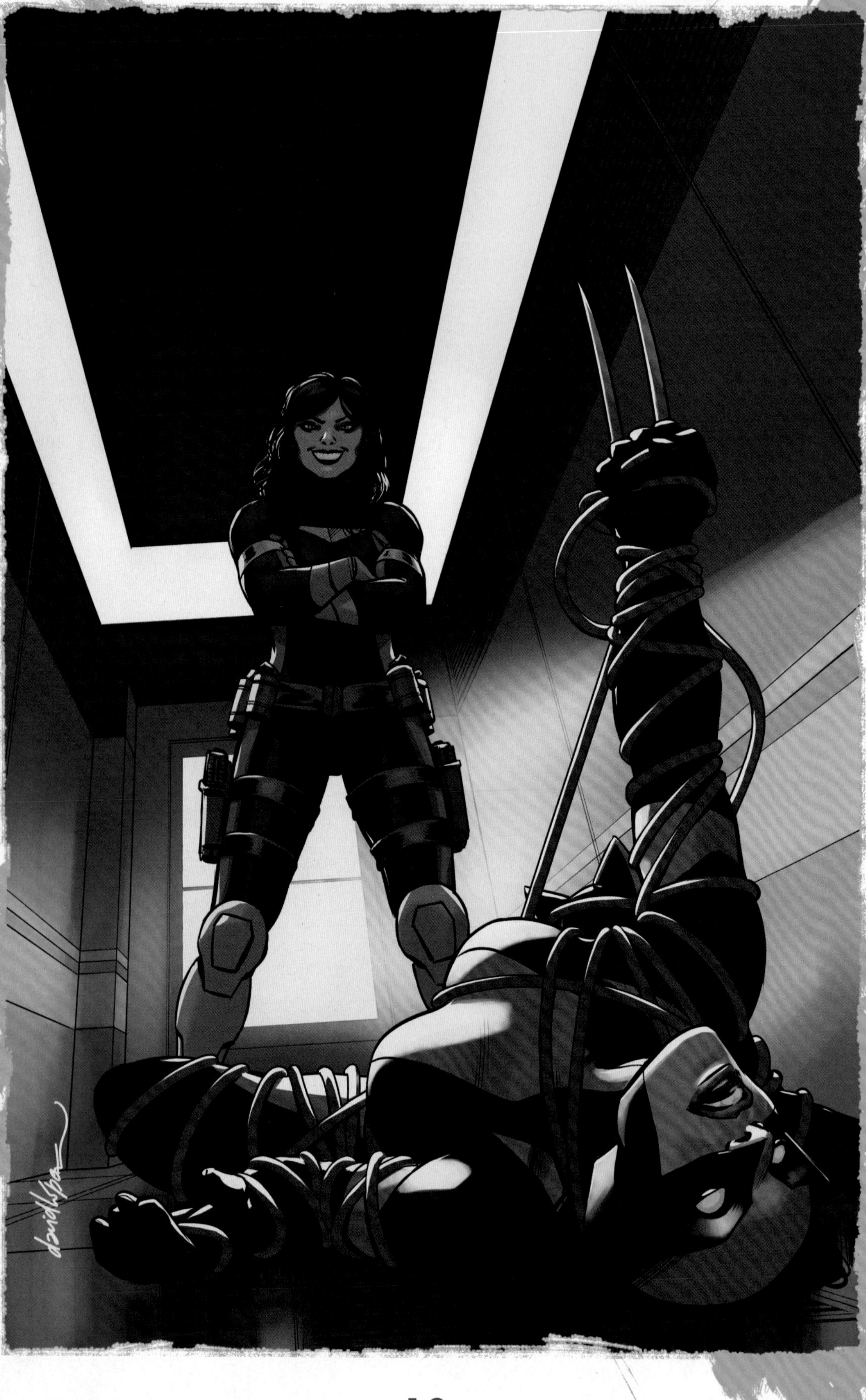

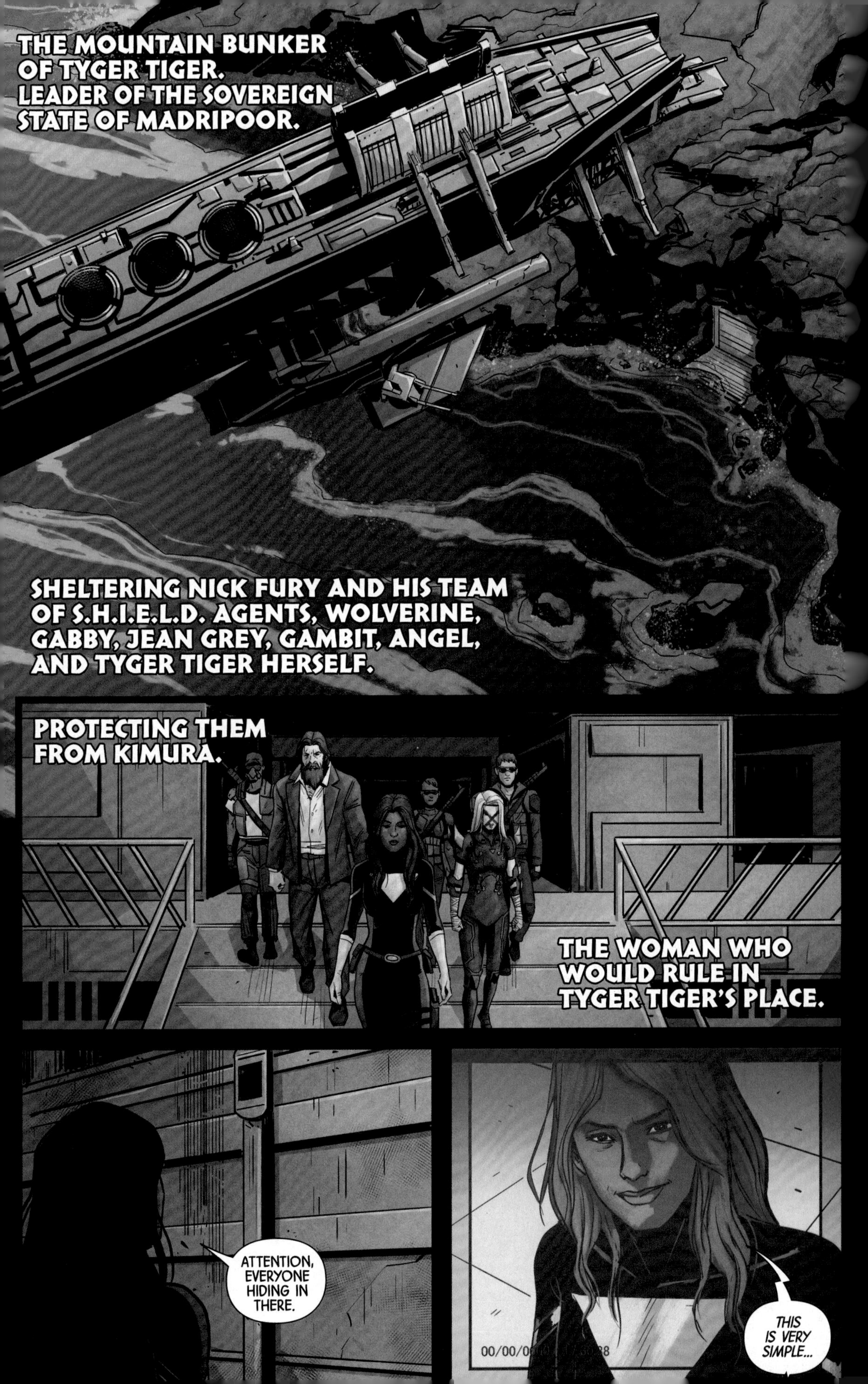
THE MOUNTAIN BUNKER OF TYGER TIGER. LEADER OF THE SOVEREIGN STATE OF MADRIPOOR.
SHELTERING NICK FURY AND HIS TEAM OF S.H.I.E.L.D. AGENTS, WOLVERINE, GABBY, JEAN GREY, GAMBIT, ANGEL, AND TYGER TIGER HERSELF.
PROTECTING THEM FROM KIMURA.
THE WOMAN WHO WOULD RULE IN TYGER TIGER'S PLACE.
ATTENTION, EVERYONE HIDING IN THERE.
THIS IS VERY SIMPLE...

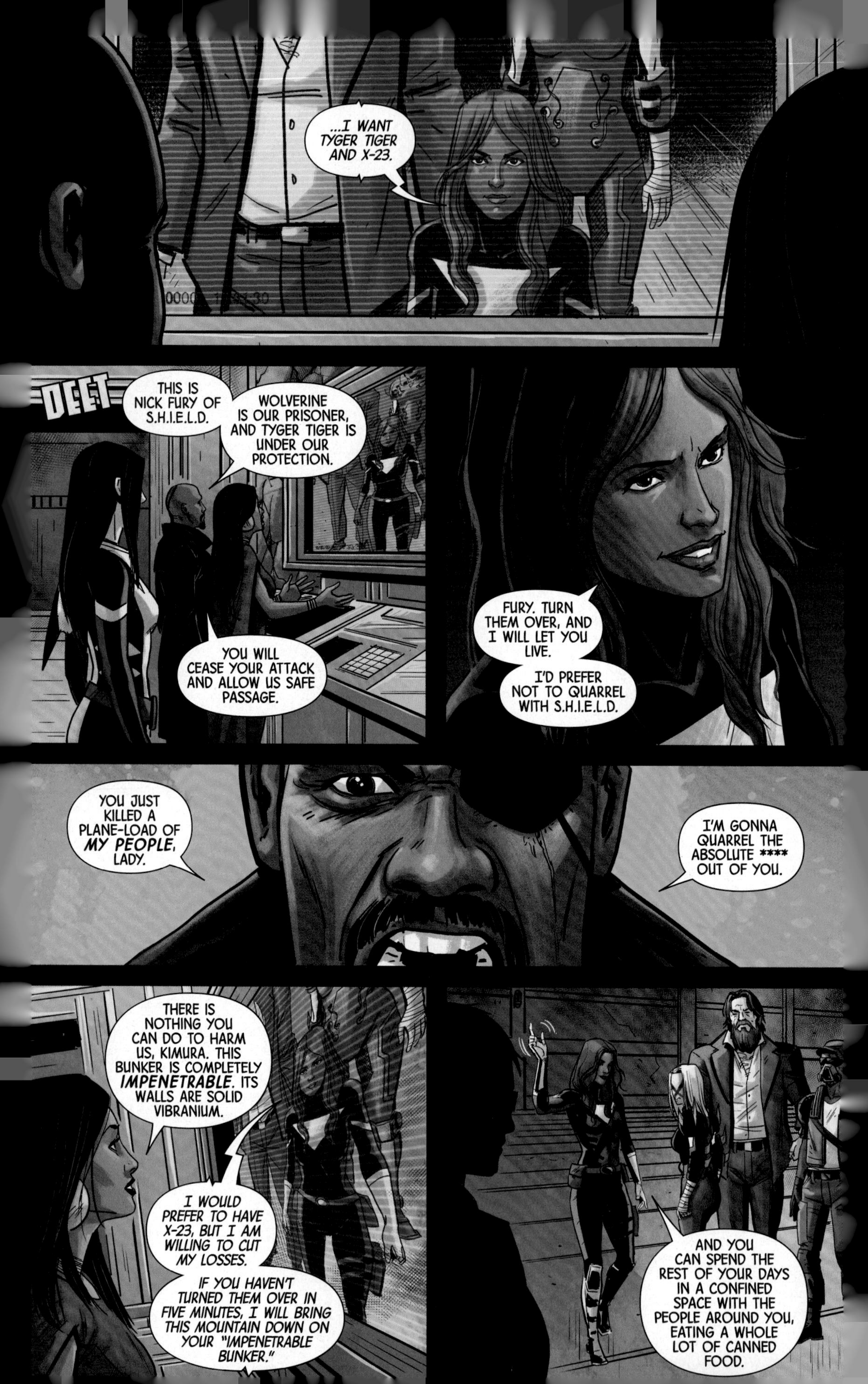
...I WANT TYGER TIGER AND X-23.
DEET
THIS IS NICK FURY OF S.H.I.E.L.D.
WOLVERINE IS OUR PRISONER, AND TYGER TIGER IS UNDER OUR PROTECTION.
YOU WILL CEASE YOUR ATTACK AND ALLOW US SAFE PASSAGE.
FURY. TURN THEM OVER, AND I WILL LET YOU LIVE.
I'D PREFER NOT TO QUARREL WITH S.H.I.E.L.D.
YOU JUST KILLED A PLANE-LOAD OF MY PEOPLE, LADY.
I'M GONNA QUARREL THE ABSOLUTE **** OUT OF YOU.
THERE IS NOTHING YOU CAN DO TO HARM US, KIMURA. THIS BUNKER IS COMPLETELY IMPENETRABLE. ITS WALLS ARE SOLID VIBRANIUM.
I WOULD PREFER TO HAVE X-23, BUT I AM WILLING TO CUT MY LOSSES.
IF YOU HAVEN'T TURNED THEM OVER IN FIVE MINUTES, I WILL BRING THIS MOUNTAIN DOWN ON YOUR "IMPENETRABLE BUNKER."
AND YOU CAN SPEND THE REST OF YOUR DAYS IN A CONFINED SPACE WITH THE PEOPLE AROUND YOU, EATING A WHOLE LOT OF CANNED FOOD.

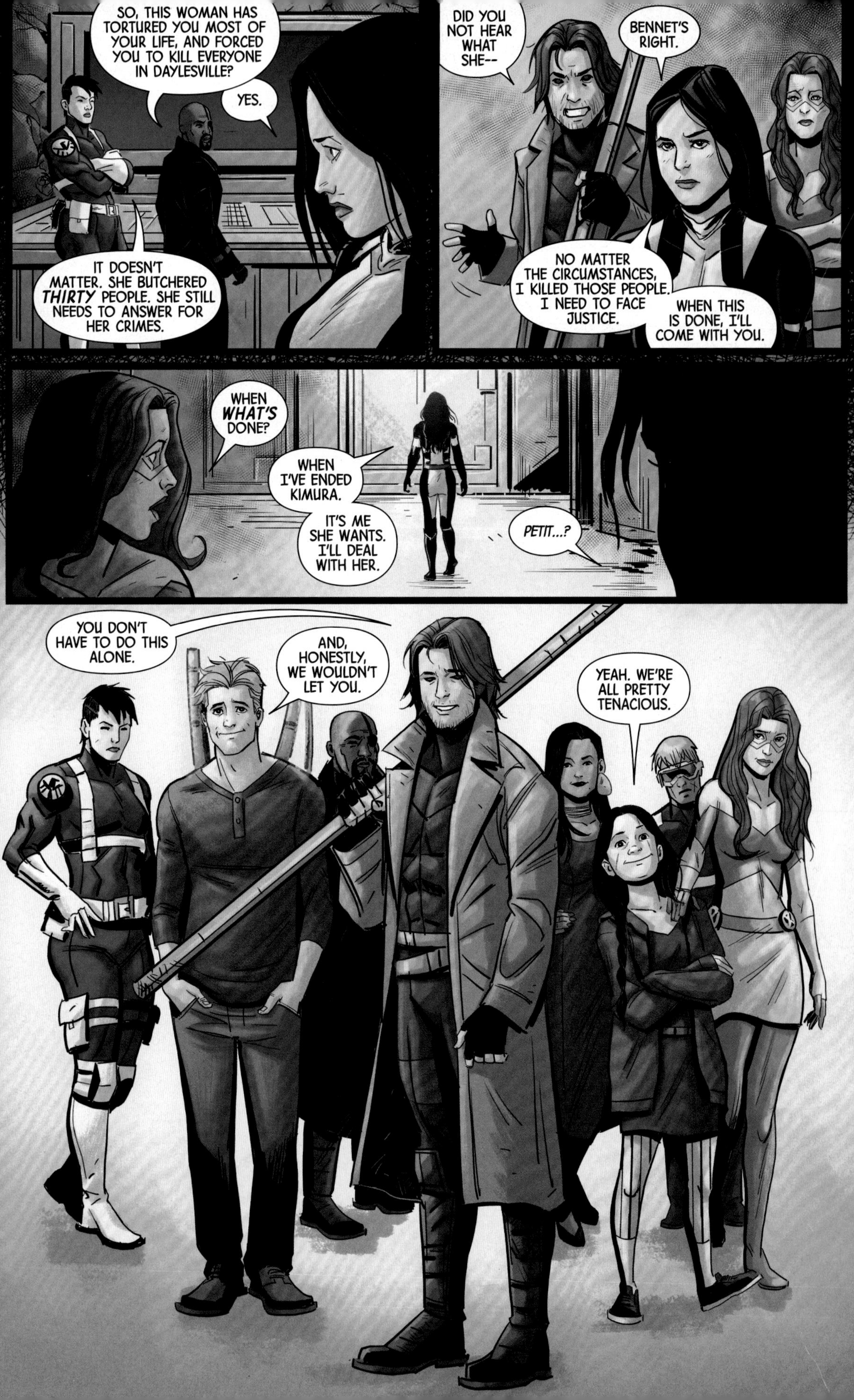
SO, THIS WOMAN HAS TORTURED YOU MOST OF YOUR LIFE, AND FORCED YOU TO KILL EVERYONE IN DAYLESVILLE?
YES.
IT DOESN'T MATTER. SHE BUTCHERED THIRTY PEOPLE. SHE STILL NEEDS TO ANSWER FOR HER CRIMES.
DID YOU NOT HEAR WHAT SHE--
BENNET'S RIGHT.
NO MATTER THE CIRCUMSTANCES, I KILLED THOSE PEOPLE. I NEED TO FACE JUSTICE.
WHEN THIS IS DONE, I'LL COME WITH YOU.
WHEN WHAT'S DONE?
WHEN I'VE ENDED KIMURA.
IT'S ME SHE WANTS. I'LL DEAL WITH HER.
PETIT...?
YOU DON'T HAVE TO DO THIS ALONE.
AND, HONESTLY, WE WOULDN'T LET YOU.
YEAH. WE'RE ALL PRETTY TENACIOUS.

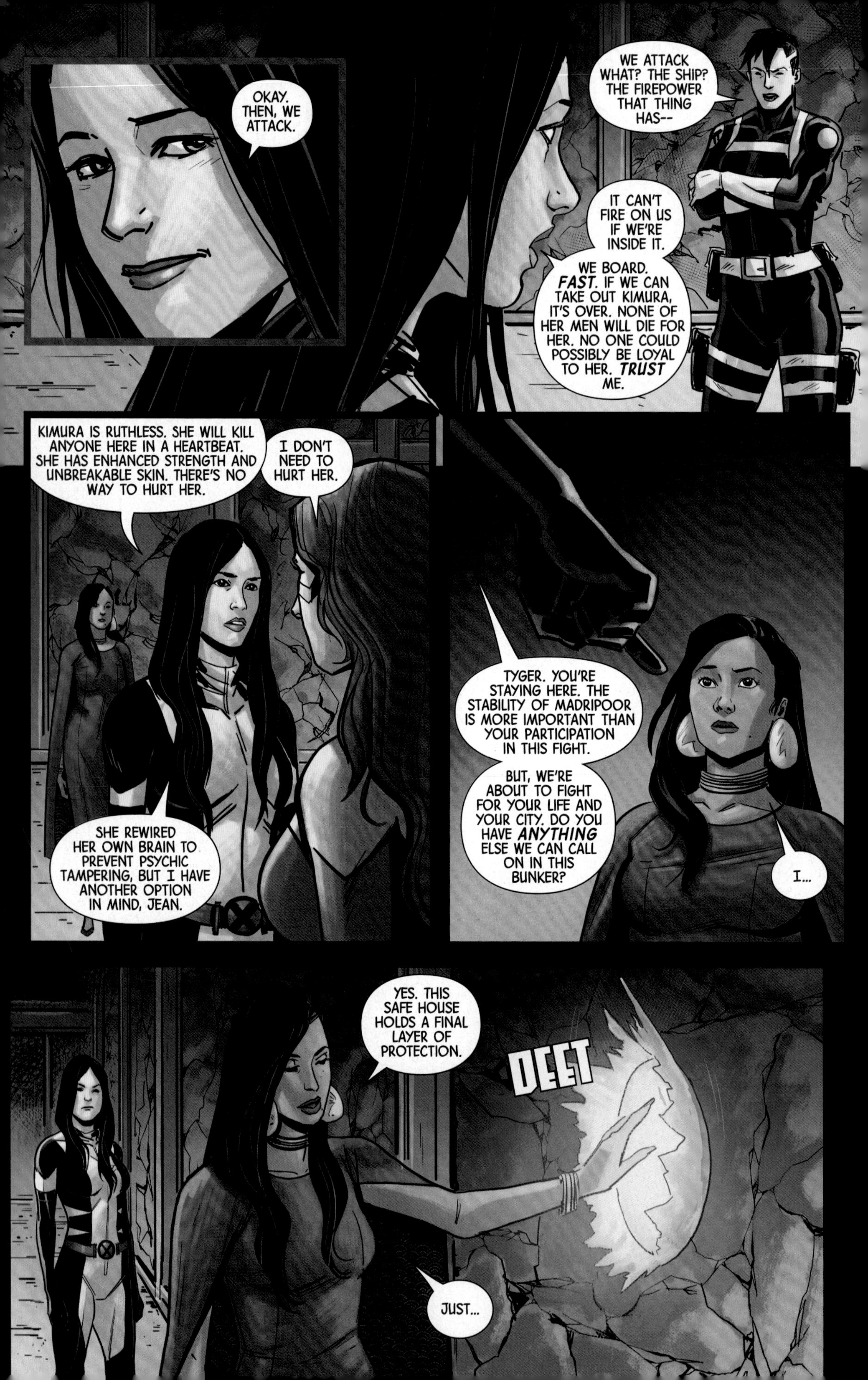
OKAY. THEN, WE ATTACK.
WE ATTACK WHAT? THE SHIP? THE FIREPOWER THAT THING HAS--
IT CAN'T FIRE ON US IF WE'RE INSIDE IT.
WE BOARD. FAST. IF WE CAN TAKE OUT KIMURA, IT'S OVER. NONE OF HER MEN WILL DIE FOR HER. NO ONE COULD POSSIBLY BE LOYAL TO HER. TRUST ME.
KIMURA IS RUTHLESS. SHE WILL KILL ANYONE HERE IN A HEARTBEAT. SHE HAS ENHANCED STRENGTH AND UNBREAKABLE SKIN. THERE'S NO WAY TO HURT HER.
I DON'T NEED TO HURT HER.
SHE REWIRED HER OWN BRAIN TO PREVENT PSYCHIC TAMPERING, BUT I HAVE ANOTHER OPTION IN MIND, JEAN.
TYGER. YOU'RE STAYING HERE. THE STABILITY OF MADRIPOOR IS MORE IMPORTANT THAN YOUR PARTICIPATION IN THIS FIGHT.
BUT, WE'RE ABOUT TO FIGHT FOR YOUR LIFE AND YOUR CITY. DO YOU HAVE ANYTHING ELSE WE CAN CALL ON IN THIS BUNKER?
I...
YES. THIS SAFE HOUSE HOLDS A FINAL LAYER OF PROTECTION.
DEET
JUST...

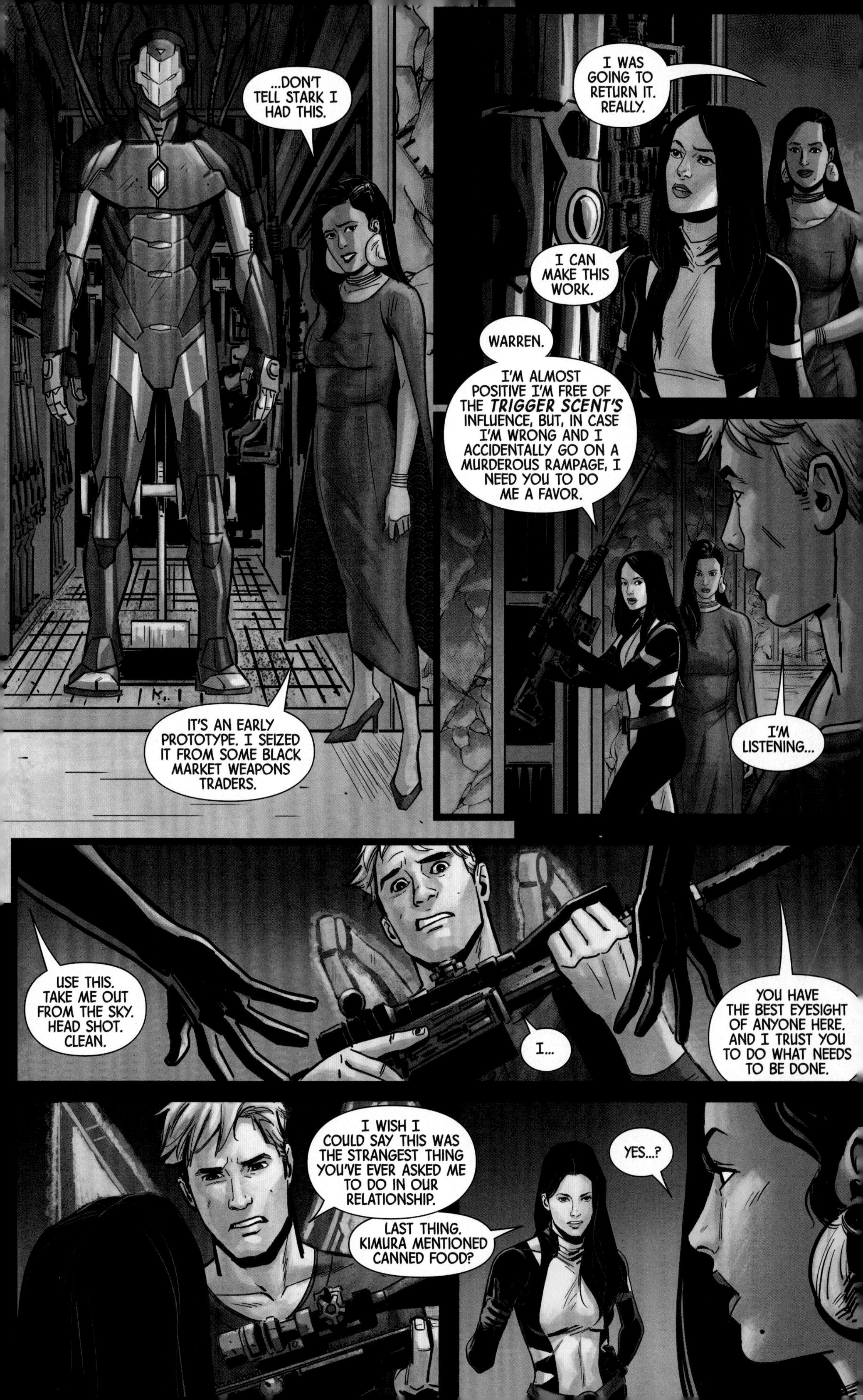
...DON'T TELL STARK I HAD THIS.
IT'S AN EARLY PROTOTYPE. I SEIZED IT FROM SOME BLACK MARKET WEAPONS TRADERS.
I WAS GOING TO RETURN IT. REALLY.
I CAN MAKE THIS WORK.
WARREN.
I'M ALMOST POSITIVE I'M FREE OF THE TRIGGER SCENT'S INFLUENCE, BUT, IN CASE I'M WRONG AND I ACCIDENTALLY GO ON A MURDEROUS RAMPAGE, I NEED YOU TO DO ME A FAVOR.
I'M LISTENING...
USE THIS. TAKE ME OUT FROM THE SKY. HEAD SHOT. CLEAN.
I...
YOU HAVE THE BEST EYESIGHT OF ANYONE HERE, AND I TRUST YOU TO DO WHAT NEEDS TO BE DONE.
I WISH I COULD SAY THIS WAS THE STRANGEST THING YOU'VE EVER ASKED ME TO DO IN OUR RELATIONSHIP.
LAST THING. KIMURA MENTIONED CANNED FOOD?
YES...?

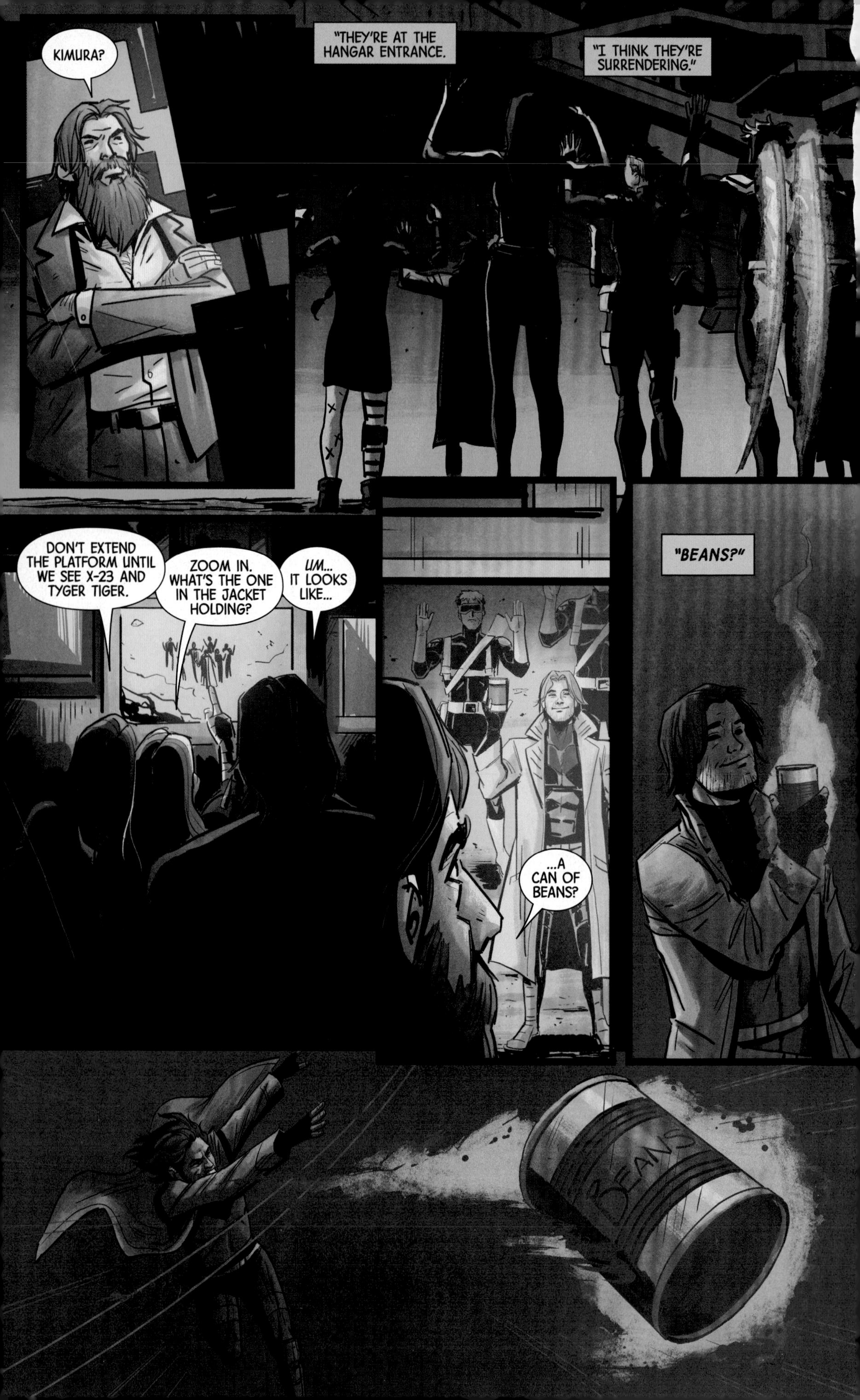
KIMURA?
"THEY'RE AT THE HANGAR ENTRANCE.
"I THINK THEY'RE SURRENDERING."
DON'T EXTEND THE PLATFORM UNTIL WE SEE X-23 AND TYGER TIGER.
ZOOM IN. WHAT'S THE ONE IN THE JACKET HOLDING?
UM... IT LOOKS LIKE...
...A CAN OF BEANS?
"BEANS?"
BEANS

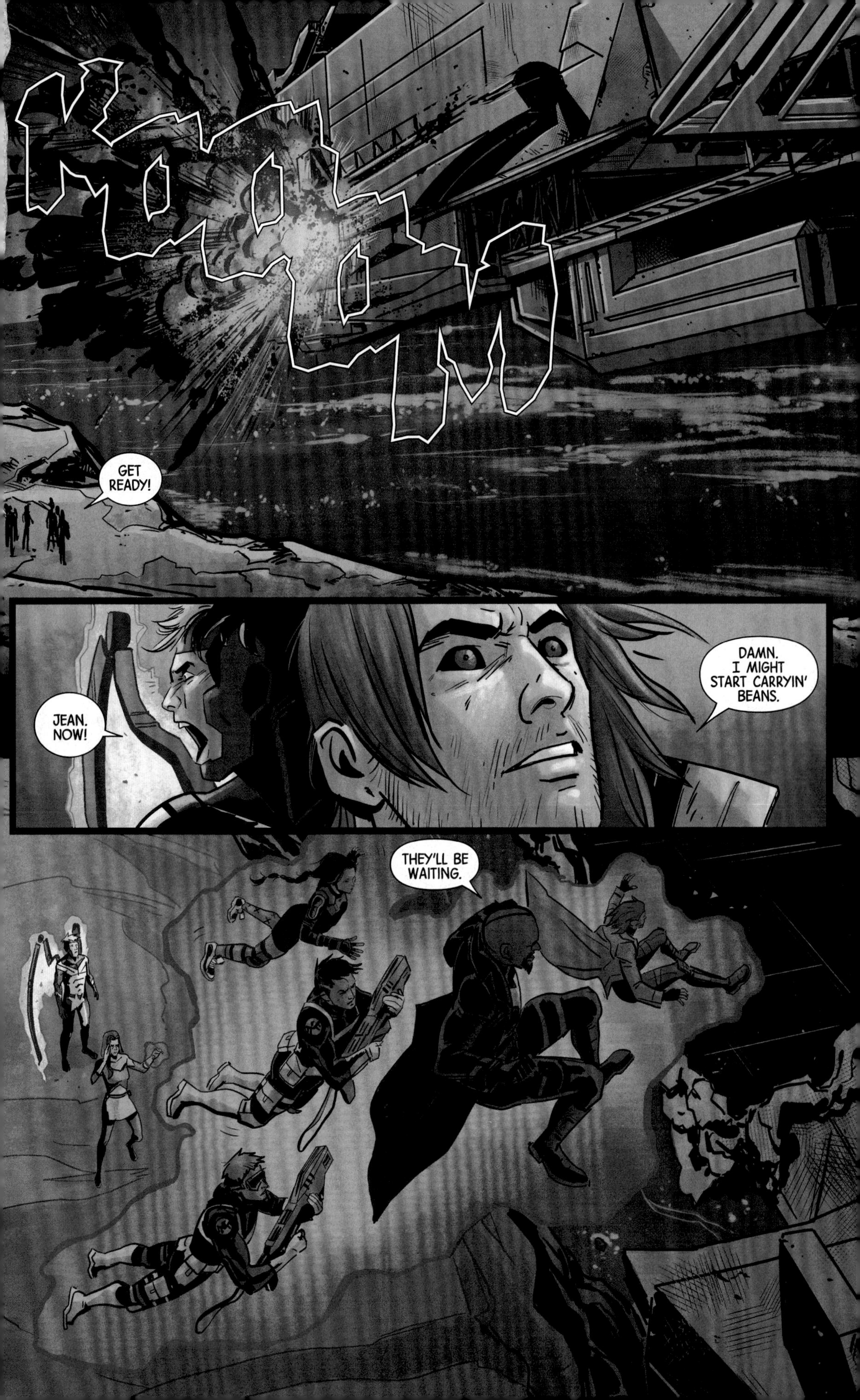
KRAKOOM
GET READY!
JEAN. NOW!
DAMN. I MIGHT START CARRYIN' BEANS.
THEY'LL BE WAITING.

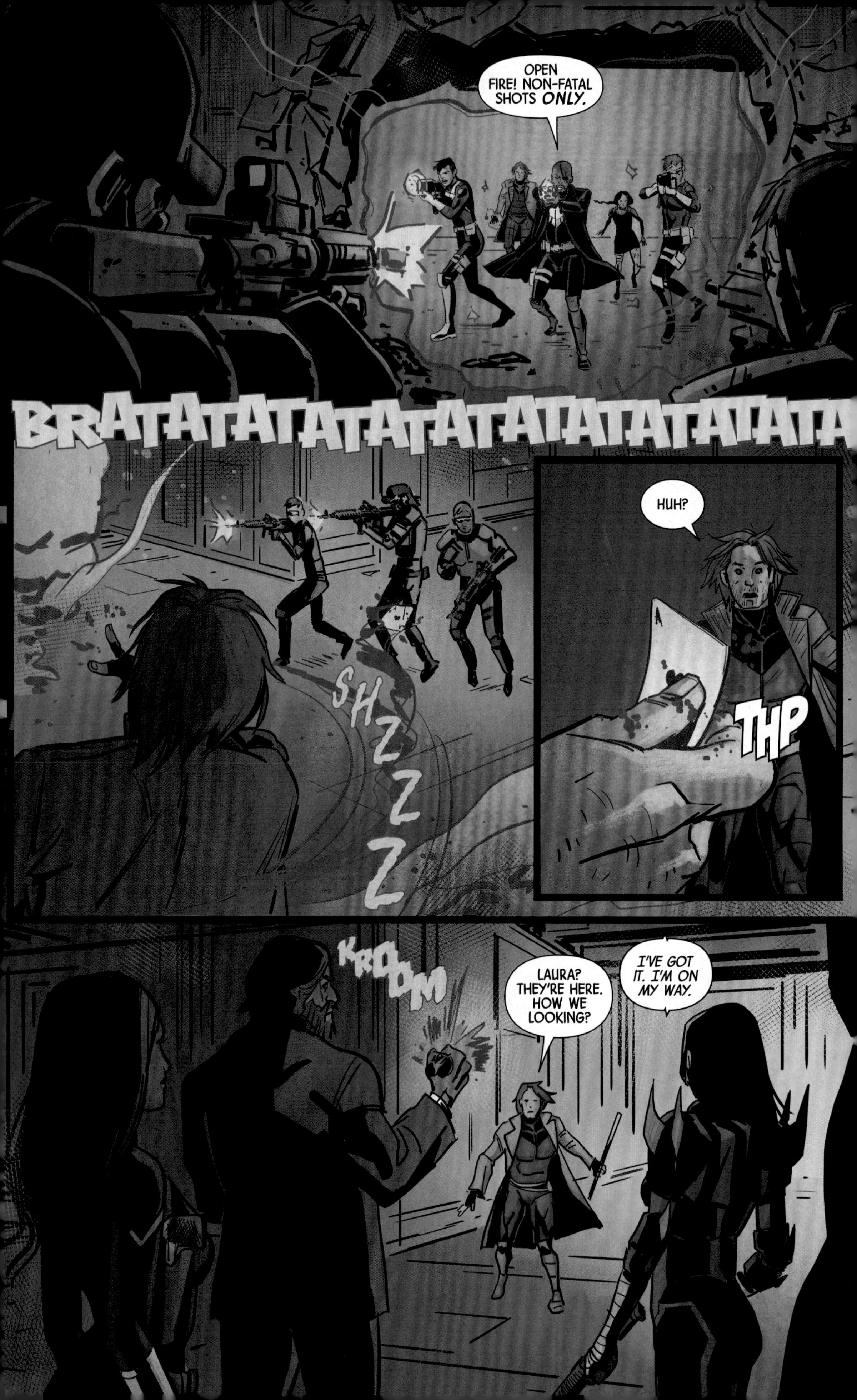
OPEN FIRE! NON-FATAL SHOTS ONLY.
BRATATATATATATATATATATATATA
SHZZZZ
HUH?
THP
KROOM
LAURA? THEY'RE HERE. HOW WE LOOKING?
I'VE GOT IT. I'M ON MY WAY.

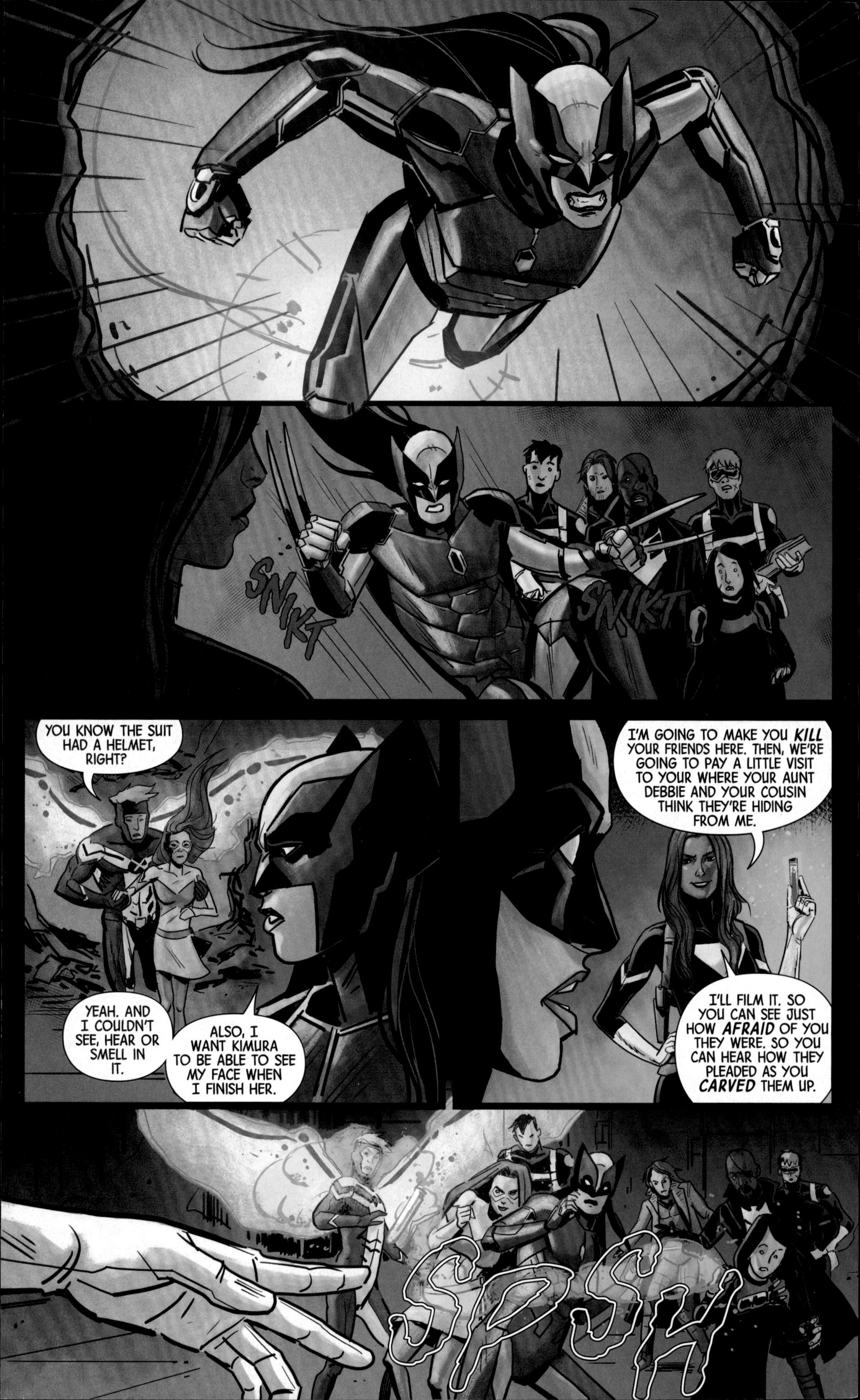
SNIKT
SNIKT
YOU KNOW THE SUIT HAD A HELMET, RIGHT?
YEAH. AND I COULDN'T SEE, HEAR OR SMELL IN IT.
ALSO, I WANT KIMURA TO BE ABLE TO SEE MY FACE WHEN I FINISH HER.
I'M GOING TO MAKE YOU KILL YOUR FRIENDS HERE. THEN, WE'RE GOING TO PAY A LITTLE VISIT TO YOUR WHERE YOUR AUNT DEBBIE AND YOUR COUSIN THINK THEY'RE HIDING FROM ME.
I'LL FILM IT. SO YOU CAN SEE JUST HOW AFRAID OF YOU THEY WERE. SO YOU CAN HEAR HOW THEY PLEADED AS YOU CARVED THEM UP.
SPSH

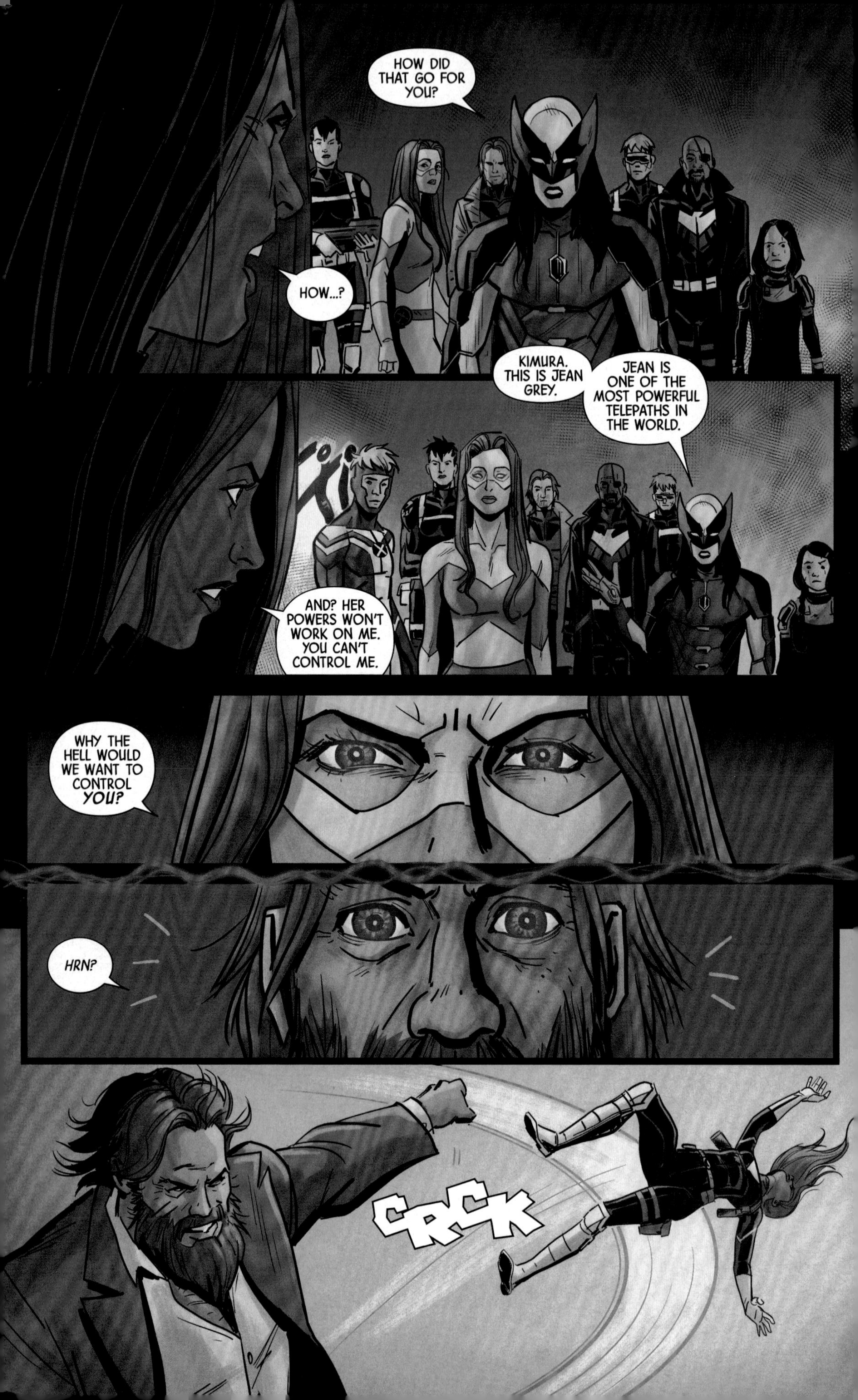
HOW DID THAT GO FOR YOU?
HOW...?
KIMURA. THIS IS JEAN GREY.
JEAN IS ONE OF THE MOST POWERFUL TELEPATHS IN THE WORLD.
AND? HER POWERS WON'T WORK ON ME. YOU CAN'T CONTROL ME.
WHY THE HELL WOULD WE WANT TO CONTROL *YOU?*
HRN?
CRCK

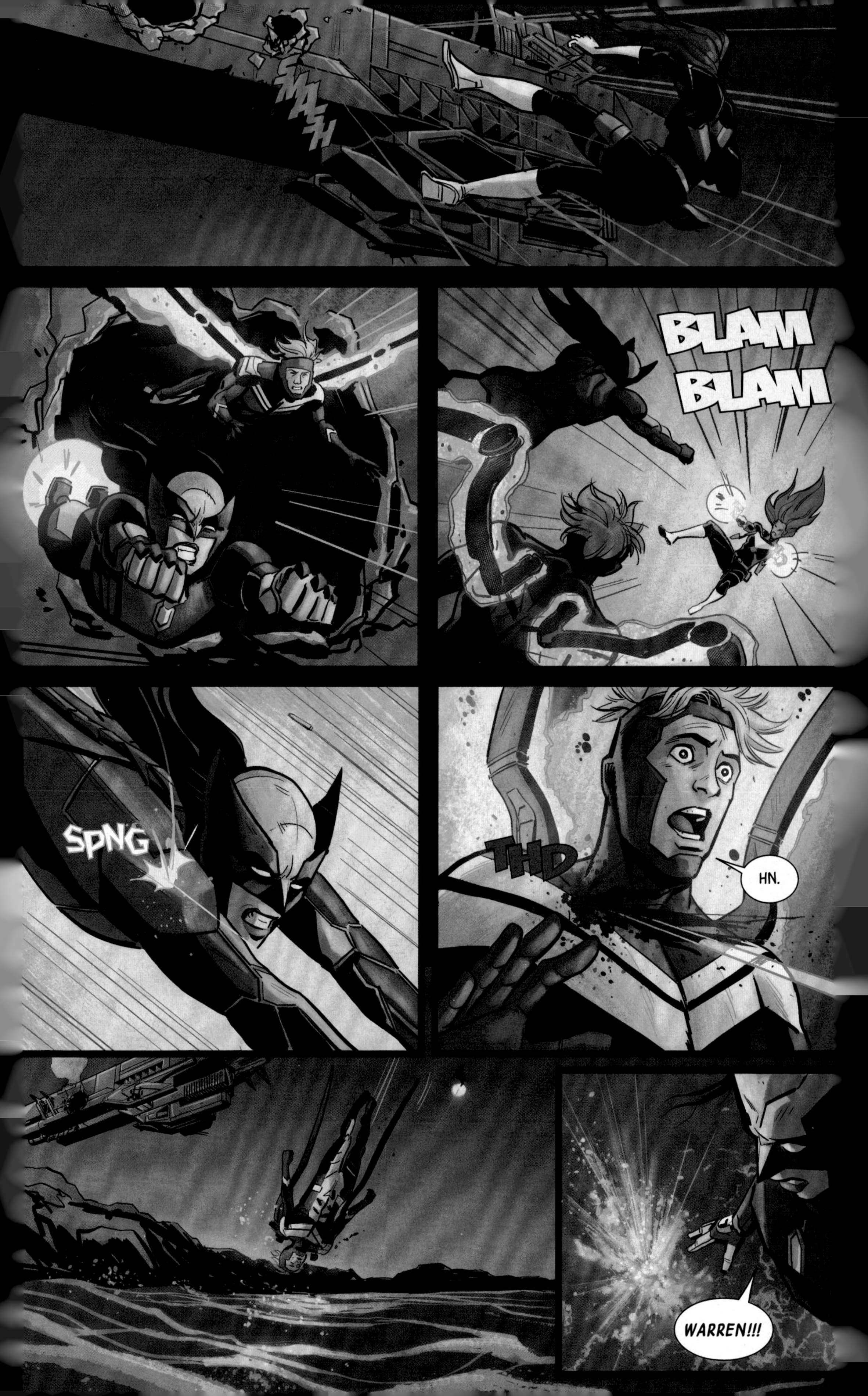
SMASH
BLAM
BLAM
SPNG
THD
HN.
WARREN!!!

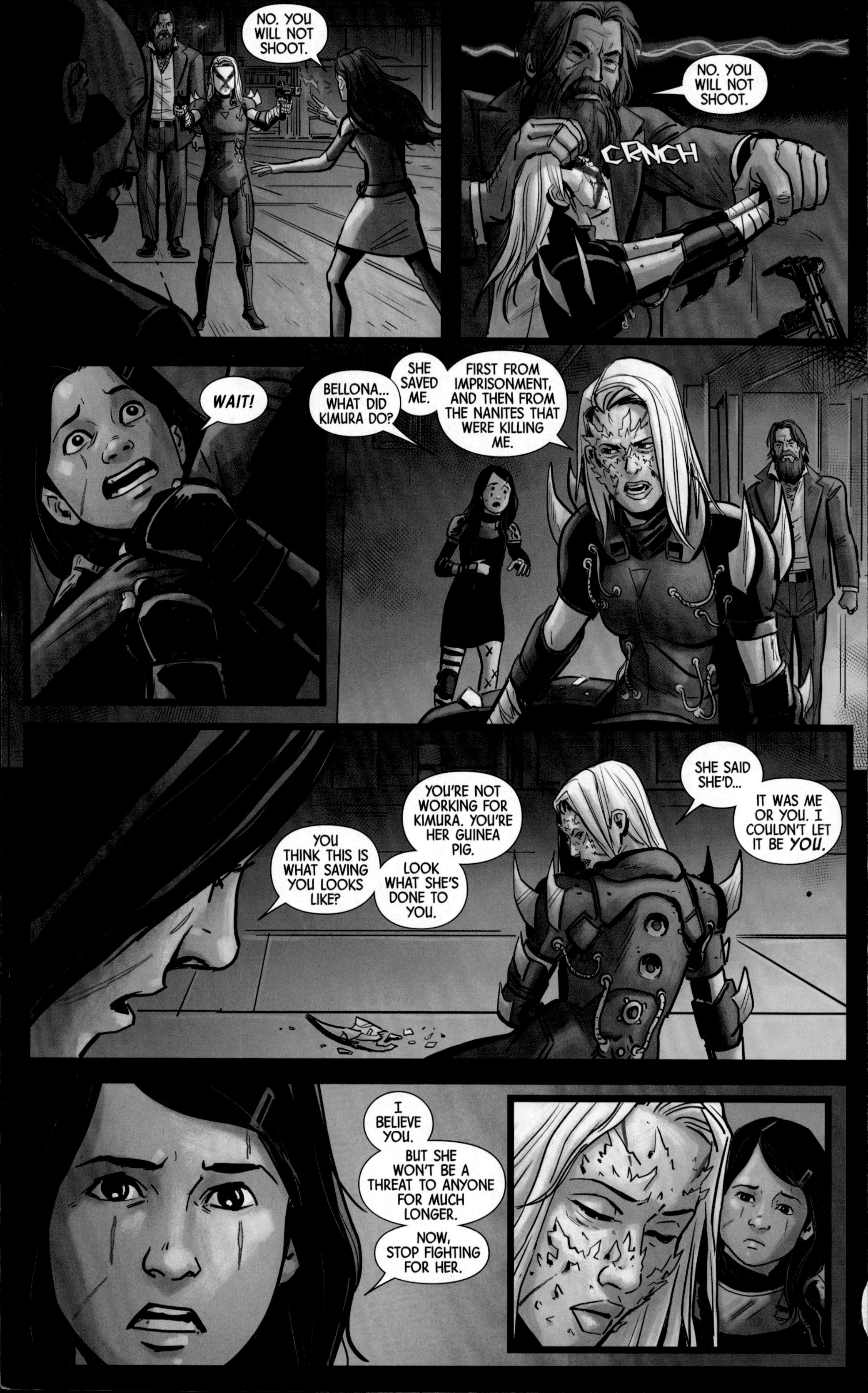
NO. YOU WILL NOT SHOOT.
NO. YOU WILL NOT SHOOT.
CRNCH
WAIT!
BELLONA... WHAT DID KIMURA DO?
SHE SAVED ME.
FIRST FROM IMPRISONMENT, AND THEN FROM THE NANITES THAT WERE KILLING ME.
YOU THINK THIS IS WHAT SAVING YOU LOOKS LIKE?
YOU'RE NOT WORKING FOR KIMURA. YOU'RE HER GUINEA PIG.
LOOK WHAT SHE'S DONE TO YOU.
SHE SAID SHE'D...
IT WAS ME OR YOU. I COULDN'T LET IT BE *YOU*.
I BELIEVE YOU.
BUT SHE WON'T BE A THREAT TO ANYONE FOR MUCH LONGER.
NOW, STOP FIGHTING FOR HER.

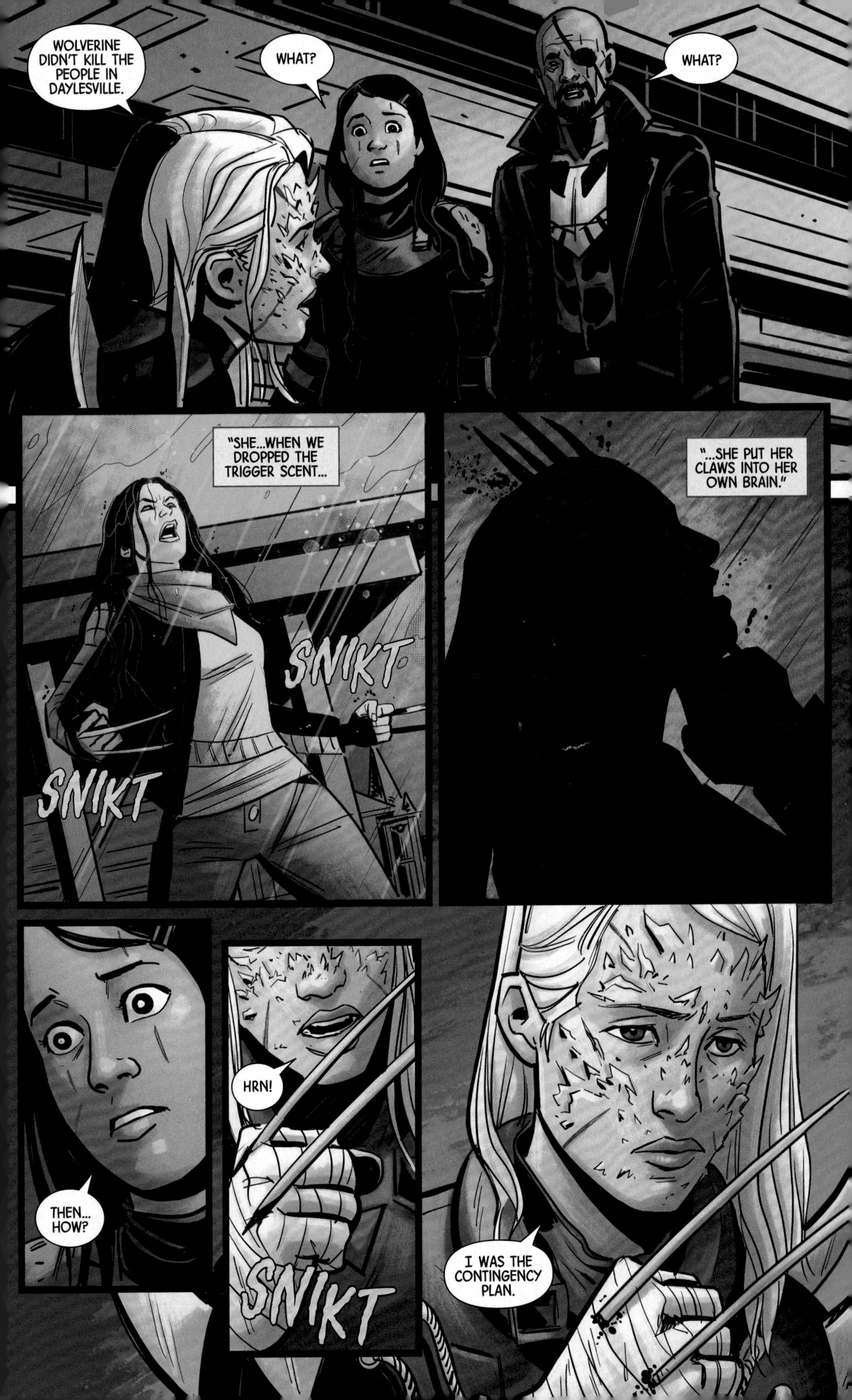
WOLVERINE DIDN'T KILL THE PEOPLE IN DAYLESVILLE.
WHAT?
WHAT?
"SHE...WHEN WE DROPPED THE TRIGGER SCENT...
SNIKT
SNIKT
"...SHE PUT HER CLAWS INTO HER OWN BRAIN."
THEN... HOW?
HRN!
SNIKT
I WAS THE CONTINGENCY PLAN.

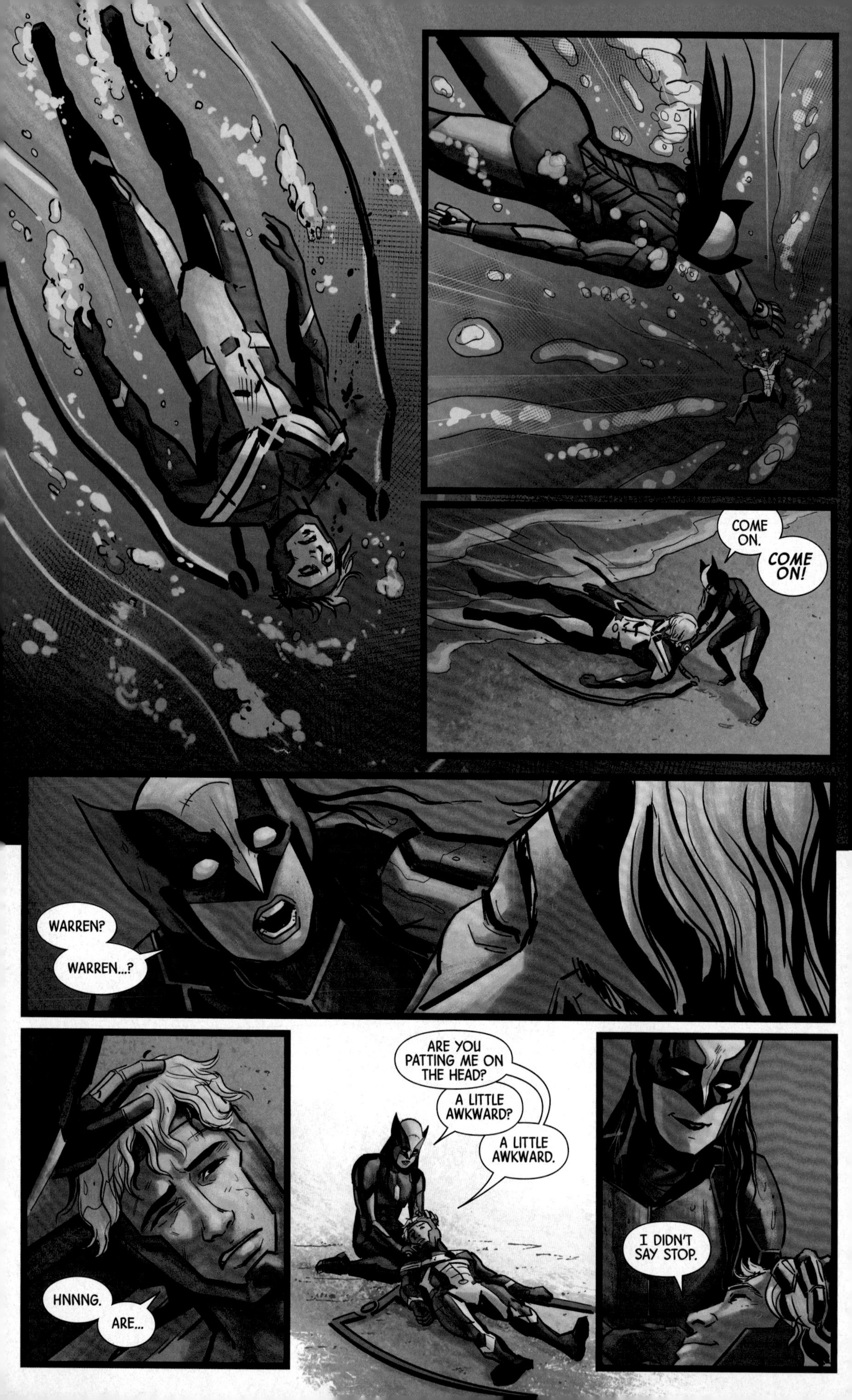

COME ON.
COME ON!
WARREN?
WARREN...?
HNNNG.
ARE...
ARE YOU PATTING ME ON THE HEAD?
A LITTLE AWKWARD?
A LITTLE AWKWARD.
I DIDN'T SAY STOP.

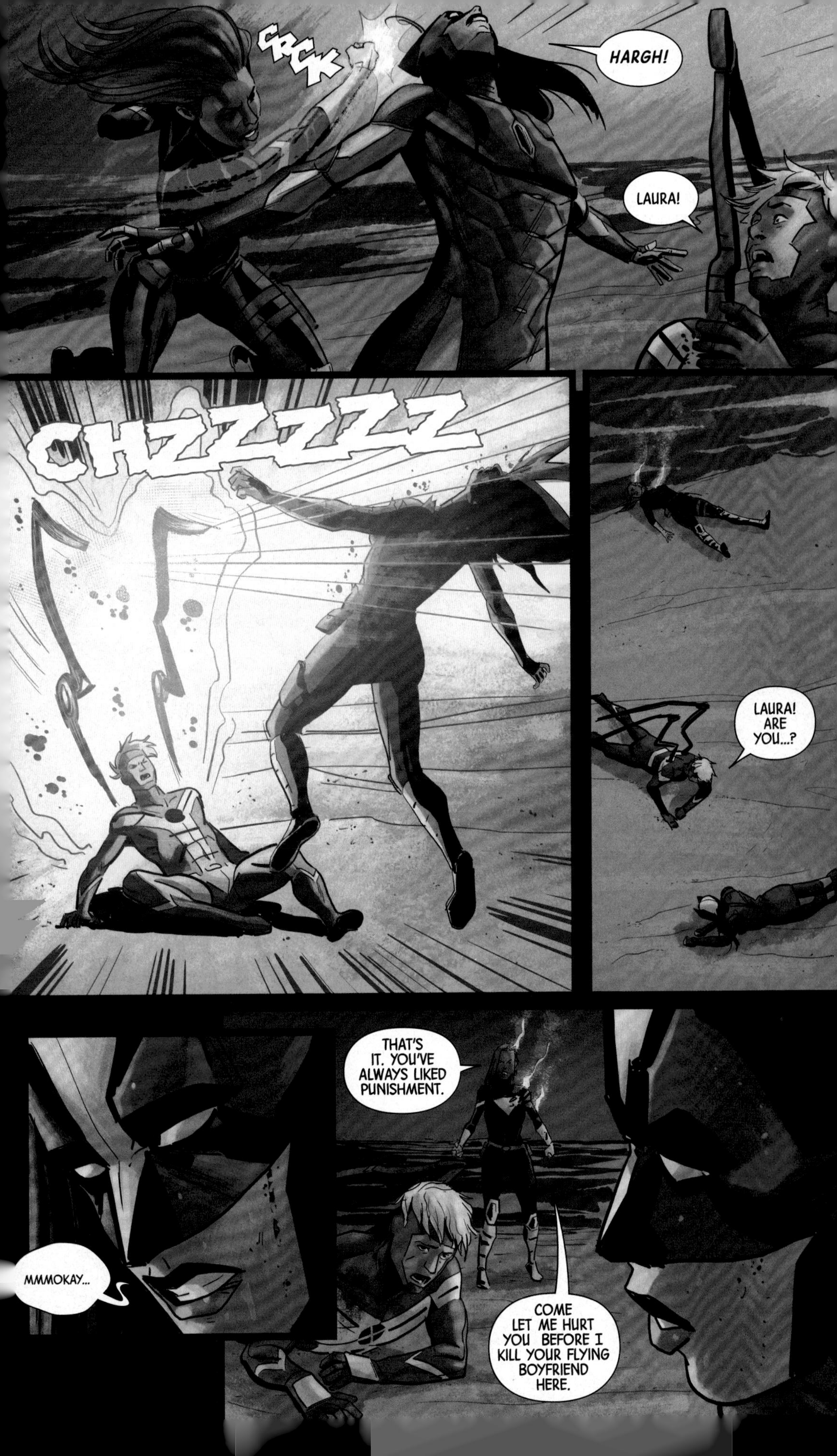
CRCK
HARGH!
LAURA!
CHZZZZZ
LAURA! ARE YOU...?
THAT'S IT. YOU'VE ALWAYS LIKED PUNISHMENT.
MMMOKAY...
COME LET ME HURT YOU BEFORE I KILL YOUR FLYING BOYFRIEND HERE.

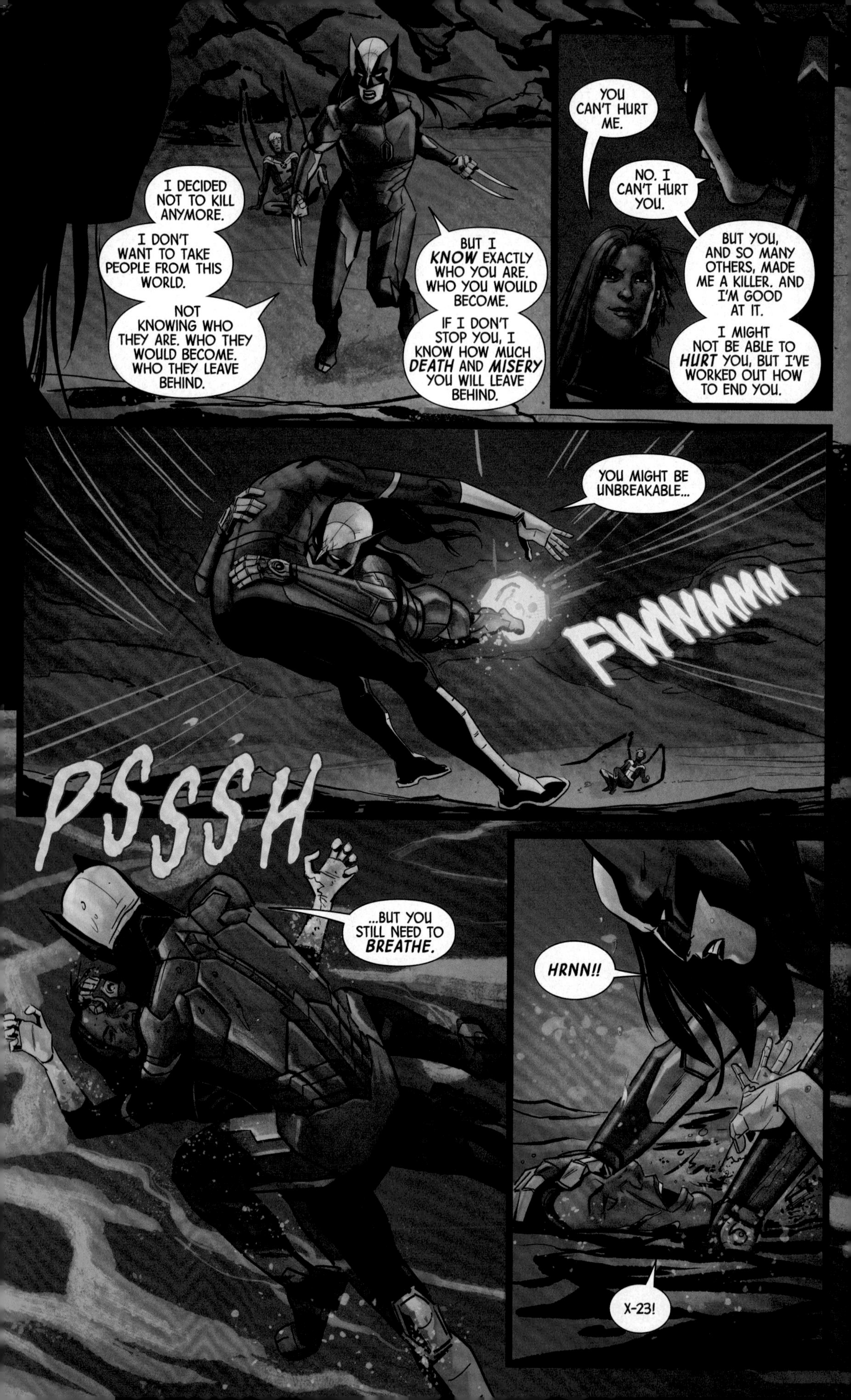
I DECIDED NOT TO KILL ANYMORE.
I DON'T WANT TO TAKE PEOPLE FROM THIS WORLD.
NOT KNOWING WHO THEY ARE. WHO THEY WOULD BECOME. WHO THEY LEAVE BEHIND.
BUT I KNOW EXACTLY WHO YOU ARE. WHO YOU WOULD BECOME.
IF I DON'T STOP YOU, I KNOW HOW MUCH DEATH AND MISERY YOU WILL LEAVE BEHIND.
YOU CAN'T HURT ME.
NO. I CAN'T HURT YOU.
BUT YOU, AND SO MANY OTHERS, MADE ME A KILLER. AND I'M GOOD AT IT.
I MIGHT NOT BE ABLE TO HURT YOU, BUT I'VE WORKED OUT HOW TO END YOU.
YOU MIGHT BE UNBREAKABLE...
FWNMMM
PSSSH
...BUT YOU STILL NEED TO BREATHE.
HRNN!!
X-23!

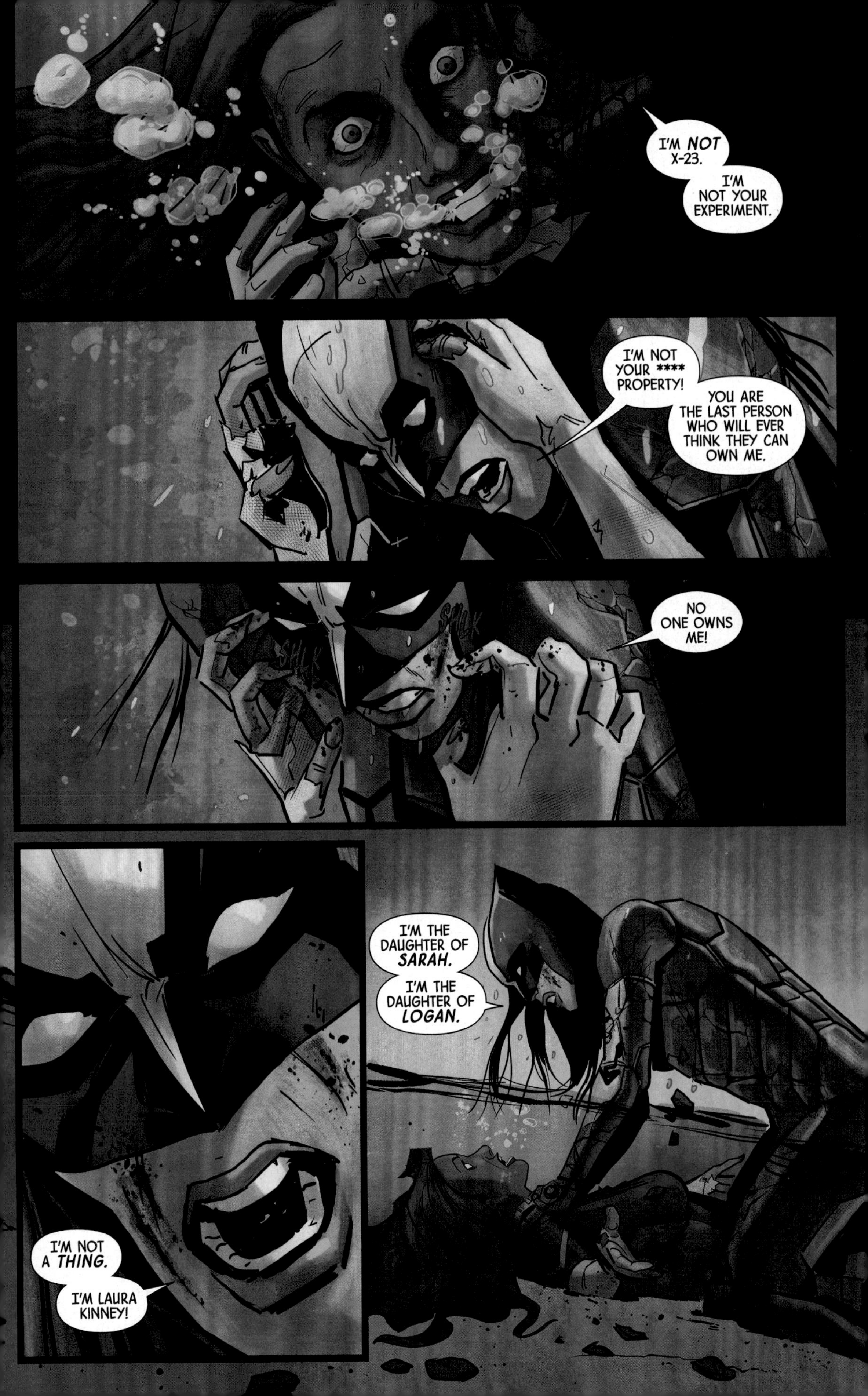
I'M NOT X-23.
I'M NOT YOUR EXPERIMENT.
I'M NOT YOUR **** PROPERTY!
YOU ARE THE LAST PERSON WHO WILL EVER THINK THEY CAN OWN ME.
SHLK
SHLK
NO ONE OWNS ME!
I'M NOT A THING.
I'M LAURA KINNEY!
I'M THE DAUGHTER OF SARAH.
I'M THE DAUGHTER OF LOGAN.

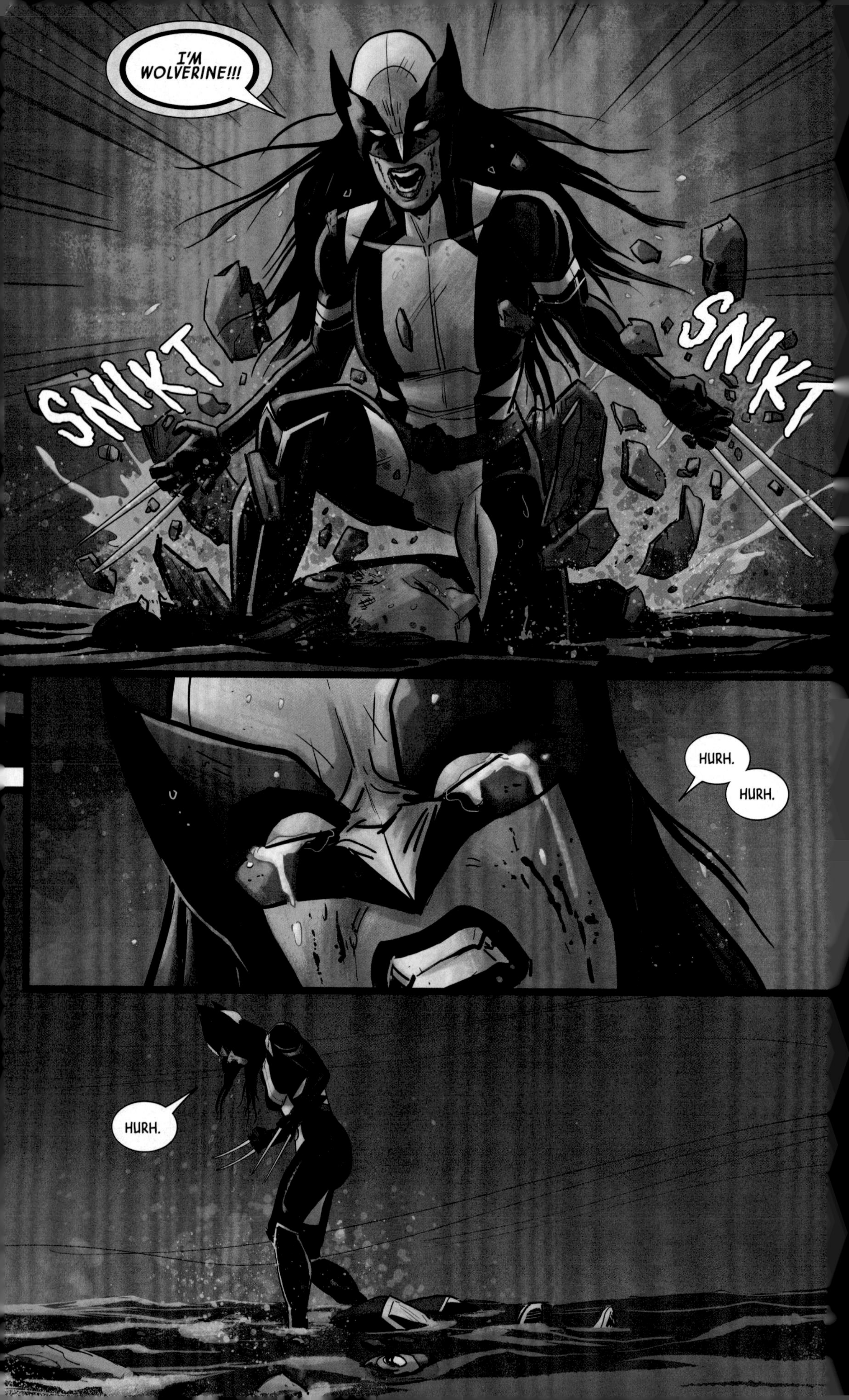
I'M WOLVERINE!!!
SNIKT
SNIKT
HURH.
HURH.
HURH.

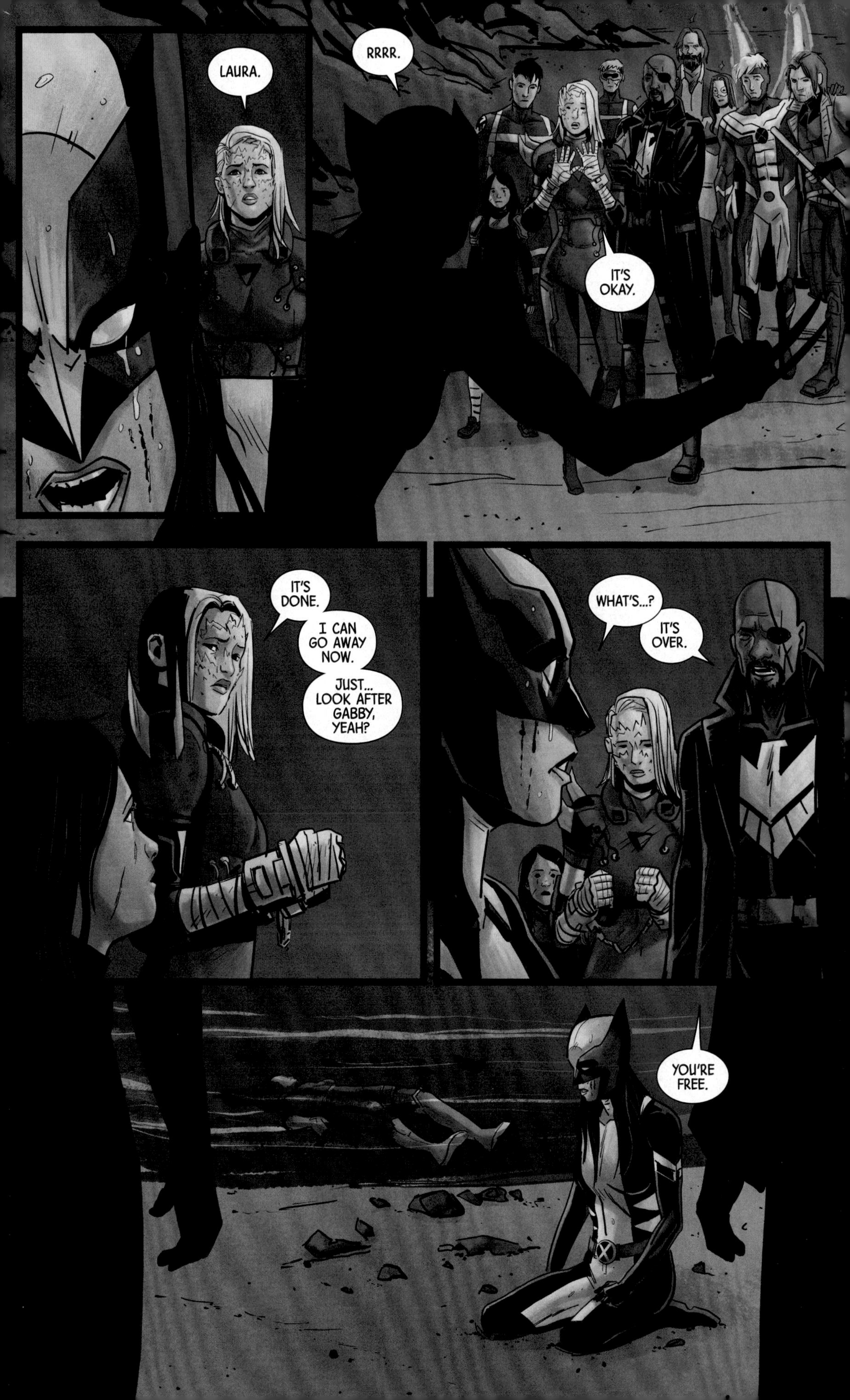
LAURA.
RRRR.
IT'S OKAY.
IT'S DONE.
I CAN GO AWAY NOW.
JUST... LOOK AFTER GABBY, YEAH?
WHAT'S...?
IT'S OVER.
YOU'RE FREE.

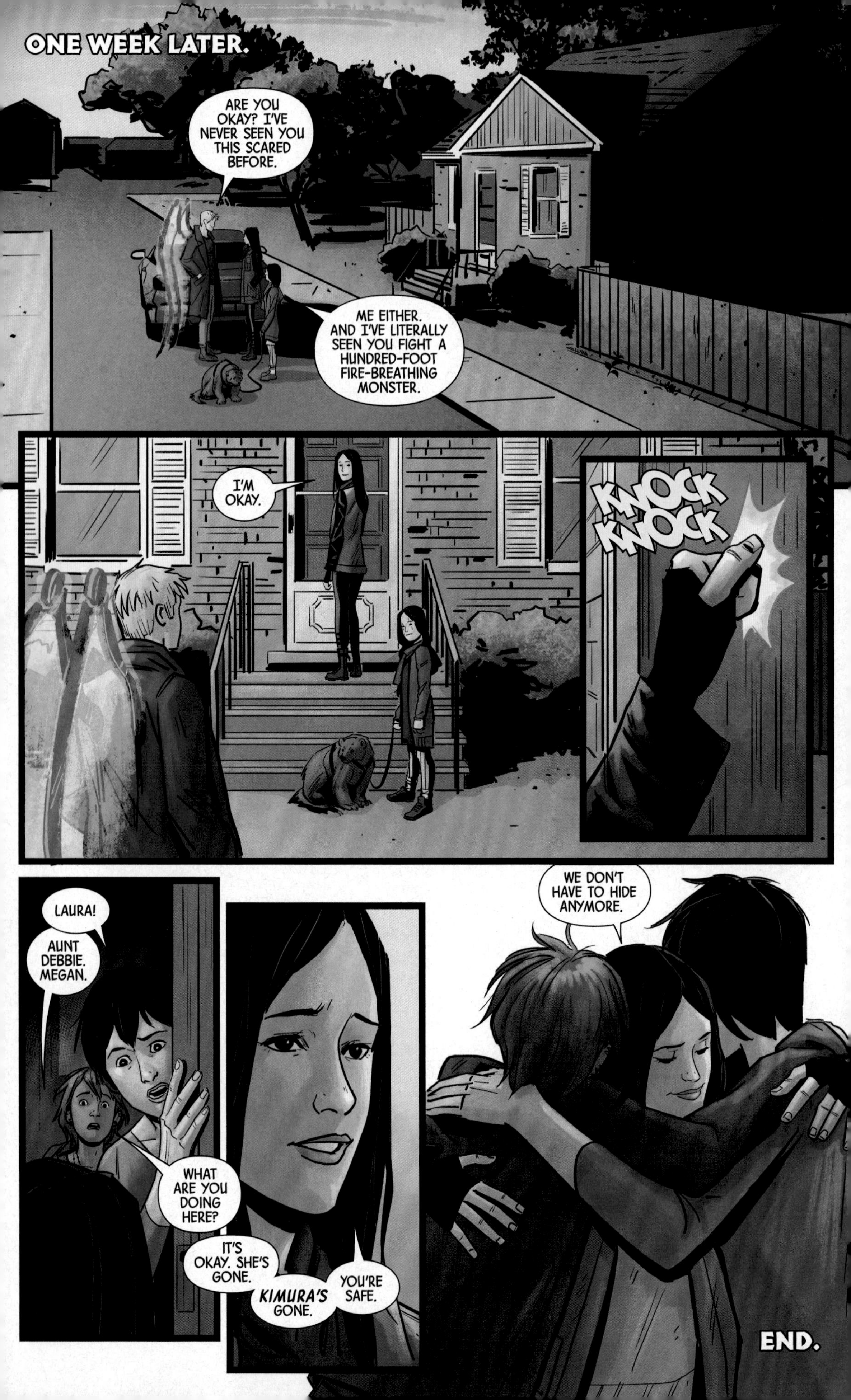
ONE WEEK LATER.
ARE YOU OKAY? I'VE NEVER SEEN YOU THIS SCARED BEFORE.
ME EITHER. AND I'VE LITERALLY SEEN YOU FIGHT A HUNDRED-FOOT FIRE-BREATHING MONSTER.
I'M OKAY.
KNOCK KNOCK
LAURA!
AUNT DEBBIE. MEGAN.
WHAT ARE YOU DOING HERE?
IT'S OKAY. SHE'S GONE.
KIMURA'S GONE.
YOU'RE SAFE.
WE DON'T HAVE TO HIDE ANYMORE.
END.

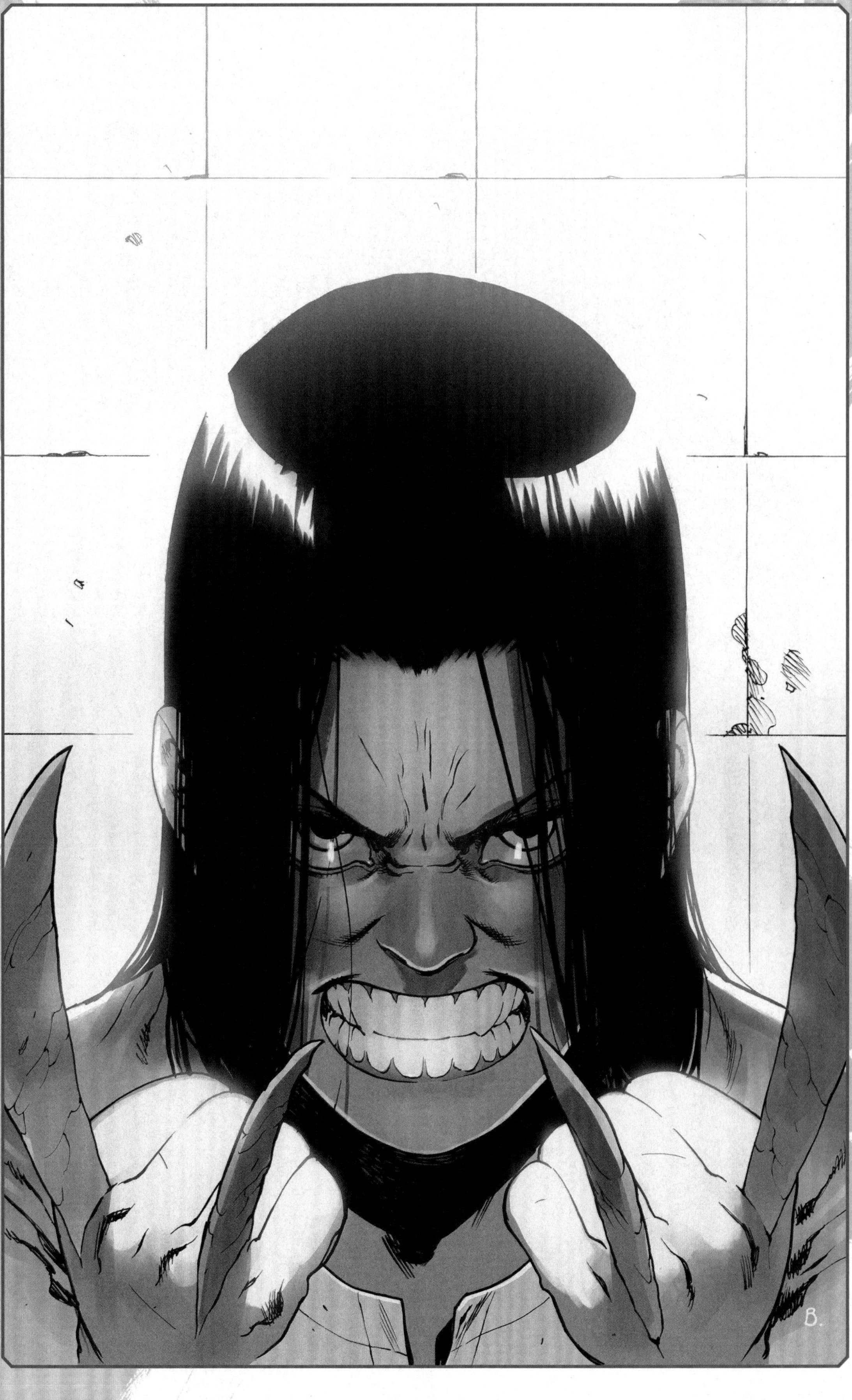

#13 variant by
BENGAL

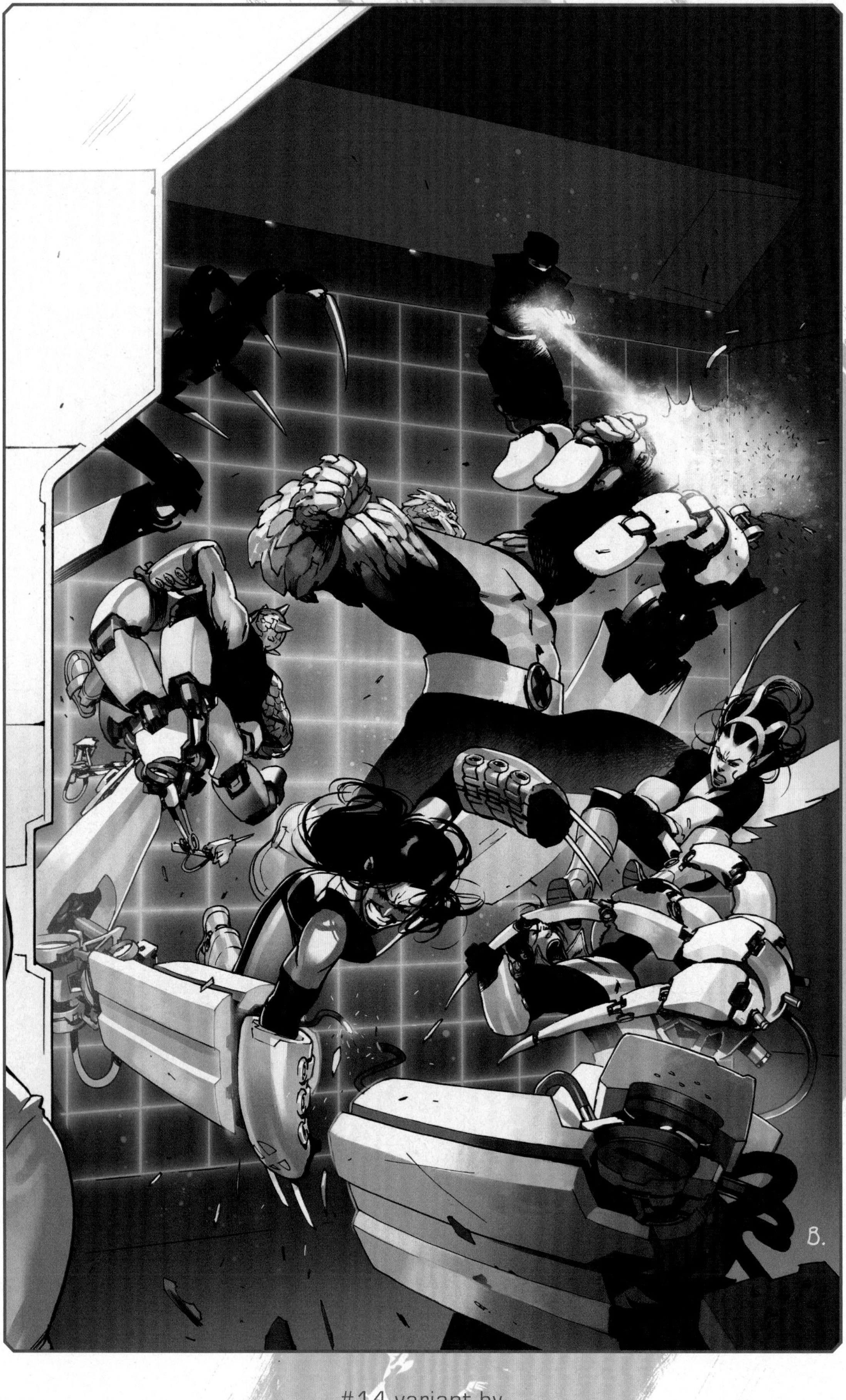
B.

#14 variant by
BENGAL

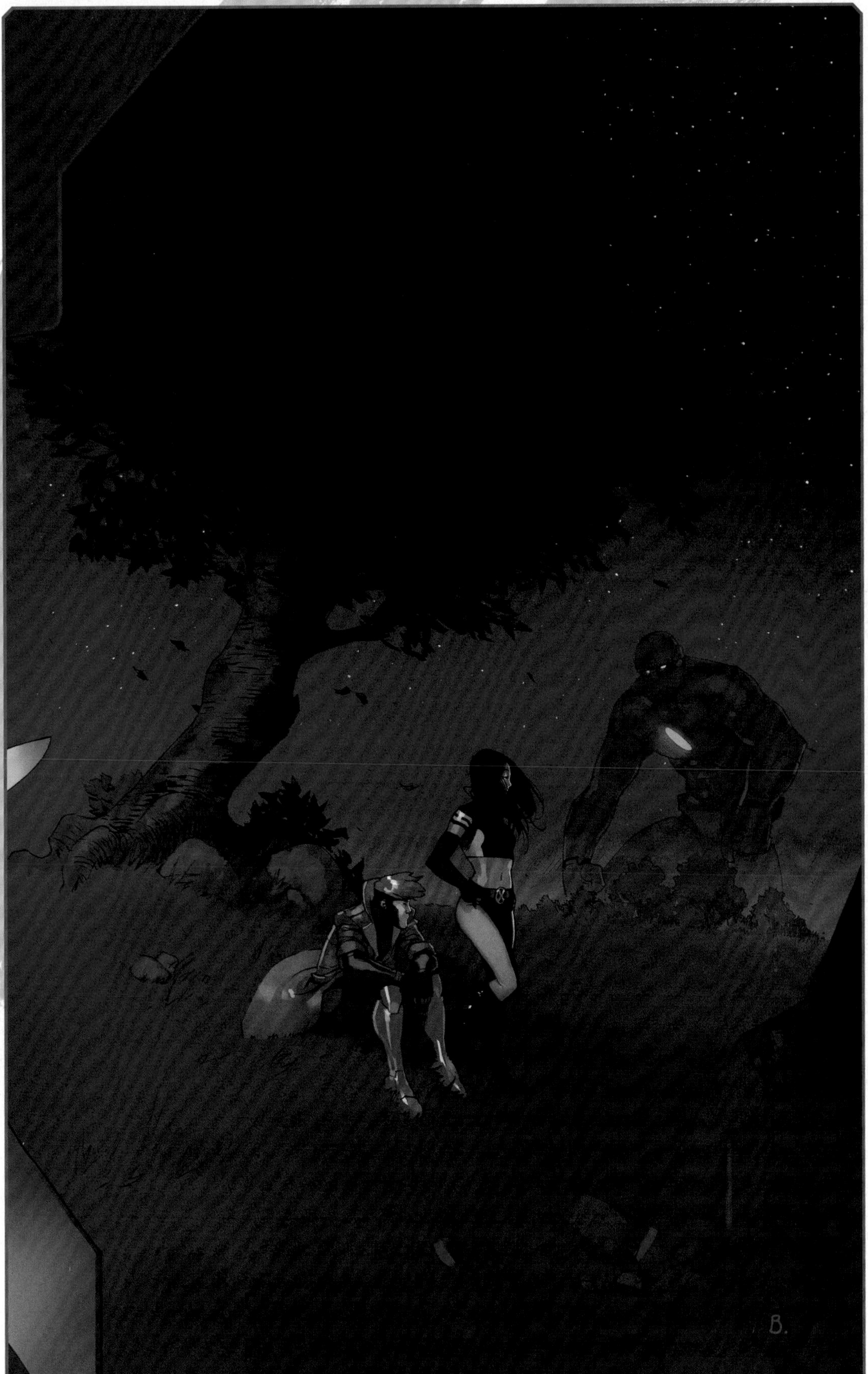
B.

#15 variant by
BENGAL

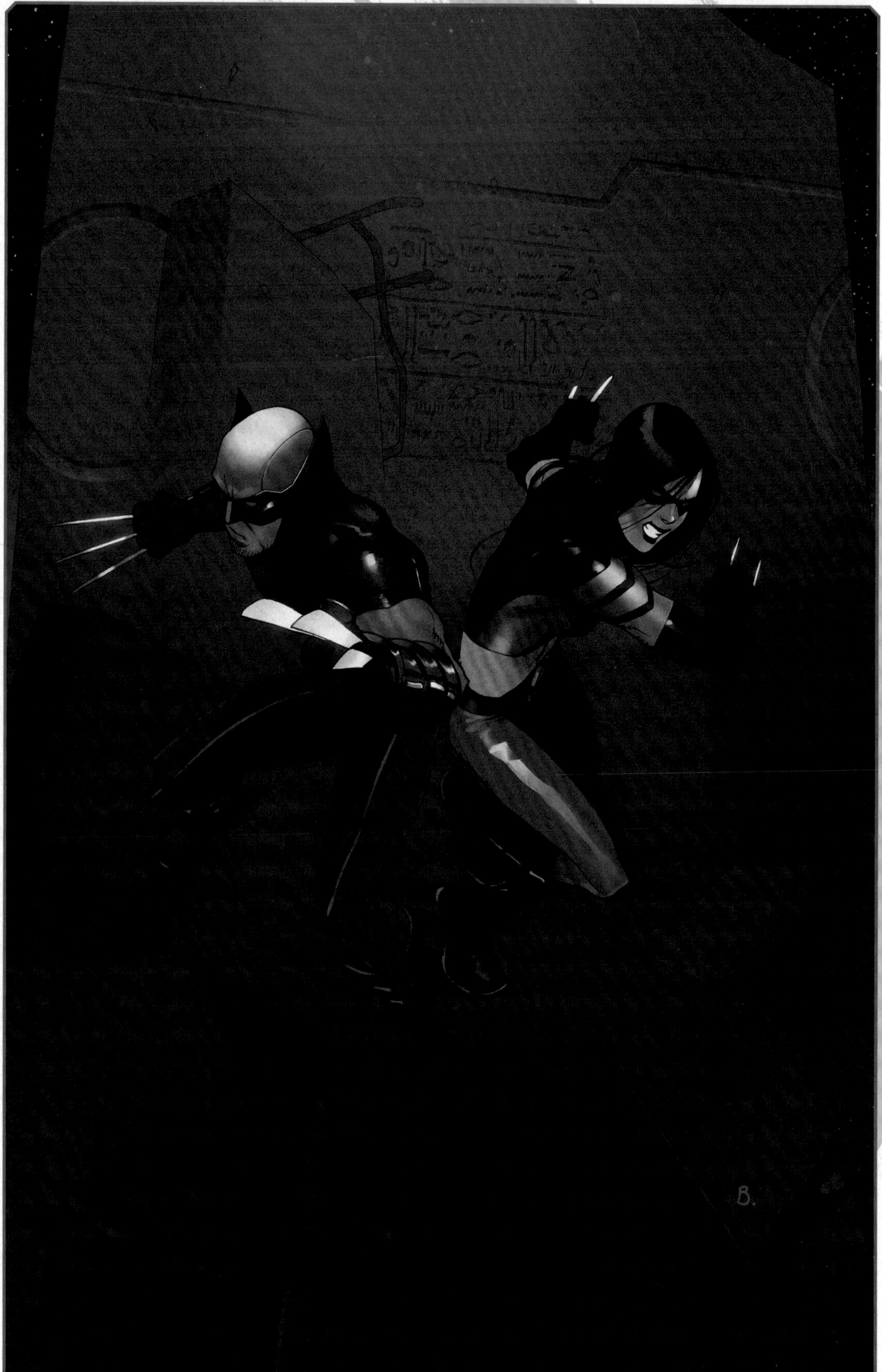

#16 variant by
BENGAL